American Psychology and Schools

A CRITIQUE

American Psychology & Schools

A CRITIQUE

Seymour B. Sarason

AMERICAN
PSYCHOLOGICAL
ASSOCIATION

750 First Street, NE
Washington, DC 20002

Teachers College
Columbia University
New York and London

Published by Teachers College Press, 1234 Amsterdam Avenue, New York, NY 10027 and the American Psychological Association, 750 First Street, NE, Washington, DC 20002

Library of Congress Cataloging-in-Publication Data

Sarason, Seymour Bernard, 1919–
  American psychology and schools : a critique / Seymour B. Sarason.
    p. cm.
  Includes bibliographical references.
  ISBN 0-8077-4088-8 (cloth : alk. paper) — ISBN 0-8077-4087-X (pbk. : alk. paper)
    1. Psychology. 2. Psychology, Applied. 3. Educational psychology. 4. Learning, Psychology of. I. Title.

BF121 .S28 2001
370.15—dc21   00-053270

ISBN 0-8077-4087-X (paper)
ISBN 0-8077-4088-8 (cloth)

Printed on acid-free paper

Manufactured in the United States of America

08 07 06 05 04 03 02 01   8 7 6 5 4 3 2 1

*This book is dedicated
to my two heroes in psychology:
William James and John Dewey*

Contents

The sources of educational science are any portions of ascertained knowledge that enter into the heart, head and hands of educators, and which, by entering in, render the performance of the educational function more enlightened, more humane, more truly educational than it was before. But there is no way to discover what is "more truly educational" except by the continuation of the educational act itself. The discovery is never made; it is always making. It may conduce to immediate ease or momentary efficiency to seek an answer for questions outside of education, in some material which already has scientific prestige. But such a seeking is an abdication, a surrender. In the end, it only lessens the chances that education in actual operation will provide the materials for an improved science. It arrests growth; it prevents the thinking that is the final source of all progress. Education is by its nature an endless circle or spiral. It is an activity which includes science within itself. In its very process it sets more problems to be further studied, which then react into the educative process to change it still further, and thus demand more thought, more science, and so on, in everlasting sequence.

John Dewey
The Science of Education

Preface

This book has long been germinating in my mind. The first half of my career was spent in research on matters that could be subsumed under the rubric of mainstream psychology. I took satisfaction from what I was doing at the same time that I was beginning to question the scope and undergirding values of the directions psychology was taking. The last half of my career has been in what was clearly not in the mainstream of American psychology: the culture of schools and its resistance to change. And in moving to the educational arena I experienced the sturm and drang of the learning and unlearning process and its dynamics. And the more I immersed myself in the educational arena, the more disappointed I became that the potential of American psychology to contribute to educational reform was not and could not be recognized or realized. The icing on this personal cake of vexation was that the educational community was mired in a conceptual mess from which were derived outlooks and practices that were confirming the adage that the more things change the more they remain the same. Throughout it all I never made the mistake of blaming this or that individual, or group, or institution as if the intractability of schools to change was a phenomenon of will. To make that mistake is tantamount to rewriting history, to project the present onto the past. There are no villains in the story. What obsessed me was to understand why the self-defeating gulf between American psychology and education seemed so unbridgeable.

How could I think and write about it without being perceived as unsympathetic to both sides or as displaying an arrogance which could be interpreted as saying a plague on both your houses? How could I do it for two audiences who hardly knew or used each other, whose relationship should be symbiotic but in reality was the polar opposite of a productive symbiosis? What was serendipitously catalyzing to my thinking about these questions was that my close friend and colleague at Yale, Wendell Garner, had written a paper, the substance of which we would discuss countless times when we would have our weekly lunch, a ritual we have honored for over 30 years. Garner's experimental research in perception—for which he has been acclaimed and honored—is as mainstream psychology as you can find. In 1972 he published a paper which challenged and transformed the conventional view of the relationship between basic and applied research. Our discussions were of help in giving to me a basis for writing this book. I discuss that paper in some detail in Chapter 2.

I am certain that what I say in this book is not the whole story. I am equally certain that it is my story, my attempt to make sense of my past experience in two fields. And, finally, I am no less certain that this book will not sit well in some quarters and with some people. If this book causes discussion and debate, I will have achieved my major purposes.

I wish to acknowledge my thanks to my dear friend, Robert Echter, a classroom teacher, for being a sounding board for my ideas.

Those who have read my previous books will know and expect that I will, of course, acknowledge my debt to and affection for Lisa Pagliaro who besides being able to decipher my handwriting—a feat that continues to amaze me—is as bright, charming, and refreshing a person as I have known, and I do thank God for very big favors. Not so incidentally, she is also very pretty! I know I am very lucky.

CHAPTER 1

The Aim and Plan of the Book

This book is an attempt to understand why American psychology has so little relationship to schools and their problems. And by American psychology I refer to the membership of the American Psychological Association, the American Psychological Society, and departments of psychology in our colleges and universities which select and train doctoral-level psychologists. There are psychologists in schools of education, but they are for the most part not at all highly respected by American psychology as defined above. But that disdain is not peculiar to American psychology because in our universities disdain of schools of education is institution wide. There is also the American Association of School Psychologists, many of whose members are not eligible for membership in the two large—the American Psychological Association being by far the largest of the two—associations because they lack a doctoral degree. In fact, one stimulus for creating the American Association of School Psychologists was that American psychology had little interest in schools. On the surface the lack of interest of American psychology in education generally and schools in particular suggests that the substance of theory, research, and practice of American psychology has little to contribute to schooling. That impression is belied by the fact that the concept of learning has always been a central one in American psychology, and up until two decades after World War II there were more than a few departments of psychology in which theory and research on learning were the dominant, identifying features of their graduate program. But the processes, vicissitudes, and contexts of learning in schools rarely or never were studied. Today the field of child development is a large, important, and intellectually fertile area in American psychology and one obviously concerned with why, how, and what the newborn learns and in which contexts, but the focus has been on the preschool years. It is not happenstance that child developmentalists played a major role in the creation of Head Start, just as it is not happenstance that very few of them subsequently sought to study the contexts of learning in schools. I say contexts of learning because if you do not describe and understand classroom and school contexts, test results are ambiguous in their meanings, at best, and mischievous and unacceptable bases for programs of educational reform, at worst.

There is an irony here, and it is that among the very small number of eminent psychologists who near the end of the nineteenth century convened to create the American Psychological Association were four who had a true interest in learning, teachers, classrooms, and schools. I refer to G. Stanley Hall, William James, John Dewey, and Lightner Witmer. The challenges and opportunities that schooling presented to American psychology were best contained in John Dewey's presidential address in 1899. And in his incomparable way William James in his *Talks to Teachers* (1900) made clear the role of the teacher in utilizing a theory of learning that distinguished between contexts of productive and unproductive learning. But it did not take long for what these people stood for to occupy a place far from the mainstream of American psychology.

As someone who has been a member of the American Psychological Association for 60 years and who came to know various departments of psychology—what they emphasized and valued—I wrote this book because of my belief that *potentially* American psychology has a great deal to offer to the understanding of schools as contexts of learning. And I am equally persuaded that the field can be rejuvenated and productively altered in its theories, research, practice, and scope if schools are seen and related to as a vehicle to meet the field's stated purpose of contributing to the public welfare. In brief, American psychology has much to give and get. And, if pressed, I would in candor have to say that it has potentially more to get than to give. And I have written this book from that standpoint.

I am not "picking on" American psychology, singling it out as a cause of the failure of post World War II efforts to redirect and alter the processes and outcomes of schooling. Anyone familiar with my previous books will know that I do not view schools of education in a favorable light, especially in regard to preparatory programs. The fact is that schools are and always have been embedded in a *system* comprised of teachers, administrators, parents, state departments of education, the legislative and executive branches of government (local, state, and national), and colleges and universities. They are all stakeholders in a system of parts poorly coordinated and frequently adversarial. That immediately confronts us with questions: How do you begin to change the system? How does one choose a starting point? Will the society be able or willing to accept the brute fact that changing a system, a very complicated, tradition bound system, will require decades, the opposite of the quick-fix mentality which has gotten us nowhere?

All human systems have a starting point, which is the same as saying that a system has an overarching purpose. The system is in the service of that purpose. What is the overarching purpose of schooling, and how does the existing system support it? It is easy to ask that question. It is by no means easy to get agreement on answers because the bulk of people, including educators, resist giving one overarching purpose, already an indication that the system will be shaped by competing purposes with a call on limited resources. Of course, schools have more than one purpose, but is there one which, if not achieved, undercuts or shortchanges all purposes? To learn basic subject matter, to learn to think critically, to learn to respect the opinions of others, to learn what it means to live in a democratic society, to learn habits of work essential to growth and independent living—these and more are the purposes people have stated to me. The one feature common to all the purposes is that they require *learning*. But when I point that out to people, they say, "of course, school is where you *learn*." And when I then ask how come so many students do not seem to learn this or that purpose, blame assignment takes over. Parents, teachers, bureaucracy, and underfunding were the most frequent objects of criticism.

It seemed to me that when people used the word *learning*, they were referring to two things: Students should want to and enjoy learning and what they learned reinforced the wanting to learn more. No one suggested that it was acceptable to require or demand learning this or that which students found uninteresting or unstimulating or unrelated to the world outside of classrooms, and having learned it put it in the category of file and forget. No one implied that learning should be a cut-and-dried, impersonal affair devoid of meaning. So, when I would ask, "When you use the word *learning* about, say, history, or math, or literature, or science, do you mean that what is learned is absorbed in the students' psychological-motivational bloodstream, so to speak, and is useable for subsequent development and growth?" No one ever answered in the negative, although some (not a few) said they never thought of learning in just that way.

And that is the point: schools are not for learning, period; the overarching purpose of schooling is to create and sustain contexts of productive learning, and if those contexts do not exist, all stated purposes are subverted. Regardless of the overarching purpose (or purposes) you select, if learning consistent with that purpose takes place in a context of *unproductive* learning, achieving that purpose will fall short of the mark, and very frequently far short of the mark.

What are the differences between contexts of productive and unproductive learning? That was the central question that William James and John Dewey, each in his own way, was posing and attempting to answer. And it is a question with which child developmentalists have been concerned, although largely in regard to the preschool years. That is why I believe American psychology, again potentially, can make important contributions to schooling. But to contribute, as in the case of schooling, requires interest and presence. That interest is not now there, and it is why I wrote this book.

Organizing this book was no easy matter because its major purpose requires discussion of issues which on the surface say little about schools but are very much part of the story. For example, Chapter 2 is about the values associated with the dichotomy of basic vs. applied research; specifically, the tendency to regard basic research and researchers as more worthy and/or important than the contributions of the applied researcher. That value judgment is by no means peculiar to American psychology. (It is a judgment already explicit in the attitude of the ancient Greeks, especially Plato, who valued the theories or abstractions the human mind can develop over the world of daily experience and appearances.) But with the emergence of American psychology at a time when the fruits of science were exciting and real, it is understandable that the founding fathers sought to insure that the new discipline would utilize the ethos and methods of science to discover the basic laws of the human mind, basic laws without which practical applications would not be possible or effective. The concept of and the imagery associated with the scientific laboratory were deemed essential for discovering laws. Practical problems had patiently to await the discoveries of the laboratory. No one at the time denied the existence and pressures of practical problems or devalued those who had to deal with them. The task of psychology was to train the basic-research researcher, not the applier of basic research. That view certainly had justification in the history of science. That one-way-street attitude, however, overlooked in that history examples where coping with practical problems altered the course of basic research. For example, wars have been occasions which stimulated and altered basic research in scientific fields. That is why in Chapter 2 I discuss a paper by Garner (1972), an eminent experimental psychologist in the field of perception, who relates how in World War II coping with practical problems in perception changed the substance and theories of basic researchers in certain fields of psychology. Garner concludes his paper with an admonition that is as justified as it is overlooked: There are problems and times when by trying to understand the nature of the problems of the practical psychologist, the basic researcher can gain a good deal; the symbiotic relationship can be a most mutually productive one, but only if it is seen as a two-way-street relationship. That two-way street has not existed and does not exist between American psychology and education in general and schooling in particular. I consider that self-defeating for an American psychology in which the concept of learning is an obviously crucial concept. For decades research on learning was done on rats in the laboratory. A decade or so ago that approach became semi-moribund. One might have hoped that American psychology would have directed attention to human learning in schools where everyone is expected to spend 12 years, a "laboratory" of unexcelled opportunities not only longitudinally to study learning but also to begin to develop a comprehensive conception of contexts of learning and their productive and unproductive consequences.

Before World War II the field of clinical psychology did not exist in departments of psychology, another instance of the unrelatedness of American psychology to important societal problems. As a direct result of World War II modern clinical psychology was incorporated into American psychology 3 years after that war. And what may be called the defining occasion of that development was the Boulder Conference on clinical psychology (Raimy, 1950). Chapter 3 discusses that conference in order to make several points, all relevant to the substance of this book. First, it predictably reflected how strongly American psychology valued basic research as its primary mission. Second, it demonstrated the degree to which American psychology was a psychology of the individual, with society, culture, and its institutions in a murky background, as a result of which the representatives of American psychology at Boulder were ignorant of and unprepared for the predictable problems that lay ahead for clinical psychology. Third, the conference never posed or confronted this question: What are the alternative ways American psychology could contribute to the public welfare other than by tying clinical psychology to the fields of medicine and psychiatry? I was a participant at the Boulder Conference, and I advocated closing the gulf between American psychology and schools. I said my piece, I was listened to respectfully, and the conference went on to mire the field not only in the repair mode (in contrast to a preventive one) but in professional wars (internal and external) that have had very mixed consequences. One of those consequences was that several decades later the basic researchers in psychology created the American Psychological Society, another indication of how American psychology divided the world into the good guys and the bad guys, leaving no doubt whom they regarded as the good guys. *And all this was taking place during decades when for the first time in our national history the controversies surrounding the blatant inadequacies of schools never were off the public's agenda; indeed they have become, together with health care, at the top of the agenda.*

In the spring of 1999 the nation was horrified at the murders at Columbine High School in Littleton, Colorado, an affluent suburb of Denver. For several weeks the mass media riveted on the incidence of school violence and what it signified about our society and its schools and what might or should be done. I, of course, cannot explain why the two troubled, socially marginal boys did what they did. But scads of people, including psychologists and other mental health professionals, directed blame to many sources they did not consider sensitive to the needs of youth. The only criticism, and it was muted, directed at Columbine High School was that it needed to relate better to students so that teachers and other personnel would have better information about troubled students in the school. For all practical purposes, the school as a large, complicated, bureaucratic social setting never got discussed by anyone, as if no one has read any of the large literature on the problem-producing features of high school, even in well-heeled suburban communities. That is why I devote Chapters 4 and 5 to Columbine High School; it serves as a setting manifesting every major problem associated with self-defeating organizations. Of all the psychologists who were asked to comment on the Columbine disaster, not one seemed to know what high schools are, the contexts of learning they sustain, the impersonality of interpersonal relationships, the huge gulf between students and staff, and how easy and understandable it is for some students to feel unknown and unstimulated. Those two chapters, as I indicated, are not intended to explain the Columbine murders. They are intended to explain why so many educators will refer to high schools as disaster areas, as do middle schools educators. That perception of middle and high schools (urban and suburban) in part explains why most educational reformers have chosen to work in elementary schools.

To some readers it may sound strange to say there is a gulf between American psychology and schools. After all, have not psychologists played a major role in developing and promoting diverse tests to be used by educators? The answer, of course, is yes, but that does not mean they were interested in contexts of school learning, the culture and traditions of schools, and how history and traditions have shaped teachers' conceptions of the nature and process of learning. If psychologists developed tests to be used and interpreted by school personnel, the fact is that they had little or no interest or experience in schools.

And by that I mean that they could not know how their tests could be used and interpreted in untoward ways, not because educators are stupid and incompetent or unmotivated, but because by virtue of their preparation for and experience in schools, they absorbed and learned conceptions of learning and development that still contribute mightily to the inadequacies of schools. To blame educators is to blame the victim. This the test developers had no way of comprehending. Psychology was in one world with its purposes and methods, and education was in another. In Chapters 6 and 7 I discuss why the use and interpretation of tests have been so predictably problematic. If tests are supposed to be of help in ascertaining the level of learning and the ability to learn subject matter, is it not crucial to study the contexts of classroom learning? Tests may be thought of as positive or negative "symptoms" of the ability to learn, but like all symptoms they have to be put in a context, or be seen as one aspect of a context, in which the symptom is but one factor. Although what I have to say in Chapter 7 and in other parts of this book is about the problematics in the use and interpretation of tests in a school or school district, I feel compelled here to bring to the attention of the reader something that exposes what can happen when those at the highest levels of state and federal political responsibility articulate policies about tests and standards that reveal abysmal ignorance of the modal contexts of learning in classrooms in particular and the school culture generally. It is a story which from its beginning to end, American psychology, test developers, and even the educational community had nothing to say. It is a familiar story in the arena of educational policy: the assumption that an articulated policy from those in Kafka's castle on top of the mountain of educational policy will have its intended effects on those in the classrooms at the bottom of the mountain. Kafka wrote novels, but they well describe the structure, dynamics, and outcomes of the educational system. I have discussed this in other books and can only summarize my position very briefly here.

The movement for higher standards and their measurement by tests began with great fanfare in the Reagan administration. One of the first actions of President Bush when he took office was to convene in 1989, again with much fanfare, a conference of governors to take actions that would make our schools preeminent in the world in regard to educational outcomes, i.e., far above their disappointing status in comparison to other countries. This led to the year 2000 policy: by that year the actions which will have been taken would have had its desired effects. I expressed the opinion that the policy was scandalously and irresponsibly unrealistic, setting the public up for another dose of disappointment and disillusionment. As I write these words in December, 1999, federal and state officials are announcing that the year 2000 goals will not be met. They, of course, give no explanation of why they were so blatantly naive or why continuation of the policy into the future are grounds for optimism. Is it possible that we have not paid attention to the differences between classroom contexts of productive and unproductive learning? That question goes masked and, therefore, unanswered, even though beginning with Comenius several centuries ago that is the question he and those who came after him put in the center of their thinking.

My practice is to write the introductory chapter after the book has been written. When I start to write a book I have a fair idea of what it will contain, but once I start to write my fair idea starts to undergo change as I realize how incomplete my initial idea was. Even so, there have been times when after the introductory chapter is written, when I have decided that enough is enough, that events take place of such relevance to why I wrote the book as to compel me to alter or to add material to one or more chapters and to write additional chapters. That is what I confronted when this introductory chapter was (I thought) finished and could be sent to the publisher. On successive days two news articles appeared in the *New York Times*. In a book which discusses tests, standards, psychologists who help develop tests, and educators who use and interpret tests, these two articles will, I hope, explain to the reader why in this book I rivet on the significance of context.

In the *New York Times* on December 7, 1999, there is an article by French with the headline "Exam Wars, Prepping and Other Nursery Crimes." The following brief excerpt explains the title.

Concern has mounted gradually for years in Japan over the downward creeping spread of school entrance exams to ever lower age groups, driving mothers to enroll their children in expensive cram schools even before they have learned to eat with chopsticks. It is said nowadays that even pregnant women here often count aloud believing that it will help prepare their children for the competition that awaits them.

Still, it took a murder in Tokyo last week to shock many people here into finally concluding that things had gone too far. Haruna Wakayama, a 2-year-old girl who had just passed an entrance exam, was killed by the mother of a classmate who had failed. The jealous mother has told police that she strangled Haruna in a playground bathroom, stuffing her body into a bag and boarding a train to take it to her parents' home 120 miles outside of Tokyo for burial.

Tokyo's newspapers have been filled ever since with accounts of the country's degeneration into a hostile society, driven by outward measures of success rather than human relationships and feelings. The killing has inspired scores of editorials about the "examination wars" that mark the progression from kindergarten to 12th grade of every Japanese child.[1]

On the following day, December 8, on the front page of the *New York Times* is a news article by Goodnaugh with these headlines:

INVESTIGATORS SAY
TEACHERS IN CITY
AIDED IN CHEATING
Report Cites 32 Schools
Answers Allegedly Supplied in
Effort to Raise Test Scores
—2 Principals Named

Accompanying the article is (1) a photo of a student's test and (2) a photo of the special investigator for New York City schools. Next to his picture is the following: "A third-grade test showing erasures and changed answers was among several tests offered yesterday by Edward F. Stancik, the special investigator for New York City schools, as evidence of cheating. Mr. Stancik charged that dozens of teachers supplied answers on reading and mathematic tests."

The article is not pleasant reading. As I emphasize in this book, I am not opposed to tests and standards. But I am quite opposed to proclamations about standards and tests which are totally insensitive to how they may be used, interpreted, and reacted to by those who have a personal or professional stake in such matters, a stake suffused with pressure and stress. But insensitivity is the least of the mistakes. In some ultimate sense the most egregious mistake is the assumption that the educational problem is a motivational one. That is to say, the reason so many students fall below standards as measured by tests is that, for one or another reason, they have not been sufficiently motivated to meet

---

1. The most instructive and interesting book on Japanese education is that by Cutts (1997), a businessman and journalist who has lived for 30 years there. He, like others, describes the pressure and terror of middle and high school students in regard to a series of examinations with which they cope because how they do determines what they will be in life. Unlike other observers, Cutts does not see the elementary school in favorable ways. He would not be surprised by the *New York Times* article. I consider his book a "must read," especially for those who use Japanese schools as ones we should model. This is not to say that their schools are without any virtues, but cross cultural comparisons, as anthropologists have taught us, can be mischievously misleading.

standards which heretofore were either too low or were ignored. By raising standards both students and teachers will be more motivated to meet new standards; if the stakes are higher, motivation will be increased. I am reminded here of the late 1950s when teacher unions *and* the general public agreed that salaries of teachers were scandalously low and that if salaries were increased so would educational outcomes increase. Neither the unions or the general public noted that this argument implied that teachers would be more motivated to help students learn because their salaries would be increased. It has not worked out that way. Even today there are people who still advance that argument as a way of improving classroom learning. Of course salaries were immorally low—below that of garbage collectors—and should have been raised on the basis of comparative equity, not on the grounds of increased motivation. Such grounds were mammothly demeaning of the bulk of teachers. Similarly, to expect that raising standards and using appropriate tests will raise motivation and scores obliterates recognition of the possibility (I would say the fact) that the modal context of classroom learning is inimical to productive learning, that that context bears the imprimatur of an educational system comprised of parts not only very poorly coordinated but frequently in an adversarial relation to each other, a system in which what is meant by learning is hardly discussed. Proclaiming more rigorous standards and their evaluation by tests is easy, it is an empty act of virtuous intent that has long plagued efforts of educational change. The hard part is thinking through why and how such proclamations will make for the changes that are desired. And when you begin to answer the why and how questions, starting with those features of contexts of school learning, you will find that starting with those contexts soon confronts you with the larger contexts in which the classroom context is embedded. I have discussed this in previous books devoted to preparatory programs of educators, parent involvement, school governance, and the relation between political leadership and educational failure, and more. This book has to be seen in relation to my previous ones. I am not plugging my books, I am just saying that improving our schools is, to dramatically indulge in understatement, more complicated than policy makers realize. Their intentions are good, their ignorance is profound, their knowledge of the history of educational reform virtually nil. I know that sounds harsh, but the stakes are too high to coat the pill of ignorance and superficiality with even semi-smooth words that pay respect to gentility at the expense of what I regard as truths.

There will be readers of this book who will question why I talk about American psychology as if I were talking about a single individual. My critique, they may say, is egregious overgeneralization. I deal with that issue in Chapter 8 and give the kind of examples that I felt justified my critique. If these examples are very personal, it is precisely because for 6 decades I have been a member of the American Psychological Association during which time my increasing interest in the educational arena made clear to me the strength of the derogation of the field of education and educators by American psychology. But, as I emphasize in that chapter, such derogation is part of the outlook of our colleges and universities wherein departments of psychology are well entrenched.

I said earlier that among the very small groups that founded the American Psychological Association were four people with an interest in education. Chapter 9 discusses them, especially William James and John Dewey. Chapter 10 concludes the book. Its contents will strike some as strange and controversial because I employ the proposal for a new high school course on the basic tenets of the major religions. I can assure the reader that my "imaginary course" allowed me to address several questions. How can you justify teaching national history and for all practical purposes leave religion out of the story? How can you understand our society *today* without discussing religious differences? If the course is, as it should and must be, to serve the purposes of education and not indoctrination, what are its implications for the preparation of educators? The crucial differences between education and indoctrination are omnipresent issues in the preparation of clinical psychologists and that is reason enough to suggest that American clinical psychology has a potential contribution to make to the preparation of teachers. But that potential will never be made until American psychology narrows discernibly the gulf between it and schools. By what criteria do we judge the educational value of a course? If you begin with that question, you are on the road to clarifying what you mean by productive learning. The course example I employ is not the central issue. The fact is that some of the most divisive issues in education today have explicitly or implicitly a religious source. We cannot afford to ameliorate issues by ignoring them.

If, as I believe, American psychology has the potential to make important contributions to schooling, the reader will be disappointed in the expectation that I will very concretely and in detail spell out what forms that potential could take. There are several reasons why I refrained from playing the role of seer. For one thing, a major change in a field's direction, especially in the social sciences, always is correlated with major changes in the larger society. Fields do not exist in a social vacuum. When dramatic changes take place in the larger society, fields relevant to the change "respond" in different ways and in differing degrees. Within each field there are always some individuals who change the direction of their professional activities (theory, research, action) in what they consider appropriate to what has become clearly a societal problem. And that happens even though the individual or the field has had little or no direct experience with that problem. But they are interested, they get involved, they act because they believe they can adapt what previously has been learned and done to the new state of affairs. *What will issue from moving in new directions is far from predictable.* Only with the passage of time does the outline of the history of the relationship between what was potential and what was contributed begin to become clear. Nowhere has this been more true than the case of American psychology.

The history of American psychology is literally incomprehensible if one does not understand how the field was changed by World Wars I and II. It was as if overnight the leadership of American psychology energetically sought to determine how the field could contribute to the war effort. At the start of World War I the very small American Psychological Association had been in existence for 25 years. The one segment of the field that potentially could make a contribution concerned psychological tests, and that potential was based on very narrow and shaky theory, research, and practical experience. The psychological problems confronting the military were serious. American psychology was unprepared. (Psychologists were a mystery to the military. What do they do? Where do you put them? They ended up in the sanitary corps.) Malingering, brain injury, psychiatric disorders, morale, personality assessment, illiteracy were some of the problems for which psychologists lacked experience. But they were highly motivated, they learned by doing, they acted. And they learned a great deal, not least the knowledge that the scope of the field had been too narrow; that they had been exposed to problems that psychology could and should not ignore. The war experience changed American psychology in regard to theory, method, and research. That was especially true in the case of brain-behavior, personality assessment, and personnel selection issues, as well as intellectual measurement. None of this was predictable in any concrete way. What was predictable was based on the millennia-old fact that war changes everything and everyone in small or large degrees, for good or for bad.

World War II was an even clearer example. No one, but no one, could have predicted on December 7, 1941, that when the war ended American psychology would embrace and develop a field that heretofore was not represented in graduate education of psychologists. I refer, of course, to clinical psychology, which soon became the largest program in graduate schools. I shall discuss this in Chapter 3. Here I wish only to note that by virtue of tradition, experience, and undergirding values American psychology was unprepared to comprehend how this new field of clinical psychology would transform American psychology in ways startling to those who had become psychologists before World War II (I being one of them).

I trust the reader will understand why in this book I refrain from predicting in any detail what could happen if American psychology should become interested in the seemingly intractable problem of educational reform, a problem fateful for the future of our society. When interest transmutes into action, and the experience of action illuminates the stimulating but sobering complexity of the culture of learning and schooling, then what has been an intractable problem will be seen in new and productive ways. That, of course, is a hope, my hope, and it is based on my assessment of what has happened in the past when psychology, however ill prepared, ventured forth into unfamiliar social and institutional arenas; it resulted in a reassessment of psychology's potential, of how its potentials for significant contributions had been seen as too parochial and impoverishing. I am not advocating action for the sake of action but rather as a way of concretely experiencing the dimensions of a state of affairs, a kind of "casing the joint" to get your bearings, to refrain from premature theorizing, judgments, and oversimplifications.

What can American psychology contribute to educational reform? I have been asked that question countless times. I had a verbalized and an unverbalized answer. The verbalized one went like this: "The more I immersed myself in classrooms, schools, and school systems, the more I saw how major fields in psychology—child development, human learning, social psychology—were ignoring the possibility that they had much to gain from seeing schools as testing grounds for their theories, research, and practical applications. I say 'gain from' because their stated aim as scientific endeavors is to arrive at conceptions which have general import. To the extent that their conceptions derive from use of unduly restricted sites and populations, that stated aim will only minimally be met. For example, it took most of the past century before it was recognized that studying rats in a maze was inadequate (to say the least) as a way to contribute to generalizations about human learning. As a result, human learning is a major focus of very few psychologists. That is a case of throwing the baby out with the bath water. My point is that what I call the culture of schools contains a challenge to the adequacy of the generalizations these fields have presented; at the same time it is an opportunity dramatically to broaden or revise or even dispose of some of these generalizations. For that challenge to be confronted requires an active immersion in the school culture. What I am advocating is totally consistent with the rationale justifying the scientific experiment: If you want to understand a phenomenon, try to change it. The consequences may be disappointing but they are always instructive, sometimes to an extraordinary degree."

My unverbalized answer is more brief: "The very fact that you ask what psychology can contribute to educational reform betrays an inexcusable ignorance of schooling. I learned what I have learned by immersion, which is another way of saying that there was a lot I had to unlearn. It will, I predict, be no different in your case. You will, like me, be puzzled, conceptually overwhelmed, and make mistakes of omission and commission. So what else is new? I do not advocate action for the sake of action but rather action for the purpose of unlearning and learning in the spirit of the self-correcting process." If there was an unverbalized answer it was because I did not want the individual asking the question to think I was targeting him or her; I was passing judgment on the field.

But there was one judgment shared by all questioners: American psychology has more than its share of bright, creative, talented people. And if there is one thing we can say about such people, it is that what they come up with when they change or move in new directions is not predictable. That is an asset that justifies me in saying that the potential contribution of psychology to educational reform is not pie-in-the-sky. But that potential will remain only a potential absent interest, engagement, and action.

Organizing this book was no easy matter, and for two reasons. The first was that I was trying to talk (writing for me is a form of talking) to two audiences: psychologists and educators. I have learned over the decades that relatively few psychologists read the educational literature, past or present. For example, I retired in 1989. After that I continued to visit psychology departments and go to psychological meetings. Believe me, I know a lot of psychologists, and many psychologists came to know me, especially in regard to the 15 years I devoted to studying test anxiety. In any event, since I retired, I have been asked by a significant number of psychologists how I have been spending my retirement years. I learned to say that I was doing some writing. Only once did my anger come through and that was to a member of the psychology department at Yale. I could not refrain from saying (laconically, I hope) that I had written 11 books on education since my retirement. I can assure the reader that although I, at least, take satisfaction from what I have written, I am quite aware that I have not said the last or the best word on anything, and that is not undue modesty. Of course I nurture (occasionally) the hopes I am wrong, my reality testing tells me otherwise.

The case of educators is even worse. I am appalled by how many educators have read little or nothing in psychology, and, to ice the cake of vexation, how little they read in their own field. For all practical purposes, for example, teachers do not read any professional journals or books. In 1993 I wrote *You Are Thinking of Teaching?* It was not written to be helpful to students considering teaching as a career but for teachers of teachers. The last chapter is titled "The Non-Reading Professional," and I make clear that teachers who do not read do not deserve to be called professionals.

So how should I talk to two such audiences? If a writer should have a good idea about where the reader is coming from, the writer owes it to the reader to tell him or her where he (in this case) is coming from. However much I did not want to go over ground I had already traveled, that turned out to be impossible. It just did not work. So what is in these pages is a compromise, and I know there will be some readers who will consider it an unhappy compromise. I hope, of course, that there will be readers who will understand the reasons for my approach.

CHAPTER 2

Basic and Applied Psychology: A Non-Symbiotic Relationship

The capacity of people to predict even fairly accurately what their society will be like two or more decades in the future has varied from seeing the future as a carbon copy of the present to seeing it as dramatically different. Both extremes, as well as those in between, have been blatantly short of the mark. We are used to hearing that in the twentieth century our world has changed beyond recognition because of scientific and technological advances. Although that is undeniable, the fact is that prior to those advances there were people, including those most knowledgeable, who did not believe those advances were possible except in a very distant future, and even then they could not predict except in the most general terms how the societal picture would change. The Wright brothers believed that it should be possible to build an airplane that would stay aloft for at least a minute and perhaps a bit more. Practically everyone else, again including the most knowledgeable individuals, thought the brothers to be, if not fools, misguided tinkerers. And when their first flight was reported in the newspapers, people did not believe it, even people who were curious and witnessed the event. If we had asked the Wright brothers to predict the pace of improved airplane design, or ways that air travel would change people's outlooks and behavior, or what would happen to the railroads and mail delivery (and more), their predictions would have contained many omissions. No doubt they would have predicted that the society would change, but their predictions would have lacked specificity. And the story would be similar for the computer, organ transplants, cloning, space travel, and walking on the moon.

In the case of atomic energy the story is similar and instructively different. When earlier in the century after the energy within the atom was theoretically and experimentally determined, physicists proclaimed that if that energy could be released, humans need never worry about a limited supply of energy; a new age would dawn. What was in the very far future, they said, was no less than the fulfillment of a fantasy. It was in the very distant future because what needed to be accomplished were three things: To release the energy, harness it, and then sustain it. To successfully solve these problems would require resources of such magnitude that at the time was totally unrealistic—truly the stuff of dreams. The advent of World War II changed all that, of course, and in ways that the scientists and everyone else did not envision. When it comes to the societal future, you are wise not to bet the ranch on your predictions, even if your predictions derive from validated scientific-technological advances.

However, a very good case can be made that non-scientific-technological advances are of equal or more historical significance in terms of how posterity has come to view their consequences. Can anyone deny that how we think and feel about the modern world is colored by religious conflict? Those conflicts, of course, have a long history spanning millennia, but who in the twentieth century predicted that as direct consequences of religious conflicts related to World War I and World War II we would today be concerned with Iran, Iraq, the Balkans, the Middle East, the republics that supplanted the defunct Soviet Union, and significant parts of Africa? Can one deny that in the United States today religious differences are an obvious source of heated divisiveness of a degree few if any predicted after World War II? Abortion, teaching of creationism, assisted suicides, public funding for religious schools, women and gays in the clergy, legalizing gay and lesbian marriages, permitting prayer in school—in all of these and more religious views play a very significant role in public and political debate. Religious divisiveness is not a new phenomenon in our country, it is an old story, but few if any people 40 or 50 years ago predicted that it would take the form it has. We today, religious or not, are aware that these issues have a dynamic future which is cloudy and unpredictable, a dynamic for which those who are near or at middle age were unprepared; their formative years were, so to speak, in another world. It should be noted that these issues are not only of a religious vs. non-religious kind but also are sources of deep conflict within religious communities. Karl Marx said that religion is the opiate of the people. Opium makes for listlessness and passivity, a retreat from the world, but the strength of that opiate has obviously decreased. Marx could say that he was using the concept of opiate figuratively, not literally. Either way, as a predictor of why, when, and how the world would change, he was as wrong as those who could only envision the positive consequences of atomic energy.

One more example. From the 1920s until a few years ago the Soviet Union was "here to stay," a presence which in one or another way influenced the policies and actions of almost every country. Particularly in the case of western countries, the Soviet Union was as dangerous as it appeared to be powerful. It is not an exaggeration that the Berlin blockade, the explosion of the Soviet Union's first atomic bomb, the orbiting of the first space satellite (Sputnik), and the Cuban missile crisis mightily exacerbated the fears of governments and their people. The Cold War, it was feared, could become a hot and deadly one. "Real politik" required that we deal with the Soviet Union as best we could. This gave rise to what was termed "Kremlinology," made up of experts in and out of government spending their days trying to figure out what was in the minds of those in the Kremlin as well as indicators of conflict among them. In the most unreflective way the Kremlinologists assumed (as if it was axiomatic) that the Soviet Union would be with us for the foreseeable future, and future meant many decades at the least. All of the Kremlinologists, as well as all people, were rendered stunned and speechless as that country began to unravel. That it was happily welcomed goes without saying, at the same time that posterity's judgment of the Kremlinologists has predictably been critical. Why did they so egregiously mislead people and government officials? Why was their "database" so frequently invalid? What were they not attending to? Had they been more perceptive and analytical could they have lessened or prevented decades of national anxiety? Should they not be judged in the same way we judge cults who predict that the world will end on this or that day? When we say that posterity is the cruelest of critics, it is meant that posterity is cruel to those who, however well intentioned, could or should have known better, who confused the world as it is with the world as it was becoming.

Another example is the 1954 desegregation decision of the Supreme Court. Most people, certainly not all, welcomed the decision because it finally recognized that a longstanding social evil would no longer be sanctioned. No one predicted that desegregation could be accomplished in 5 or 10 or even 20 years. But neither did people expect that by the end of the millennium urban schools would be more segregated than before. The Supreme Court decision said that desegregation should proceed "with all deliberate speed." The Supreme Court justices were not social scientists, and they can be pardoned for suggesting a pace that vastly oversimplified the obstacles ahead. But what about the social scientists? After all, we expect—we certainly should expect—that social scientists would have, as a consequence of such a momentous decision, alerted us to the individual and institutional obstacles desegregation would encounter. They did not. It was not because social scientists were ignorant of the fact that throughout our national history—before and after the Emancipation Proclamation—there were more than a few individuals who had written incisively and eloquently about the price that was being paid and would continue to be paid for slavery and then racial prejudice. Myrdal's book *An American Dilemma* was published in 1944, just 10 years before the Supreme Court decision. I find it interesting and instructive that it was two foreigners (Myrdal, 1944; de Tocqueville, 1835–40/1956), separated by a century, who saw the race problem in its complexity and who, I believe, would have been astounded by the phrase "with all deliberate speed." My own explanation of the unpreparedness of American social science was that it viewed segregation as basically a moral issue and when that moral issue received the appropriate legal-political resolution, implementation would not encounter, except perhaps initially, serious obstacles.

Of course at the root of segregation was a moral issue, but it was one that over several centuries not only shaped the organization and practices of institutions (religious, political-legal, educational) but the attitudes of individuals, including many of those who in principle were against slavery and then segregation. You can hold and proclaim moral principles (like the Ten Commandments), but when put to the test of actions consistent with principles, especially when they require behavioral change, you become aware that your principles come with a personal price you may not wish to pay. I consider it to be a glimpse of the obvious that the Supreme Court justices and the jubilant supporters of their decision virtually ignored or vastly underestimated, which is why they expected/predicted that the goals of desegregation would be achieved in the relatively near future.

Some personal experience is relevant here. But first I have to say that I am no seer. My training and education in psychology were utterly inadequate in preparing me to understand how institutions were (among other things) shaped by and in turn shaped the psychology of their members. Psychology was and still largely is a psychology of the individual. This does not in any way mean that such a focus has not contributed to knowledge and its applications. What it does mean is that beginning with World War II and then in the following decades, many psychologists found themselves dealing with problems of organizational structure, purposes, culture, traditions, and decision making. These were problems for which their training and education had not prepared them. They learned, to the extent that they did, on the job. Some were able to unlearn conceptually handicapping theories and ideas about individual behavior, some were not. Learning is always accompanied by unlearning and that process can be destabilizing or liberating, or both. When it is largely destabilizing, the person may seek to leave the site and return to a role in which he or she feels more comfortable and adequate. For example, beginning with the sizzling sixties a large number of academic psychologists (and other social scientists) spent varying amounts of time consulting to diverse governmental agencies. In more than a few instances they took a leave from the university to spend full time, up to 2 years in some cases, in a governmental agency. My sample is small but during that decade I estimate that I had long discussions with 30–40 people (from different universities) about their governmental experiences. If I was curious, it is also the case that they wanted to talk. The average response went like this: "I was not prepared for what I encountered. There were so many vested and divisive interests. Turf, power, status, infected everyone. They were bright, serious, dedicated people for the most part who, whether they liked it or not, felt compelled to be competitive, to be recognized, to play the zero-sum game, to win allies, to put their mark on policy. When I would talk with the policy makers, they would say their staff does not really understand what they have to contend with those higher-ups in other parts of the system and they have limited freedom to do what they think best. It was a wonderful experience, I learned a lot, I influenced little if anything, but I am glad I am home. Never again."

The world of public and private institutions is not comprehensible within the confines of a parochial individual psychology, nor is the thinking and behavior of those in these organizations. That is not to say that an individual psychology is useless but rather that it is of limited value in comprehending why and how the organization is what it is and shapes the thinking and actions of its participants. Let me now discuss some personal experiences relevant to what I have said above.

My first job after completing graduate school was in a spanking new state residential institution in Connecticut. I had been in complicated institutions from the time I started public school to when I went to graduate school. I say complicated *now,* but during all those years I did not see them as complicated. To me they were *places* divided in diverse ways; they were not an organized collection of people whose roles, obligations, and relationships were of relevance to me. So, for example, in graduate school I knew that in any department a professor had more status than an associate or assistant professor, just as I knew there was an undergraduate and graduate dean, a provost, a president, and a board of trustees. If asked how faculty were selected, how promotions came about, how a chairman of a department was selected and by whom, what the powers of the president were, and what decisions a board of trustees could make, I would have needed less than a page to write my answers. If asked to describe sources of conflict among faculty members of my department, given the rumor mill among graduate students, I could have written at length, and it all would have been about the personalities of the individuals and their different psychological theories, as if that sufficiently explained everything about interpersonal rivalries and conflicts. You can say that I was naive, and you would be right, of course, but you would be wrong if you attributed such naivete to the kind of individual you might think I was: someone unable or unwilling to go beyond appearances. But let us assume there is a kernel of truth to such an attribution. If so, it is a kernel possessed by all graduate students I have ever known. For 3 years before I retired I asked advanced graduate students to write briefly about the process by which a person is recruited, selected, and formally appointed to a faculty position at Yale. Their ignorance was profound.

The fact is that the source of such ignorance is deliberate. Deliberate in that faculty and administrators zealously protect knowledge about what they do and why; students are considered to have neither the knowledge nor experience wisely to comprehend why the system has the features it does. I am not referring to issues of confidentiality but to the history and philosophy undergirding how and why a university has become what it is: a very complicated institution. It robs the university of an opportunity to educate students about the brute fact that students and faculty do and will increasingly work in large, complicated organizations each of which intersects with similar ones.

The above explains why I was not prepared for my experience at the Southbury Training School. I met many friendly people, I luxuriated in the beautiful, bucolic surround and the striking revolutionary architecture (it looked like a new college campus), and I plunged into the obligations of my first professional job. But it did not take many weeks before puzzlements began to plague me. Why did department heads seem on the surface to like each other but in talking to a newcomer like me made critical, barbed comments of each other? Why did they seek to enlist my support for a particular policy they thought important and had not been adopted? Why at meetings of department heads was it obvious that the superintendent reacted very differentially to what different members said or suggested? Why was it equally obvious at these meetings that the superintendent had made policy decisions prior to a meeting based on talks with one or two departmental heads? Clearly, there was a pecking order of power not explainable by me in terms of size or responsibilities of departments. And why were teachers, cottage attendants, and maintenance personnel so quick to criticize "higher ups"? Why is it that almost no one asked my opinion about anything? Why, as I quickly learned, was the superintendent considered a frustrated architect who knew next to nothing about mental retardation? Why, when the board of trustees came for their monthly meeting, did they make no effort to get to know department heads? What was the function of the board of trustees? Was it to rubber stamp the policies of the superintendent? How could they make policies without knowing, even at some superficial level, the opinions of department heads, let alone the largest group who spent the most time and most directly influenced the lives of the residents? I refer, of course, to the cottage personnel who received no training whatsoever and nothing you would call supervision; some of them were truly nice people (some were not) but with, for practical purposes, no understanding of the residents who ranged in age from 6 years to 50, came from very diverse backgrounds with dramatically diverse physical and mental conditions.

The dominant impression of those early months was of a rumor mill, its speed and substance. It is too easy to say that people like to gossip, some more than others, as if an explanation in terms of individual differences is sufficient. What I and everyone else ignored was that we were living together in the middle of rural nowhere and there were very few things to distract us from cloistered living. We were unaware how much we needed each other to let off steam, and a lot of steam certainly makes for murky and distorted perception and understanding. It is noteworthy that everyone at Southbury, whether patient or employee, divided the world into "here" (the institution) and the "outside," and the latter was not visible or perceptually salient except as a symbol of personal freedom. And all this was taking place during World War II when gasoline was rationed and the Flying Eagle bus line stopped to take on or discharge passengers three times a day.

When I left Southbury to go to Yale, I initiated a research project on test anxiety in several school systems. I spent a lot of time in a lot of schools. I spent a lot of time with individual teachers and principals. Although my focus was not on schools as organizations, I began to be aware of two things. First, a school was part of a system of schools, a pyramidally shaped system with layers of management. At the top of the pyramid was the superintendent and the school board. And, just as at Southbury, those at the bottom of the pyramid, the teachers, felt powerless, unrecognized, and unrewarded, which is why a few years later teachers ambivalently signed up as union members. When the unions began to be a factor, administrators would tell me that salaries were scandalously low and that the powers that be would have to do something about it. What they were utterly insensitive to was that teachers felt unrespected, unlistened to, and very expendable. Yes, salaries were abysmally low but so was the feeling of not being respected. Teachers did not have to be told that one does not, should not, live by bread alone; administrators to the contrary not withstanding.

The second thing I learned was ironically identical to the first, but it had to do with how students perceived teachers and vice versa. I was appalled by the docility and conformity of the students. They rarely said anything in class or asked a question; they did what they were told to do. They were not dumb, they just did not seem all that interested and motivated. Teachers, on the other hand, saw students as empty vessels to be filled with information and to learn how to regurgitate it; and the more accurate the regurgitation, the "smarter" the student was. From our interviews with parents we learned that it was frequently the case that how parents described their children's behavior and style differed starkly from how we saw these children in their classrooms; that was not explainable by an individual psychology. Crucial confirmation of this came from what students said about themselves on our test anxiety scale; 10–20% reported a high load of test anxiety, 30% a moderate level, and the rest little or no anxiety. When we would show the distribution of scores (not using student names), most teachers seemed unwilling to take the results seriously or having potential practical value for their teaching. As one teacher said, "You can't put much stock on what students say about themselves on a questionnaire." Their reactions were somewhat surprising but what forcibly struck me was their conception of children: little folk whose inner life was uncomplicated, or unformed, or did not play a major role in school learning. As a group, parents, of course, described their children very differently.

It was during the years of the anxiety research project that I became aware (again) of the obvious. Neither students, teacher, and administrators were comprehensible only in terms of their individuality; they were embedded and socialized in an organized, bounded, non-porous system which overtly and covertly affected their thinking, attitudes, and behavioral style. The obvious was unsettling to me if for no other reason that as a psychologist, let alone a clinical one, I was unprepared to deal with such concepts as culture and system. *Riveting on individuals with problems needs no defense.* But the Achilles' heel when one goes that route is that you miss the forest for the trees. And to me the single school and the system of which it is a part was a forest I did not know how to begin to traverse.

In part the above explains why in the early 1960s I started and directed the Yale Psycho-Educational Clinic (Sarason, 1971; Sarason, Levine, Goldenberg, Cherlin, & Bennett, 1966). It was not a clinic to which problem children could be referred by schools. Our explicit goal was to develop ways to be of help to teachers in their classrooms; our implicit strategy was to use those ways to become knowledgeable about the culture of schools and school systems. I knew from my clinical experience that the offer to help and the process of helping inevitably encounters resistance in the troubled person, regardless of how much he or she says change is wanted and necessary. We treasure our symptoms, they serve a purpose, which is why changing our ways of thinking, feeling, and acting is so difficult. I felt secure in assuming that school personnel as individuals and as collectivities, such as complicated organizations and school systems, would be equally revealing in their reactions to the process of change in regard to the thorny (too weak a word) problems with which they were confronted.

The glimpses of personal experience I have presented are no more than that: glimpses, abbreviated descriptions, not for the purpose of being revealing, but rather to present enough to allow me to buttress my critique of an American psychology that ill prepared me for what I encountered in the modern world of organizations-institutions. I now consider myself an expert on the *sturm und drang* of unlearning as a necessary and sufficient precondition for new learning. It was not, is not, and never will be easy.

So what? Aside from learning a lot and having a helluva sense of intellectual growth, what did I think I contributed to psychology as theory and practice? If you go by what is taught in graduate department courses in theory and practice, the answer is: nothing. Whatever status I have had in psychology was based on research which met the conventional criteria of "good" research. That is to say, the research had a very clear focus, its methodologies were reasonably objective, statistical analysis was appropriate, and the results were capable of and indeed were replicable. What I have done and written in the past 3 decades is known only to those psychologists with an interest in education, and no one has to tell them that being identified with that field immediately marginalizes you in the psychological community. Indeed, these psychologists feel far more at home in the American Educational Research Association than they do in the American Psychological Association; and it is also the case that most of them have appointments not in psychology departments but in schools of education, and it is not a secret in the university that schools of education are very low on the totem pole of respect. Educational psychologists are labeled as applied psychologists who have nothing to contribute to psychological theory, to a "basic" psychology which alone can provide a basis for justified applications. What I have said here is captured in a paper I wrote in 1975 with the title "To the Finland Station in the Heavenly City of the Eighteenth Century Philosophers." That was written when I was still regarded as a card-carrying, respected psychologist, albeit one who from time to time wrote polemics about psychology's parochialism and its undergirding and unexplored values.

The reader would be quite wrong if he or she concluded that these words are being written by an aged psychologist disappointed and roiled because what he considers to be important work has had little or no impact on or recognition in the psychological community. The fact is that in the process of creating the Yale Psycho-Educational Clinic, I knew full well that what I was going to do would have no impact. For example, I twice sought grant support from the National Institute for Mental Health (NIMH) to help start the clinic. On both occasions I was visited by a group of institute consultants who were respectable and well-known psychologists (and one psychiatrist). I, like them, was not unknown in psychology. They were troubled by several things in our grant application. First, my conception of the culture of the school was murky. Second, the rationale for the way we would experience and study that culture was very subjective. Third, we did not and could not say what would constitute evidence for whatever conclusions we would draw from what we experienced. Fourth, however much the two groups respected my previous work, it would be difficult to justify support for what seemed to be a fishing expedition. I liked them, they liked me, but they were puzzled by the fact that although I said loud and clear that I understood and *even largely agreed with their reservations,* I could not be more concrete and specific in regard to a problem that had been discussed only by Waller in 1932. If it had some of the features of a fishing expedition, I was certain of one thing: We would catch fish, conceptually nutritious fish. We did not receive support, and I knew then that whatever we would learn and write about would be regarded as at best "applied research" and at worst as possessing all of the drawbacks of the anthropologist's ethnography he or she writes after spending months in some exotic culture; from the standpoint of science personal experience has very dubious (if not mischievous), theoretical, practical, generalizable value. Having said that, I should say that I am aware of and agree with the caveat that it is hard to be completely wrong.

There was another factor that convinced me that whatever we would accomplish at the clinic would be hard for the psychological community to take seriously. What truly appalled me about the two visiting teams was how near totally ignorant they were about schools. If I did not overevaluate the extent and depth of my knowledge about schools, compared to them I was a walking encyclopedia. There was an unbridgeable gulf I knew I would have to live with. I never allowed myself to indulge high hopes. Did it initially bother me? Yes. Has it ever bothered me since? No.

Let me now briefly answer the question I asked earlier: What did *I* personally consider my contribution to be to understanding learning and schooling and to psychological theory and method? The answer is in several parts.

1. In 1965, 3 years after the clinic had started, I gave an invited address to educators at the University of Maryland. In it I predicted why the educational reform movement was and would continue to be a failure, a prediction that was 100% correct. That paper was the basis for my 1971 book *The Culture of the School and the Problem of Change*, a book that continues to be influential in educational circles, although in "real life" it has changed nothing. In 1990 I wrote *The Predictable Failure of Educational Reform* enlarging on themes in the earlier one, this time on the basis of an ever-increasing number of published accounts of failed reform efforts. In 1996 I was asked to "revisit" the 1971 book and to add approximately 100 pages on what changed over 25 years. That book was titled *Revisiting "the Culture of the School and the Problem of Change"* (1996). Little or nothing had changed, and again I predicted that the reform movement would go nowhere. A carping critic could say I was right for the wrong reasons, but *no one* in the educational community has ever said that. Some people, perhaps many, may have thought I was too pessimistic, but they did not question the thrust of my diagnosis and conceptualizations.

2. Generally speaking, schools—in terms of their traditions and style of organization—are inimical to the creation and sustaining of contexts of productive learning. They are contexts of unproductive learning. None of this is comprehensible only by observing children and teachers in classrooms. Classrooms are embedded in an organization and system, tradition and culture, and undergirded by a conception of learning that insures that as students go from elementary to middle to high school their interest in and level of motivation for learning decreases. American psychology, particularly the field of child development, can be given credit for illuminating some of the variables that facilitate or hinder productive learning but primarily in preschool contexts markedly different from the features and goals of pub-

lic school classrooms; even then, contextual-organizational influences are only superficially described or analyzed. When it comes to the school-age child, developmental theory has little to say. When on those infrequent occasions psychologists meet to discuss the fecklessness of schools, they have never addressed this question: What are the features of a context of productive learning and to what extent are they honored in school classrooms? For an answer one has to go beyond an individual psychology and ask: Why are schools and school systems non-self-correcting institutions? That is a question the answer to which requires a theorizing quite different from existing psychological theorizing. If I take satisfaction from anything I have done in regard to education, it is the substance of my argument that schools have not and cannot change and improve until we take seriously the features of contexts of productive learning, features I have tried to describe and clarify in all of my books. I do not, thank God, suffer from a sense of grandiosity. My track record in prediction over the last 4 decades has been pretty good; which is why my 1998 book on the latest educational panacea is titled *Charter Schools: Another Flawed Educational Reform?* The conceptual rationale for that book stems directly from my 1972 book *The Creation of Settings and the Future Societies,* a book which says very little about schools even though it was in part written at a time when I was trying to make sense about why the scads of efforts to create and sustain new educational sites and programs died or fell far short of their mark. If it contained little about schools, it nevertheless was totally relevant to schools. Charter schools were not then on the horizon. I did not and could not have predicted that in 20 years charter schools—as clear examples as you will find of the creation of a new setting—would be one of the foci of a campaign debate between two presidential candidates (Clinton and Dole). That is why the charter school book has the pessimistic subtitle it does. Since the publication of that book, my pessimism has deepened.

3. There is no way that contexts of productive learning can be created and sustained for students (really for anyone) if that kind of context does not exist for teachers, which it does not. There is no way that desired change and improvement of schools can take place absent a radical transformation of the preparation of educators.

4. The history of American psychology has been characterized by (among other things) the value judgment that "basic" research is in some ultimate sense more inherently productive and worthy than "applied" research. There is a kernel of truth to that, but it is a kernel. The historical record demonstrates it to be at best incomplete and at worst inaccurate. Basic research is and should influence and direct applied

research. But it also has been and is the case that applied research has changed the course of basic theory and research.

All that I have said thus far has been prologue to a discussion of a paper I consider seminal for understanding a long festering "value" conflict within American psychology. It was not written by an applied psychologist but by a hard nosed "experimental" psychologist who has received every award such a psychologist can be given. I refer to Wendell Garner's 1972 paper titled "The Acquisition and Application of Knowledge: A Symbiotic Relationship."

Garner begins by noting that "There are many meaningful distinctions which scientists make concerning the research process—the acquisition of knowledge—and one is more important to one person, while another is important to another person. There are at least five meaningful distinctions that need to be made."

1. "A most common distinction is between pure and applied research. The term 'pure' is certainly intended to have a morally favorable connotation, while the term 'applied' may or may not have an unfavorable connotation, depending on the user. In these days, the alternative word 'relevant' is frequently substituted to give the right moral tone to the process. This distinction between pure and applied is one that I always have disliked, just because of the evaluative connotations of the words used. I feel more comfortable with the term 'basic' because it has less of this moralistic connotation, but it still produces a dichotomization that seems to me to miss the essence of the problem."

2. The second distinction is between general and specific research. "This distinction is more to my liking because it cuts more directly to the heart of the problem. Research should be evaluated on grounds of efficiency; and the knowledge obtained on grounds of breadth of utility. General knowledge is more valuable than specific knowledge, but this statement is true whether the knowledge has been obtained from pure or applied research. Pure research can be as specific as applied research, and the assumption that pure means general and applied means specific, even though frequently made, is tenuous at best."

3. A third distinction is between experiment and observation. "Experiments are what happens when the scientist manipulates the world in order to gain knowledge, while observation is what happens when the world is left as is, insofar as possible, but observed. Research can be of either type, however, and this is true whether the research is basic or applied."

4. "A fourth distinction is between laboratory and field research. Laboratory research is done under constrained circumstances, often leading to the study of phenomena in environments quite different from the natural habitat of the phenomenon. Field research is done under circumstances as like the natural habitat as is consistent with other goals of the scientist."

5. "A fifth distinction is between analytic and wholistic research. In analytic research the scientist tries to break the phenomenon to be understood into component parts, usually with the hope of studying the component parts separately. With the wholistic approach, the characteristics of the phenomenon are left as intact as possible while their nature is studied."[1]

Garner's argument does not rest on logical analysis alone. Selective attention, space perception, speech perception, pattern recognition, absolute judgments—for each of these psychological processes he indicates how basic research and theory were mightily changed by researchers confronting practical problems for which knowledge did not exist or was inadequate or simply wrong. It is not happenstance that in all of these examples it was practical, circumscribed problems the military encountered in World War II that affected basic research and theory. I cannot refrain from giving one example, that of space perception.

The topic of space perception is almost synonymous with the name of James Gibson these days, so when I want to talk about concepts and research in space perception, I cannot do so without talking about James Gibson's research. He was well established as an authority on perception before World War II, but his experiences during that war, working on some applied problems, changed the nature and direction of his theorizing considerably. Specifically, his experiences led him to his "ground theory" of space perception as described in *The Perception of the Visual World*. As Gibson describes experience in that book, he and some other psychologists were trying to understand how aircraft pilots estimate the distance to the ground when they are landing an airplane. He found that the

---

1. It is interesting that in 1959 a group of very eminent basic researchers (Garner, Hunt, and Taylor) in psychology were asked to prepare a report on research training in psychology. Garner was the senior author of that report. It is not happenstance that one of the points in that report is that the picture of the research process conveyed by research publications bears little relationship to what goes on from the beginning to the end of the process; that is not to call into question the validity of the results or the appropriateness of their interpretation but that the published report omits phenomenological, intuitive, social-contextual, even irrational features of the research process. The image of the researcher conveyed in publications is a fable.

traditional cues for depth perception, listed without fail in every introductory textbook on psychology, simply failed to explain the perception of
depth at the distances required in flying and landing an airplane. He furthermore found that experiments had to be done in the field to get at the
process, that laboratory experiments changed the nature of the process
too much. So into the field he went. It was from these experiments that
Gibson came to the conclusion that the prerequisite for the perception of
space is the perception of a continuous background surface—thus the
"ground theory" that evolved from this work.

The important point for the present article is that Gibson's whole way
of thinking about the problem of space perception changed when he was
faced with the problem of understanding how pilots in a real-life situation
actually land their airplanes without too many crashes. His theoretical no-
tions were changed by his contact with people and problems. He did not
develop these important ideas by a continuous relation to his previous
work. Rather, his research and thinking, according to his own report, took
a decided turn for the better as a result of this experience.

For Garner his argument is a glimpse of the obvious, the historically
obvious. Why was it not and still is not obvious, if you go by textbooks
in psychology? Garner provided the answer at the beginning of his paper: Psychology has been suffused with the value judgment that those
engaged in what was labeled pure or basic research were more worthy
than psychologists who were not.

The thrust of Garner's paper was not reflected in the thinking and
actions of those at the Boulder Conference, which shaped the substance and direction of modern clinical psychology. To them, clinical
psychology had to be suffused by the substance, ethos, and values of
basic psychology, which was the goose that laid the golden eggs. That,
potentially, clinical psychology could influence basic research issues
was inconceivable. The intellectual, informational highway went in
one direction. Such a highway has borne some important fruit, but it
has its impoverishing limitations. That is why Garner concludes his paper as follows:

> My point, however, is that the quality of the basic research is im-
> proved by communication between the basic research scientist and the
> people who have problems to solve. Thus, for scientists to engage in goal-
> oriented research, research aimed at solving problems already known to
> exist, is both to perform a service to society and to improve the quality of
> the basic research itself.
>
> I am not arguing that these real-life problems should be attacked as
> emergencies, since such research frequently leads to very specific infor-
> mation, of little use in solving later problems. The doing of good basic re-

search requires a reasonably long time perspective, and this requirement should not be forgotten as the scientist undertakes to talk to the people who have problems. But if the scientist will talk to people with real problems and, just as important, if those people will talk to those of us who are scientists, then both those who acquire knowledge and those who apply it will benefit. The relation is truly symbiotic.

In 1948 American psychology took a step that I will discuss in the next chapter, a fateful step that set the stage for radical changes in the field that few people anticipated and which centered around the basic–applied dichotomy Garner later wrote about. I refer to the Boulder Conference which put its imprimatur on the introduction of a modern clinical psychology into American psychology. Before World War II clinical psychology did not exist as a formal part of graduate training. It was a conference, as I shall indicate, that exposed the shortcomings of theory, research, and practice of American psychology, and it also mammothly reduced the possibility of a symbiotic relationship between American psychology and education in general and schools in particular. The virtually non-existent relationship between these fields, before and after World War II, is not comprehensible unless one understands the substance and consequences of the Boulder Conference: more specifically, how the values and traditions of American psychology were obstacles to a realistic appraisal of the alternate ways psychology could have a fruitful symbiotic relationship with a field like education containing problems and opportunities that could enrich theory and research in psychology. So, when I discuss how clinical psychology was brought into American psychology, it is not a detour; it gets at the heart of the matter of the non-symbiotic relationship between American psychology and schools.

CHAPTER 3

The Boulder Conference: American Psychology at a Choice Point

From the time more than a century ago when psychology became an academic discipline, psychological theory has always been about the *individual* psyche. That should occasion no surprise because the term *psychology* is defined as the study of the psyche: its development, structure, dynamics, pathologies, its underlying and/or concomitant relationships with the palpable brain. But, to continue with glimpses of the obvious, theorists did not have to be told that the psyche from the moment of birth was in constant transaction with a social surround. The features of that social surround—its contexts and history—served at best as an amorphous background for conceptualizing and understanding the individual psyche. Several things contributed to a relative lack of interest in the social surround. The first of these antedated the emergence of psychology as a formal, academic discipline; I refer to what is wrapped up in what we call the nature-nurture controversy. What features of the human psyche were genetically determined and explained individual and group differences? The proponents of nature marshaled their evidence which they interpreted as downplaying the role of social surround. The proponents of nurture had little or no quantitative evidence but rather based their counter arguments on what to them at the time was a gross downplaying of the fact that our society was so structured as to differentially allocate resources and opportunities to groups within the society.

The second thing, related to the first, had to do with controversies surrounding immigration, an arena of controversy today as it was in bygone eras. It is relevant here to note that every immigrant group that came to these shores was judged as a threat to the existing social fabric. There was no attempt to understand them in their terms, in the context of their cultures. They were seen as different, clannish, and inferior; their obligation was to become "Americans." Predictably, there were culture clashes (an understatement) in which it was quite clear that Americans were no more disposed to examine the nature of their own society then they were of the immigrants' cultures.

The third factor contributing to a most superficial conception of individual-societal transactions was the emergence of psychology as a formal discipline, a body of theory and research. It would be more correct to say that this factor has to be seen as a reflection of, as well as a contributing factor to, such superficial conceptions of the substance and power of those transactions. For the first 6 decades of the twentieth century psychologists riveted on the nature of human learning, an obviously central problem to a discipline whose goal is to explain how people develop and acquire the overt and covert mental and behavioral repertoires they do. But psychologists did not start with humans but rather with *rats*. I expand on and qualify this point in Chapter 5. I emphasize rats because research with that animal increasingly occupied theorists of learning. No department was lacking a well-equipped laboratory to house the animals. One reason for this strategy was the assumption that the fundamental laws of learning were as applicable to lower organisms as to humans. A second reason was that those fundamental laws had to be established according to the highest standards of scientific experimentation, methodologies, and the canons of objective, quantifiable evidence. Although the assumption and the strategy had its opponents and critics, animal learning was the major preoccupation of very eminent psychologists. Everyone getting a doctorate in psychology had to know the learning literature on much more than a superficial level.

I shall make no attempt to discuss the criticisms of the learning theorists and researchers because I have referred to them in order to make a point relevant to my assertion that psychology has long been an individual psychology that for all practical purposes has ignored or downplayed the structure and dynamics of the social-societal surround. And that point can be put in the form of these questions: Why did these researchers put only one rat in the maze? Why not two, three, or more? Is learning ever a solo affair? Are the "laws of learning" the laws of *asocial* organisms? Those questions were not asked, and I would argue they could not be asked because these theorists had absorbed a tradition in which the individual psyche was center stage and all else an off-stage, noisy chorus. In their personal lives they knew full well that that chorus was complex, impactful, and structured. They were not fools; they were highly intelligent, perceptive parents, citizens, and teachers. And, yet, they devoted their professional lives to studying the individual rat in a maze.

I said above that they had absorbed a tradition. The concept of absorption, unlike that of learning, suggests that the ways we think about things have sources of which we are frequently unaware. We pay them no mind, so to speak, because our minds did not have to pay for them in order for them to become part of our psyche. Let me illustrate some aspects of this point.

For several years before I retired, I would ask each entering class of graduate students this question: "Very briefly list the major influences on your life." There were 15 or so students, two fifths of whom were female. *In the first class no student listed their gender as a major influence; in the subsequent two classes two students, both female, listed gender.*

You could say that the students took their gender for granted, an obvious fact of their lives. Would we or they deny that it was, is, and will continue to be an organizing fact in their lives, shaping their psyches and how they view others and the social world? Would we or they deny that they had absorbed or assimilated stances, attitudes, expectations (and more) that not only defined their sense of personal identity but also their conception of the opposite sex? Would we or they deny that being male or female in America was radically different from being a Spanish or French or Italian or Russian male or female? Would we or they deny that being a male or female at Yale (and all that connotes) was a different cup of psychological tea than being a male or female in a community college? Would we or they deny that what they would define as their maleness or femaleness was not learned primarily in any formal way—as rats learn in a maze or students learn in a classroom—but in very subtle and yet impactful ways? Finally, would we or they deny that their society, or the slice of it in which they grew up, had structure, history, traditions, that it was not a randomly organized social, political, economic surround?

These students wanted to become psychologists, but they had a conception of psychology that was as superficial and incomplete as their conception of the origins and development of their gender. They took it for granted that psychology was not sociology, or economics, or political science, or anthropology, let alone history. Yes, they knew that psychology was a social science, but "social" primarily meant the interpersonal in dyadic or small group contexts, not in terms of culture, social structure, national history, regionalism, and religion. I mention religion because I had occasion (Sarason, 1993b) to examine 15 of the leading textbooks in child development for what they contained about the role that religious or non-religious background, beliefs, and adherence played. In 14 of the 15 books their indexes did not contain anything about religion. In the one book it did appear in the index. The reader was referred to a page containing one paragraph that essentially said nothing. Are religious or non-religious beliefs or ways of living without consequences in the psychological development of individuals? Can you understand America and Americans today and leave religion or the lack of it out of the picture? You, like me, may not be religious, but that is no warrant for ignoring that being religious or not is a difference that makes a difference in the lives of people. What would you think of a member of the Democratic party who wrote a book about contemporary America and never mentioned the Republican party?

I shall return to the issues raised in these introductory remarks at the end of this chapter. Let me now turn to when psychology changed; indeed it would be correct to say when psychology as a formal academic discipline very self-consciously *decided* to change. It assumed that it knew where it had been and where it wanted to go. The problem, as we shall see, was that where psychology had been remained unexamined, just as the graduate students "forgot" to list their gender as a major influence on their lives. What went unexamined had predictable but unintended consequences for the field; I see no reason to believe that those unexamined assumptions and traditions have received the scrutiny they require and deserve.

I shall list very briefly some background factors which set the stage for the Boulder Conference:

1. The attack on Pearl Harbor by Japan on December 7, 1941, made it almost immediately obvious that the World War II would be a long one and that its outcome—given that Europe was being overwhelmed by the Nazis—was by no means clear, let alone certain.

2. The casualty rate would be frighteningly high. In the course of the war approximately 15 million people in a total population of 150 million entered the armed services.

3. The existing Veterans Administration (VA) would be for all practical purposes totally unable to deal appropriately with such a casualty rate. Not only was the then-VA providing second- and third-class professional services and care, but its physical facilities tended to be in the middle of nowhere, unconnected with medical schools and centers of medical research.

4. A radically new VA would be confronted with the brute fact that the variety of professional personnel required to give a high quality of service and care were and would be in short supply, to indulge in understatement. And, in addition, such a quality of service and care demanded the development of a research base and program under the aegis of well-qualified professionals.

5. It was as predictable as the sun rising that the number of psychological casualties would be enormous. Prior to the war, clinical psychology as a formal program for practice and research did not exist in departments of psychology. If you got a Ph.D. in psychology and could not get a job in a university, you "became," as some did, a clinical psychologist—university positions were scarce during the Great Depression, and if you were Jewish, your chances were near zero, and they were certainly not better if you were a woman. (Parenthetically, can you write a history of American psychology and hardly if at all discuss religion, race, gender, and ethnicity in its pre-World War II phase? It was done, as I and others of my generation of psychologists can attest.)

6. During World War II plans were drawn for a total overhaul of the VA. In the case of the mental health professions (psychiatry, psychiatric nursing, psychiatric social work, and psychology), that would mean funding new and improved programs as well, to attract many more people to enter these programs; quality and quantity would be crucial. Money would not be a problem. (Yes, a grateful nation was prepared to spend whatever it took to insure quantity and quality of service, care, and research.)

7. Unlike the other mental health fields, psychology as organized and represented in the university before the war had a research tradition, not a clinically applied one. For psychology to develop and assimilate a field of clinical practice consistent with its research tradition would be as difficult as it was socially necessary.

The Boulder Conference took place over 2 weeks in 1949. It was funded by the VA and the new National Institute of Mental Health. All but a few of the major departments of psychology were represented, together with representatives from psychiatry, nursing, and social work. Victor Raimy (1950) from the University of Colorado edited and summarized the proceedings the following year.

Two things can be said about the psychologists who were participants. The first is that they came to the conference already persuaded that psychology departments should develop graduate programs in clinical psychology. Many of them had been in the armed services or had been intimately involved as consultants to different parts of those services. They had encountered thorny practical problems for which psychology as an organized body of theory and research was ill-prepared to deal with or with which they never had to deal. And, yet, at the same time they became convinced that psychology potentially had a good deal to contribute. The second thing was that they took for granted that in some ultimate sense psychology's contribution would be in the research contributions clinical psychologists would make, what was called the research-practitioner model. Psychology would play to its major strengths as basically a research endeavor. Researcher first, practitioner second. Put in another way: psychology would not, must not, change by incorporating programs in clinical psychology. Although no one doubted that psychology would change, and not in some superficial way, that change would in no way alter psychology's basic traditions; psychology was responding to social needs, it was reaching out to a society in ways unimaginable before the war, it could no longer be criticized as a field unconnected or irrelevant to that society.

What were the predictable problems the changes presented? What had psychology "learned" about the variables influential in human behavior? What had social psychology taught us that was relevant to the new course on which psychology was embarking? How might the change be influenced by features of American society and culture? Can institutional change ever take place without threats to or altering power relationships?

Let us start with a predictable problem that is at the root of the other questions I raised. It is a problem—really a set of related problems—that emerges from the fact that aside from three or four participants (I was one of them) the conference took it for granted that clinical psychology would be allied with medicine in general and psychiatry in particular. The internship for students in clinical psychology would be in a medically administered setting, and these students would be encouraged or required to take medical school courses in physiology, neuroanatomy, and psychopharmacology. Aside from three or four participants, all the others unreflectively favored the alliance. I say unreflectively because the institutional implications of such a decision were hardly discussed. In fact, one of those implications was that the training and education of clinical psychologists would be radically different from psychology students in other areas of psychology. Let me put it concretely as I did in my autobiography (1988).

> Why was I opposed to affiliating the Yale program with the VA? The general answer was that the rationale for clinical training advocated by the VA, and the fact that a significant number of students would be trained in the VA, were inimical to the development of potentials of this new field for the society generally; that is, in some ultimate sense, the public welfare. That the government had legitimate needs I, of course, did not question. But if the training rationale of the VA became dominant in the new field, it would be putting it in a conceptual, service, and professional straight-jacket, constricting its potentials at its birth.
>
> The specific answer to the question was in several parts. First, I considered it unduly restrictive that a VA trainee had to have his clinical experience in a VA facility. Second, that experience would give the trainee

almost no exposure to women. Third, it would give him no exposure at all to children. Fourth, it would restrict the trainee to two functions: diagnostic tester and researcher. Fifth, precisely because the VA facility would be under the control and direction of the medical-psychiatric community, the clinical psychologist would be a second-class citizen, a member of an underdeveloped colony, so to speak, of a remarkably imperialistic medical profession. The contrasting experiences I had at Worcester State Hospital and the Southbury Training School were not lost on me.

There was another part of the answer, which over the years became clearer to me and required that I put my money where my mouth was. If departments of psychology adopted the VA rationale, it meant that they were treating clinical students differently from those in other areas of specialization. For example, graduate students in social or developmental psychology are directly educated, trained, and supervised by faculty in their specialization. They are not farmed out to sites and psychologists outside the university, except in very limited ways, to obtain experience crucial to their specialization. That is precisely what the VA rationale entailed: the forging of the identity of mental health professionals outside the university; that is, the role models for the clinical trainee would not be the clinical faculty of the department. Those faculty would serve as consultants to the outside facility, which would mean from time to time they would visit and discuss with trainees and staff how things were going and what problems were being encountered, the frequency of visits depending on variables of distance and amount of consultant funds.

The university consultant was not, obviously, a clinical role model for the trainee. The process of consulting can be helpful and fruitful to both trainee and site, but that should not be confused with the functions of being an observable role model for clinical behavior. What did it mean to say that a department had a clinical faculty that had relatively little to do with the clinical student during the crucially formative internship experience? What did it mean to say that a clinical student would get a Yale degree while his identity as a clinician had not been forged at Yale? My questions had nothing to do with the quality of VA staff. Generally speaking, in those early years the VA psychologists were serious, mature people of quality. And, I must emphasize, my concerns in no way questioned the need of the VA for clinical psychologists. What I opposed was cooperating with a program that required that the student do his (mostly his) internship in a VA facility. And included in my criticism were departments of psychology that clearly had not thought through the educational and professional implications of what they were willingly agreeing to. Why agree to something in regard to clinical students that not in a million years would they apply to any other type of graduate student? (p. 273)

What made this situation more problematic was that the curriculum the Boulder Conference recommended meant that clinical students would not see a patient until his or her third year in a program. How do you learn to think about and do research on clinical problems when you have no or little clinical experience? Before the war graduate students in psychology engaged in research with a faculty member not very long after entering graduate school. If you quizzed faculty about the wisdom or underlying "theory" for such early immersion, they would in one or another way have said "you learn by doing," and they could point to a research literature justifying the practice. The fact is that the proposed curriculum was not in any deliberate way informed by this or that theory or conception of what makes for a context of productive learning. Yes, they were going by their past experience as individuals and psychologists, unaware that they were creating an educational context inconsistent with what they espoused and had done in the past. They were unprepared for what soon happened: When clinical students were put into the clinical situation, they had great difficulty in identifying and formulating a doable clinical problem to which could be applied what they had learned in courses in research design, statistics, and personality theory. Indeed, many clinical students found these courses to have been unhelpful. The reader may find it instructive to read the most frequently used textbooks of those times for these courses. To the student beginning "real" clinical work, these texts were minimally useful, if at all. It was not that these students were anti-scientific or anti-research. What disturbed them was how to do clinical research that was scientifically credible but not at the expense of diluting its clinical significance. More than a few students decided to do their dissertation research on a non-clinical problem, or one which was tangential, which did not have the features of messiness, conceptual ambiguities, and complexity of clinical problems.

I said earlier that clinical programs did not exist before the war and that said a good deal about the value judgments of faculties most of whose members saw as their obligation, if not mandate, to train basic researchers. In those pre-war days there were two classes of psychologists: basic researchers and applied psychologists. The label "applied" was not what you would call a badge of honor. It was not that applied psychologists were not respected but rather that in some ultimate sense what they contributed to psychological knowledge was of limited value. That kind of value judgment was then (as today) taken as a glimpse of the obvious. His name escapes me, but an eminent psychologist wrote a paper in which he said that the introduction of clinical psychology into the field ran the risk of "killing the goose that laid golden eggs," leaving the reader in no doubt that clinical psychology would divert attention away from the vigorous pursuit of basic research. He was well reflecting what many academic psychologists feared would happen. It should be noted that although all participants at Boulder were psychologists representing their departments, there were more than a few who had never had clinical experience and spoke often and long about the absolute necessity of insuring that clinical students assimilated the ethos of the basic research endeavor. They were mightily influential in regard to the curriculum the conference proposed, a curriculum one participant characterized as an acceptable 8-year graduate program.

What I am saying here is that although many academic psychologists of the time sincerely believed that psychology should be responsive to an obviously important social need, they truly feared that embracing this new field might well have negative, unintended consequences. That ambivalence is absent in the report of the conference's proceedings. But that ambivalence was articulated in the informal, social, interactions that took place evenings and weekends.

The fate of the strength of ambivalence depends both on the context in which it is elicited and the subsequent contexts which may sustain the initial strengths of the two poles or increase or decrease one of them. How would this ambivalence play out in departments of psychology as they developed and initiated clinical programs? It did not take long before controversy, polarization, and divisiveness came to characterize departmental atmospheres. Those features manifested themselves differently in different departments, of course, but I know of none where they were absent. There were cold wars and hot ones. Let us leave aside the fact that the introduction of clinical psychology in a department would in one or another way affect decisions about resources, space, and the "socialization" of a new "kind" of faculty and students, nitty-gritty matters which can alter the poles of ambivalence. And let us also leave aside the fact that when on a percentage basis the size of an organization is discernibly increased, problems arise, some of which exacerbate problems antedating the increase. Increase in size is never a neutral factor in existing power relationships.

Predictably, the most problem-creating factor concerned training for research, its substance and quality. What was an acceptable thesis topic? How well designed was it? Was the thesis problem amenable to appropriate statistical analysis? Was the problem embedded in or logically deducted from a clearly stated theory?

Henry Kissinger is reputed to have said that the reason academic controversies are so raucous is that so little is at stake. Well, there was a lot at stake in those days because it concerned a long past, traditions, and a commitment to an altered and ambiguous future. Those who had been intellectually reared in what psychology had been had good reason to worry, to be supervigilant in protecting the research tradition. That, I should emphasize, was not disputed at Boulder or for more than a decade thereafter by the clinicians seeking a place in the academic sun. They were not ambivalent. They "wanted in," and they saw no serious problems ahead.

What was there in psychological theory and research to alert the Boulder participants to predictable serious problems? That is not an unfair question to ask of a field concerned with the nature and vicissitudes of human beings in their transactions with each other and their social surround. Of what class of events was Boulder an instance? Was it a singularity in human affairs and history? A case of $N=1$? Let me start with two brief answers to these questions. The first is that Boulder contained all of the seeds of a clash of cultures, no different in theory and "real life" from a clash between an immigrant group and the established ones. The second is that there was precious little in psychological theory and research to allow psychology to label, to see, Boulder as an instance of a familiar and large class of instances all of which contained predictable phenomena. So let us start with the first day of the conference.

The Boulder conference began with a brief introductory statement by Dr. Robert Felix, director of NIMH, an energetic, idealistic psychiatrist who was "liberal" in that he vigorously advocated an important role for the clinical psychologist. He was more "liberal" in private conversation than in his public statements. Robert Felix (1988) was an astute politician-statesman, and he well knew how zealously the American Psychiatric Association guarded its leadership in the mental health arena. So let us listen to an excerpt from his opening remarks:

> If my experience as a medically trained person is worth anything, I would say that, although the best possible didactic and laboratory training is very necessary, the technique and attitudes learned in clinical clerkships, wardwalks, internships, and residencies leave a lasting impression and are the shapers of attitudes and concepts which, for better or for worse, last a lifetime.
>
> Although I recognize the dangers involved in discussing problems outside one's field of competence, nevertheless, because of my firm conviction regarding the critical role to be played by the clinical psychologist, I hazard to enumerate here a more detailed listing of the functions of the clinical psychologist as I see them. It seems to me that the diagnostic function includes much more than the determination of intellectual status. I, for one, in my clinical practice of psychiatry have never been too concerned about the numerical figure supplied me by a psychometrist to in-

dicate the intellect of a patient. Were this all I wanted in a diagnostic way, I would not use a psychologist at all. I can tell to my own satisfaction within reasonably broad limits, whether an individual is very dull, dull, of average intelligence, or above average.

If I wish a somewhat finer determination, I can either do my own intelligence testing or have it done for me by a psychological technician. There are other diagnostic data that I need and that the properly trained clinical psychologist is peculiarly prepared to: (a) supply me, (b) interpret for me, and (c) confer with me in planning the treatment of the case in the light of his findings. I refer to procedures for the evaluation of personality structure and dynamics and for the exploration and appraisal of vocational interests and potentialities. Much of this information does not come as much from test material as from the clinical experience and judgment of a psychological diagnostician—the properly trained clinical psychologist. As we move into the broad field of mental public health, however, there is another diagnostic role that the clinical psychologist must be adequately prepared to fill. It is essential that we know the size of our mental illness problem in order to lay strategy to attack it, and this means the proper identification of mental disorders that exist in a community undetected until a special effort is made to identify them.

The identification of mental illness or emotional problems in a community, while of scientific interest, is in many ways a disservice to a community if reasonable facilities are not available to deal with the problems discovered. This means the utilization of all therapeutic skills available and the development of potential skills to the point at which they can be useful and relied upon. The fulfilling of this function, it seems to me, involves the treatment of psychological disorders and the promotion of the mental health of the individual or the group by the utilization of appropriate and established psychological techniques and principles of therapy under psychiatric direction. As more and more clinical psychologists enter active working relationships, in hospitals, clinics, and elsewhere, the psychiatrists and other mental health personnel there have naturally developed some conflicts and problems centering about the specific functions of each. As this relationship continues, and each learns to know the other better and to understand his sphere of competence, and as all grow to understand the tremendous scope of mental health work, these conflicts will inevitably decrease. (pp. xvi–xvii)

My heart sank when I heard these remarks. Although he did not intend it (I think), he described the clinical psychologist as tester in the service of the psychiatrist. He also left no doubt that the clinical psychologist should receive his training in a psychiatric setting, that training being modeled on what he regarded as the virtues of medical-clinical training. Although he had the courage to say that there were and would be professional conflicts in regard to functions and roles, he had no doubt that the curative aspects of the passage of time, together with goodwill, would "inevitably decrease" these conflicts. That, I knew, was an indulgence of wishful thinking exacerbated by ignorance of the history, traditions, and realities of American medicine. I geared up for battle. That was not easy, because I was at the conference as a young upstart, a nontenured associate professor who was inevitably in awe of the well-known, influential participants who were there. I took a stand on several issues. Why was the proposed curriculum weighted in favor of such elective courses as neurophysiology, pharmacology, and neuroanatomy? Why should clinical psychology be tied to a setting that would not expose its members to such areas as mental retardation, schooling, criminality, physical handicap, and vocational planning and adjustment? What about prevention? Did not Dr. Felix rightly emphasize the importance of the community, early detection, secondary prevention?

These issues were raised and joined, and the outcome was predictable. Only a handful of people at Boulder took the position I did. I do not think I ever expressed it at Boulder, but I know the following thought crossed my mind: If the funding for the development of clinical psychology was coming from other sources with no strings attached, would clinical psychology move in the direction it was going? In some vague way, I knew that the conference was not confronting the age-old maxim that the hand that feeds you is the hand that can starve you, that money as an incentive is almost always powerful and frequently, unwittingly corrupting. And by corrupting, I mean that dependence, in whole or in part, on a funding source facilitates rationalizations that constrict one's thinking about alternatives more congruent with one's initial values, expectations, and capabilities. The problem is made more difficult when one is part of a professional field the internal policies of which reinforce the tie with the external funding source. By virtue of the nature and details of the origins of modern clinical psychology, it is not surprising that one of the characteristics of its development has been concern with achieving independence from and a kind of parity with psychiatry. This concern catapulted the field into the arenas of politics, legislation, lobbying, and public policy. It was a move to gain and preserve independence, not to change the conceptual substance of mental health policy. It was a move considered as good as and as financially deserving to "us" as to "them." It was not a move that challenged the underlying conceptions of public policy; for example, its focus on the individual organism deriving from an asocial psychology. Nor was it a move that stemmed from an attempt to identify past conceptual mistakes. Self-scrutiny has never been a notable characteristic of professional organizations. I should amend this statement, however, by saying that professional organizations do scrutinize their political-organizational mistakes, but only when their status is threatened. The recognition that a field may have based itself on faulty conceptions of the nature of its subject matter always reflects sea-swell changes in the society, affecting the field along a time dimension quite different from our usual experience of time.

What happened in the subsequent decades was predictable. Far from the battle between clinical psychology and psychiatry lessening, the conflict increased. It also widened in the sense that it went far beyond the confines of clinical settings and the two national associations to the courts and the halls of legislatures. And central to the conflict was who, professionally and legally, was entitled to practice psychotherapy? That became the all-engrossing issue. The conflict around that issue became exacerbated by the economic dynamics of the growth of health insurance: no less than the psychiatrists, the clinical psychologists expected and sought to be reimbursed for their therapeutic efforts as individual practitioners. No one has yet seen fit comprehensively to describe, dissect, and explain how the battle was fought. It was really a war with many battles in many places, costing large sums of money, involving thousands of people, many casualties, and an endless stream of articles, pronouncements, position papers, and vituperative rhetoric. Although no armistice has ever been declared, and certainly no peace treaty has ever been written, for all purposes the clinical psychologists have emerged as victors. They have established themselves as independent clinical practitioners.

Wars always have intended and unintended consequences. And it is always the case, especially in prolonged wars, that memory of their origins becomes faint or markedly transformed. So, for example, if you read the proceedings of the Boulder conference, it is apparent that the consensus was that the arena of psychotherapy should not be off limits to psychologists; that is, the issue was joined, albeit subtly and politely. But it is no less apparent that most, if not all, of the participants did not look with favor at the possibility that any significant number of clinical psychologists would become independent practitioners, and for two reasons. First, the major obligation of the clinical psychologist was to his or her discipline: to contribute to its substantive and methodological base. There were many ways one could do that, but common to all was the obligation to contribute to strengthening and improving the discipline. This obligation could not be discharged by the private practitioner unconnected with or isolated from research or training centers. Second, in the future as in the past, psychology as a basic or applied activity should be practiced in societal institutions devoted to the public welfare. Psychologists were not and should not be economic entrepreneurs. Indeed, the willingness with which psychology brought clinical psychology into its mainstream was in part because it was envisioned that these psychologists would work in public institutions: VA facilities, state hospitals, and community clinics. It is fair to say that the bulk of the participants at Boulder looked with disfavor and unease at the possibility that clinical psychologists, like the physician in medicine, would become private practitioners. You did not go into psychology to make money! If that sounds strangely idealistic, you must remember that most of the psychologists at Boulder were academics who had grown up in the field, a small field, when it was primarily ensconced in the university. The point of this is that the professional war between psychology and psychiatry did not begin and heat up around the issue of private practice or even salary differentials (which were large) but rather around the question, who owned psychotherapy?

I never envisioned a time when clinical psychologists would be in private practice to any significant extent. It was not that I was in principle opposed to private practice but that I felt that psychology's obligation was to society and its major institutions, to the reform and improvement of those settings in which the less fortunate of our society were to be found. It is probably the case that my attitude on this score derived from my political history. As I have said earlier, I was critical of psychology because its substantive concerns seemed so far removed from societal concerns. And I enthusiastically greeted the possibility that by becoming part of American psychology, clinical psychology could force the field to a more realistic understanding of our society. To me, clinical psychology, like any other organized field, had an explicit or implicit political agenda. It was inevitably embedded in and reflected a political context. It could not avoid using and being used by the political system. To me, clinical psychology was more than an endeavor to repair individual misery. It was also an endeavor to identify and influence institutional contexts that engendered and reinforced that misery. Clinical psychology had to be, broadly speaking, a social psychology. To the extent that clinical psychology tied itself to medicine and psychiatry, its ties to the social sciences becoming weak or nonexistent, it would become another in the category of lost opportunities.

Within a few years after Boulder, during which time psychologists began to flee from the VA and the state hospitals, it became apparent that psychiatry was beginning to lose its claim to ownership of psychotherapy. And in challenging that claim, the new issue in the professional war became the right of clinical psychologists to engage in private practice. This change in issues was facilitated by two interrelated facts. The Age of Mental Health manifested itself in many ways in many parts of the society, as any analysis of the mass media would confirm. Lying on the analyst's couch became a status symbol. And flocking in droves into graduate programs in clinical psychology were students who had assimilated the ideology of the Age of Mental Health. Psychotherapy was the strongest magnet attracting these students, and the personal satisfactions and financial rewards of private practice were slightly less strong magnets. Before World War II, clinical psychology did not exist as a field in American psychology. Within 2 decades after World War II, clinical psychology became the largest field. Before World War II, only a handful, so to speak, of psychologists were outside of and unconnected with the university. Within three decades after the war, a majority of psychologists were outside of and unconnected with the university.

If the funding for the development of clinical psychology had come from other sources with no strings attached, would clinical psychology have moved in the direction to which Boulder moved? Let me rephrase the question: If psychology had the opportunity to use its accumulated knowledge base to better understand and remediate problems of disordered living, personal misery, and wasted lives, what was the universe of alternatives it could and should have explored? The fact is that exploring that universe did not occur at all at Boulder because the initiative for the conference came from governmental sources (especially the VA) with their own vested, understandable, specific goal and what appeared to be a lot of money—more correctly, there was a lot of money and the *appearance* that those funds would be available for a long time to come. Psychology's stance at Boulder was reactive, not proactive. It was reacting and accepting one way of defining the goal: the so-called researcher-clinician model.

There is an irony here. What if we had asked the eminent learning theorists of the time this question: What have we learned from learning theory and research which is applicable to and important for the upcoming Boulder Conference? Is there a feature of learning and problem solving that the Boulder participants should be aware of? Aside from looking at us with staring disbelief at our display of innocence mixed with ignorance, they would have said one or both of two things: The question involved mixing apples and oranges, and that psychology was not yet at the point where it could provide anything resembling a helpful scientific answer. To the first part of their reply, we could have answered that we know that confusing apples and oranges is a no-no, but why do we put them in a class we call fruit? Obviously, they look, taste, and feel very differently, but somewhere in the history of the pursuit of knowledge someone provided a basis for putting them and a lot of different objects in the same class. To the second part of their answer, we could reply with a rhetorical question: Is it not strange that psychology has nothing to offer to *individuals* at Boulder who will be making important individual decisions that will have long-term effects, desired or undesired? I italicize individuals because that was what psychology had been studying.

The irony inheres in the fact that researchers of learning-problem solving, especially those using rats, employed the concept of *choice points.* Indeed, one eminent learning theorist said that when he tried to make sense of a rat's learning of a complicated maze, he imagined himself as a planning, decision-making rat encountering choice points.

Boulder was a choice point in the history of American psychology. But it was not a choice point that psychology had, so to speak, sought, just as the rat does not seek to be put in a maze. Yes, there were respected and influential people in psychology who worked hard to make the conference possible, but the decision to have and fund such a conference was made by individuals in different layers of government, many of whom were not psychologists but decisively influential. Why was it that nothing like Boulder took place in Canada, England, and France and other countries faced with similar consequences of the war? Why did psychology departments in those countries not embrace clinical psychology? It was not because these departments of psychology contained individuals with a weak sense of social responsibility or that they were opposed in principle to training clinical psychologists. They were not asked to embrace the new field. They had no choices to consider. They put up no opposition to developing such programs in other sites. Do we have any basis for saying that the clinical psychologists trained in those countries are less competent than those we have trained?

I am not rewriting history when I say that if psychology (departments and the national organization) wanted to be responsive to problems in the larger society, it had several alternatives. One was that it move to forge a relationship with education in general and schools in particular, and to do so in terms of both research and practice. What passed for educational research and practice in those days *by default* had become a responsibility largely of schools of education, a placement that ran counter to Dewey's 1899 plea that education and educational psychology be seen as a part of the social sciences. Then, as today, schools of education were at the bottom of the academic totem pole: criticized and devalued. Psychology viewed the educational arena as an applied one just as in the pre-war era it had judged clinical psychology. Historically (and ironically) psychology had more of an empirical base from which to move into the schools than it had in moving into the clinical-medical-psychiatric community. It should be noted that in his 1899 address to the American Psychological Association Dewey said that what was needed in education was a "middleman" whose role would be to translate and disseminate to teachers the findings and implications of psychological research relevant to practice. Dewey recognized the gulf between psychology and education and implicitly was predicting that if psychology did not deal with that gulf, the society would pay a high price. Was he ever right!

What I have said above I said at Boulder. *I was not arguing then against the development of clinical psychology but for the proposition that these new programs be encouraged and permitted to give students a meaningful exposure to research and practice in schools.* Why couldn't a clinically enriching and research stimulating internship year be in schools? But, as I said before, by the time of the Boulder conference the ties with medicine and psychiatry were firmly in place. I said what I had to say, I was listened to respectfully, and the conference went on to its predetermined agenda.

Another alternative is wrapped up in the question, What were psychology's actual and potential assets in regard to the prevention, the primary prevention, of personal misery, wasted potential, and intergroup conflict? What Boulder did was to base clinical psychology on a stance of repair, the so-called medical model in which problems occur and then you try to repair them. You can call such repair efforts as instances of secondary and tertiary prevention but repair they are.

No one who engages in repair needs to defend what they do. When something is wrong with you, you need, expect, and deserve a competent clinician. But one thing is for sure: over time, repair does not hold a candle to primary prevention. One reason I took the stand I did at Boulder was that I regarded schools as sites both for primary prevention and repair. I do not want to convey the impression that the issues surrounding the two alternatives (schools and primary prevention) were clearly formulated by me. What was clear was that there were alternatives that in some ultimate sense would not mire psychology in professional wars, in turf and status conflicts within psychology itself, and in the worst aspects of market economics.

If I had to state in the most succinct way why psychology took the road it did, I would say that clinical psychology was tailor made for an American psychology that riveted on the individual. If you think that is an exaggeration or an overgeneralization, I suggest you peruse the leading texts on personality theory in the prewar period and for the decade or so after the war. Allport's and Murray's books had many stimulating virtues, but they were theories of the development, structure, and dynamics of individuals. But can any theory of personality be independent of the history, structure, and dynamics of the local and national society and their cultures? Let me be concrete. Does it make any theoretical sense—is it theoretically justified—to explain the personality of any Boulder participant and not seriously take into account that he or she was (possibly with one or two exceptions) born and reared in America? What do we mean when we say that Americans are different from the French, English, German, Russian, or Serbian people, just as they are in no doubt whatsoever that they are different from Americans? We and they know that by virtue of being born and reared in our countries we have absorbed into our psychological bloodstream axioms, attitudes, world views, self-views, an absorption so thorough that we are unaware of the contents and processes of that absorption. I have never met Americans who after their initial trip abroad were not startled by the recognition that they were Americans and how American they were! They found it difficult to pinpoint wherein their Americaness inhered, but they now knew that how they thought, felt, and acted "back home" was inexplicable apart from having been born and reared in America.

Personality and child development theory say next to nothing about this matter. They are general statements specifying how certain variables play basic roles in the emergence and vicissitudes of psychological content, structure, and dynamics. The concept of an external environment is taken seriously, of course, but it is a local, restricted environment consisting, among other things, of Americans unaware of how their Americanness is being transmitted to others as if what is right, natural, and proper is independent of country and era. A telling exception brings us back to immigration. We are used to hearing that we are a nation of immigrants, and we take pride (as we should) that immigrants were welcomed to these shores. What we are not told and do not like to hear is that the welcome mat had and has its revealing downside: Their new country expected and pressured immigrants to become Americans in dress, appearance, thought, language, values, and outlooks. If those expectations were grossly insensitive and unrealistic, as soon became apparent, the focus shifted to the children of immigrants and the schools of the time (before and after compulsory education became universal) and saw their mission to be to insure the Americanization of children of immigrant parents. Probably several thousand novels and plays have been written about the sources of intergenerational turmoil and conflict in those families. Nobody had to tell these immigrant families that what was at stake was the brute fact that their children would be estranged from them, that their children would become unfamiliar to them, that their ways of thinking and acting would over time show less and less remnants of the "old country," that they would become American while the parents remained what they had always been. If parents did not understand the nature, force, and ubiquity of the Americanization process, they did understand that their children were being transformed into an unfamiliar breed. These parents understood something about being an American, a *real* American, that personality and developmental theorists have never understood or have taken account of: The process of Americanization is one that is bedrock for understanding Americans because that process suffuses all aspects of psychological functioning, however silent and unlabeled those consequences become. Personality theories are intended to be applicable to all people everywhere. Theorists, of course, know that countries differ in how the variables in their theories get played out but *they rarely discuss their research findings in terms of a "country variable," a crucial and universal variable.* Theories are tested for two purposes: To determine the degree of validity of the theory and to improve it in one way or another not least of which is to add new variables which enlarge the significances of the scope of the theory. Just as in the industrial arena a new product goes through a Model A ⟶ Model B ⟶ Model C process, personality theories are expected to traverse a similar self-improvement process, an enlarged capacity to explain and interrelate psychological phenomena. By ignoring the "country variable," personality and developmental theorists are robbed of the possibility of incorporating a variable which may put psychological phenomena in a new or altered light.

So what does this have to do with Boulder? I said earlier that the Boulder participants had no basis in psychological theory and research to conceptualize what the conference was an instance of. Nor could they ask this question: in regard to whatever decision we make, should we not take into account that we are deciding at a particular time in a particular country which has a distinctive history, culture, political system, and economic values and system? You did not have to ask the participants if they were Americans and if they thought that what they were deciding would be influenced by that glimpse of the obvious. Their answer would have gone like this: it is the best of American tradition to do whatever needs to be done, to use all of its resources, human and material, to give the best of service and care to those who have been psychologically and bodily injured in a war fateful for America and the rest of the world; therefore, as a field of scientific inquiry psychology is obligated to play a role, to make a distinctive contribution that will benefit society and the field. That was a sincere answer, but it was an egregiously incomplete one in that it neither implied nor said anything about what was distinctively American and how that distinctiveness was in varying degrees and ways in all of us at the conference. So, for example, all of us had lived through the Great Depression and some of the older participants had experienced the shock of the 1929 stock market crash, both of which forced people to ask: How could this happen in America? What allowed us to be blind to those catastrophes? What had we been unreflectively assuming about America that was wrong? Why did we see our world in such simplistic and unrealistic ways? How much must we change our thinking to prevent crises? Is it enough to say as President Coolidge did that "The business of America was business"? If we know anything about the decade before World War II, it is that the psychology of Americans was changed, a degree of change unimaginable before 1929. To my knowledge only one American psychologist saw the significance of these catastrophes for psychology, and that was J. F. Brown (1936) in his book *Psychology and the Social Order.* One does not have to agree with Brown's embracing theory—heavily influenced by Marxism—to appreciate his effort to indicate how being American meant that you saw yourself and the world in distinctive ways.

If, again, I had to state succinctly the central omission at Boulder, I would say that it was as if to its participants the "outside world" had no distinctive traditions, structure, dynamics, and ideology. They, of course, would have denied this, but the fact is that they proceeded as if they were ignorant of the obvious or, more likely, that the obvious was beyond psychology's domain. What they could not see was that from its earliest days the field was almost exclusively concerned with individuals in at best a very circumscribed social context. It was a very circumscribed outside world. That is not at all to suggest that such an emphasis was not productive of important knowledge of human behavior but that it was very incomplete in terms of theory, research, and practice. It was an incompleteness that in its silent way virtually guaranteed that they were unprepared to give due weight to decisions which would require confronting and being embroiled in American society and culture as never before. I should also note that at approximately the same time of the Boulder conference, a similar conference of American psychiatry under the same governmental agencies took place. What I have said about Boulder applies to that conference as well. If anything, the incompleteness was more evident.

The issues I have raised were long a preoccupation of anthropologists interested in culture and personality. What are the relationships between culture and personality, and how do those relationships vary and why in different cultures? For example, was Freud's assumption that the oedipal conflict was universal tenable? Did certain child-rearing practices have the same predictable consequences as this or that theory asserted? What did these studies of exotic cultures say about personality and life-long development in American culture and society? The field of culture and personality was a very small one before World War II. It was a small and vibrant field in anthropology. The absolute number of anthropologists concerned with culture and personality was very small, and this in anthropology departments which were among the smaller departments in the university. Nevertheless, the publications of the culture-personality anthropologists received a good deal of attention and respect, if only because they stimulated discussion of American society and culture. As a direct consequence of World War II and the assumption by America of guardianship of numerous South Pacific societies about which relevant federal agencies, military and civil, had neither knowledge nor understanding, anthropologists became, so to speak, hot commodities both for research and administration. The field of culture and personality grew in terms of interest and number within anthropology and psychology. At the end of a decade or so after the war, that interest and growth ceased; in fact, in psychology the field of personality theory and research lost much of whatever central focus and identity it once had. It became an unrelated, balkanized melange of topics.

There are two reasons I have brought up culture-personality relationship. The first is that the ethnographies of the anthropologists were valiant attempts to understand individuals in terms of the main features of the society: its political and economic systems, educational practices, social stratification, religion and cosmology, gender roles, kinship system, climate and geography, rites of passage, and more. These features were not conceptualized as circumscribed variables but as parts of an encompassing mosaic into which the individual was born, lived, and died, a mosaic without which understanding the psychological makeup of the individual would be incomplete or wrong. That is why so many ethnographies are so long; they aimed to see things whole. That they inevitably fell short of the mark is not the point. The point is that they did not seek to understand individuals in the narrow way to which American psychologists are accustomed.

The second reason has to do with why psychology lost interest so quickly in the transactive relationships between culture and personality, and why interest in them discernibly waned in anthropology. I do not pretend to know all the different reasons for the waning. Certainly one of them was that funding for that kind of research began to dry up. After World War II the research communities in all parts of the university believed that funding and increases in funding would be the order of the day into a distant future. That belief was held by almost all Boulder participants. By virtue of my early political affiliations and having lived through the Great Depression, it is understandable if I considered such expectations as at best rampant optimism and at worst a manifestation of an unbelievable ignorance of our economic system and American history. (I suppose that I am a textbook case of what I say in these pages. It would not surprise me if I was the only participant at Boulder who knew what it was when my parents had no food for us. Anyone interested in my personality dynamics would be grievously wrong if they did not appropriately weigh the intimate relationship between me and America during the Great Depression.)

An additional, and perhaps the most important part of the answer, is that the culture-personality issue did not lend itself at all easily to psychology's emphasis on clear-cut research designs and quantitative analysis. If you take seriously what is involved in thinking about, let alone investigating, how individuals absorb aspects of the larger society, you realize two things at least: America is a very complex society, and to pursue the issue requires knowledge that you have not been exposed to in your graduate education. The university is a balkanized community of parochial departments, and in this age of increasing specialization the boundaries among departments are not porous. (Need I tell readers who are faculty members in a university about non-porous boundaries *within* departments?)

Anthropologists studied small, usually encapsulated societies, devoting at least a year to their efforts. But let us not gloss over the fact that the word *studied* meant living in that culture 24 hours a day, everyday—a kind of total immersion. To study American schools in that way for the purpose of enlarging our understanding and conception of sources of individual development and behavior would take a lot of time. Given the publish or perish caveat so sedulously observed in our universities, no academic psychologist without tenure is likely to tackle the problem. And by the time you achieve tenure you are likely to want to continue to do the kind of research which got you tenure. I can illustrate the problem of time by asking: Why have there been so few longitudinal studies? The answer has nothing to do with the importance of such studies, an importance no one denies. Indeed, there are many psychologists who know that a longitudinal methodology would be the very best way to study what they are interested in.

It would be very wrong to say that American psychology has no interest or stake in longitudinal studies. It would not be wrong to say that American psychology has no interest in schools if by interest you mean a willingness to understand the traditions and culture of schools. Such a willingness would be testimony to the recognition that in addition to being a context for human learning and development, schools shape attitudes, relationships, and understandings (right or wrong) of the world students experience. It would be testimony that, like anthropologists, psychologists seek to understand schools because they are complicated contexts in which everyone in the society spends years; and to gain such understandings they are ready to immerse themselves to a meaningful degree in the school culture. You cannot understand the school culture from your academic office and laboratory, let alone by theories of learning derived from studies in contrived rather than naturally occurring situations.

The next two chapters discuss the reactions to and the interpretations of the murders in 1999 of students and a teacher by two very troubled boys at Columbine High School in Littleton, Colorado. That tragedy could have been an opportunity to deepen people's comprehension of the school culture and its regularities, raising the question: What do students experience and learn in school besides subject matter? That opportunity was missed in a welter of suggestions that diverted attention away from the school itself. And among all the professionals who offered explanations and suggestions, psychologists, as individuals or their professional organization, essentially had nothing to contribute except some generalizations about mental health services. In the case of Columbine High School that was a clear case of misplaced emphasis. For my purposes in this book, the significance of the Boulder Conference is that it reinforced and widened the gulf between American psychology and education. Of course, Columbine said a lot about mental health issues, but we knew about those issues before the tragedy. By riveting on those issues, however, we cannot entertain the possibility that our schools have features that have untoward and unintended consequences for the psychological development and status of all who are in schools. Those consequences are far less obvious than dramatic incidents of violence, but they are frequent and fateful in the lives of individuals and the social health of the society. For the most part they are silent, unrecognized consequences.

Columbine consisted of two tragedies, the obvious one concerning the two murderers and those they killed. It was not the classical tragedy where we know the starting point in which the grisly ending is contained and foretold, an unfolding of the inevitable, a process and dynamic the ancient Greek dramatists so brilliantly understood and described. From my standpoint there was a second, somewhat more classic, tragedy in that the killings aroused a riveted national audience to ask: How can such killings be prevented in the future? Where have we gone wrong? Who and what are to blame? Once I got over the horror of the affair I found myself saying, "We are fated to learn nothing. There will be school killings in the future, as much or more school violence of different types and degrees, we will appease malevolent fate in this or that way, and when our actions prove ineffective, we will come up with new appeasements." I stayed glued to the TV, especially any program where experts proclaimed their understanding, diagnosis, and course of preventive action. I read as much as I could of discussions in the mass media, again especially articles by educators, psychologists, and similar professionals. And I learned what I feared I would learn: vague generalizations, platitudes, bromides, superficialities, irrelevancies. And the worst offenders (to me, of course) were educators and psychologists because what they said betrayed their ignorance of schools, especially high schools. The ignorance of psychologists did not surprise me, but that of the educators did until I recalled a point I had emphasized in my 1971 book *The Culture of the School and the Problem of Change:* Generally speaking, school people have a very incomplete and distorted sense of how the culture of the school shapes their lives and that of students. Schools, like other institutions, seek to socialize their inhabitants, with the intended result that they will regard what exists as right, natural, and proper, and that alternative ways of thinking about learning, organizational structure, and purposes are regarded as alien, off limits. Columbine was an opportunity, an unfortunate one, but it quickly became a lost one, despite subsequent killings and other forms of school violence. As the eminent philosopher, Yogi Berra, said, "It's deja vu all over again." And it was also Mr. Berra who in regard to how to go from here to there said, "When you come to a fork in the road, take it." The educational reform movement in the post World War II era seems to have encountered many forks, with the result that it still is trying to determine how to go from here to there.

CHAPTER 4

American Psychology, the Man from Mars, and Columbine High School

What are the ways posterity's judgments get reflected in its historical accounts? That question rests very solidly on (at least) several taken-for-granted assumptions. The first is that the received past is more complicated than it was thought; the past should always be revisited, judged, and revised in small or large ways. In any past era, individuals and collectivities possessed world views containing, again in small or large ways, self-fulfilling, self-serving prophecies; or they held unexamined axioms and values the validity of which was dubious or simply wrong on factual or social-moral grounds; or they had little or no doubt that posterity's judgments would be benign; they, like us today, were prisoners of their time; or all of these. The obligation of history, especially of the national genre, is to seek knowledge and understanding of the past on the basis of an implied superiority of knowledge and, it is hoped, wisdom, even though the historians know (or should know) that their contribution will be revisited and revised by their posterity. History is not written, it is rewritten. History does not literally repeat itself. Generally speaking, history is an "again and again" account of the assets and deficits of the imperfect human mind in a social world in which "lessons" are "learned," forgotten, and then learned again. (The attraction, among many other things, of religion's heaven is that re-learning will not be necessary, mortal time has ended.)

So how will posterity judge American psychology, which in its organized form celebrated its centennial in 1993? I can assure the reader that I am quite aware of the pitfalls my answer encounters. For one thing, psychology in its organized form is comprised of well over 150,000 members clustered in more than 50 interest groups. Even though I restrict myself in this book to those interest groups primarily concerned with human behavior in personal and social situations, I will still be characterizing most psychologists. For another thing, I know that by generalizing I am not doing justice to a very complicated diversity of interest groups. Also, I know that by passing judgment on what psychology has been as well as predicting how posterity may judge the field, I am but one person whose attitudes and values may not be shared by others who, unlike me, have not lived 81 years of the twentieth century. Finally, having said all that, I feel justified in indulging the right to be found wrong even though I will not be around when posterity's judgment will be handed down.

Psychology is by its ethos and educational-training programs an ahistorical field. I am reminded here of when in the late 1940s the American Psychological Association began to certify graduate programs. The visiting team talked with students and faculty. One of the team, whom I knew well, said he was bothered by a student's response to the question: "Have you read Köhler's *The Mentality of Apes* (1925)?" The student, who in later years became president of the American Psychological Association, replied, "That's old hat. No one reads that anymore." I would not be surprised if all but a handful of graduate students today would reply, "Who is Köhler?" For several years before I retired in 1989, I asked classes of all graduate students if they had ever read anything by William James. No one said yes. I would then ask the same question about John Dewey. One student said yes, and he was one who had shifted from education to psychology; except for that one student, no one knew who John Dewey was. Of course, no student knew that James and Dewey were founding fathers of the American Psychological Association. That William James almost single-handedly created and sustained what today we call cognitive psychology is not a dry fact, nor is it a dry fact that after he wrote his books on religion and pragmatism, psychology pigeon-holed him as a philosopher, and that was not praise. Nor is it a dry fact that Dewey's paper (1963) on "The Concept of the Reflex Arc in Psychology" exposed the narrowness of an emerging behaviorism. That paper is as relevant to psychology today as it was back then. In the 1960s we were used to hearing that you could not trust anyone over 30 years of age. That's the way psychologists regard the history of their field.

To give the reader some idea of the point of this chapter, I start not with what is clearly a complex psychological problem but rather one that has come to occupy the attention of the medical-scientific community and every society on earth: AIDS. No one blames that community for initially not recognizing that the AIDS virus was not like any other virus it had encountered. Early on there were critics who said that it was wrong, misleading, or misguided to associate the virus primarily with male homosexual activity; the course and spread of the virus precluded such a simple explanation. Where and how did the virus originate and spread? That question went beyond the confines of the medical researcher and clinician who were diagnosing, treating, or experimenting with treatment of a patient or group of patients. It was an epidemiologist who found that the AIDS virus was not an American phenomenon, that its occurrence and spread varied greatly from country to country. (Epidemiologists are housed in schools of public health and are viewed by medical researchers as a type of applied researcher whose statistical group findings are not all that helpful to those who spend their days with individual patients.) There were other factors which made a complex picture even more so. One was the belated recognition that because the public had been given the impression that AIDS was associated with homosexual practices, and given public disdain for homosexuals, many of those who were HIV positive or who showed the symptoms of AIDS were reluctant to be identified, a psychological factor that could contribute to the spread of the disease. AIDS was not the run-of-the-mill transmittable diseases. It had consequences of a social, legal, economic, and social-ethnic nature. It had also political and governmental repercussions. Political because by the time the spreading incidence of the disease was comprehended, its economic and public health implications made it obvious that governmental outlays for research and treatment would have to be dramatically increased. It also galvanized action to pressure the Federal Drug Administration to change its rules and procedures for determining when new medications could be approved for use by physicians. If you had AIDS and had learned that there were new drugs in the FDA pipeline for which further evaluation was deemed necessary to protect recipients from untoward side effects, in the face of an early death you would want the opportunity to gamble, to try anything even though it fell far short of certainty in outcome. Still another factor was the ethical one: How do you justify the extraordinary cost of the new and approved drugs, which meant, of course, that the large majority of those with the disease were not able to be treated with those medications? And AIDS had implications for international relations because there were parts of Africa and other countries where the incidence of HIV and AIDS was somewhat astronomical. AIDS was no respecter of national borders or oceans; the much heralded emergence of the "global village" had its price. AIDS is not like chicken pox, polio, or other infectious diseases. In its potential to affect whole societies, it is similar to what the bubonic plague had been in the thirteenth and fourteenth centuries.

There are things to be learned from the AIDS story. First, when a field is confronted with new and puzzling phenomena, the odds are very high that it will seek to understand them in ways that were productive in the past. Second, that understanding will, for varying lengths of time, turn out to be very oversimple. Third, the approach to the problem will markedly downplay the ways the phenomenon has cause and effect transactions with existing social attitudes, different interest groups, and a host of other types of collectivities and institutions. Fourth, predicting the course or spread of a new phenomenon considered a threat to the public welfare has a large margin of error. We do and should attempt to predict the future. I would say the word *attempt* is wrong, if only because as organisms born into and reared into a social world, we are socialized to predict, it is part of our second nature. If that is so, and I consider that a glimpse of the obvious, it is also the case that as demonstrably imperfect organisms, our hour-to-hour, day-to-day, month-to-month, year-to-year predictions are, to indulge understatement, far from possessing robust validity. And that is especially true when we make predictions in regard to phenomena that are strange or puzzling.

I did not start with AIDS because it is in all respects analogous to what I shall be discussing in the pages which follow. But there are correspondences most of which can be summed up in two statements: The problem is far more complicated than was initially thought. The more you know, the more you need to know. Knowing cause (or causes) is not to be confused with knowing its (or their) percolating consequences in a world we far from fully comprehend and we should be humble enough to say that we do not control. One of the reasons posterity is the cruelest of critics is that it relentlessly exposes how those in the past ignored what was and is knowable and took their world, as they saw it, for granted.

In April 1999, two high school students entered their school, shot and killed 15 students and one teacher, and then killed themselves. For the next several weeks what took place in Littleton, Colorado, occupied every form of communication medium, and from the president on down officialdom proclaimed their horror, concern, and a call for action. Within days after Littleton the media reported that schools in other states had suspended students who were found to have guns or had been heard saying that they were going or wanted "to blow up" their school. Several weeks after Littleton a student in Georgia shot several students in his school. At the time I am writing this (May, 1999) hardly a day goes by without a newspaper or a TV program referring to Columbine High School in Littleton. It was noted (but not stressed) that one reason Littleton gripped and held national attention was that it served a middle-class, if not affluent community in a Denver suburb. One Black spokesman said that if it had occurred in an urban school, it would have received less sustained attention because the incidence of criminal attack by students on other students and school personnel have been and are, relatively speaking, very high there. Predictably, professionals considered to have expertise about schools and youth were asked to express their opinions: educators, psychologists, psychiatrists, social workers, law enforcement personnel, and more. And if you go by letters to the editor, op-ed columns, call-in TV shows, and televised focus groups of parents, there was a high degree of overlap between the experts and non-experts. Although everyone had some kind of a very general explanation for what Littleton signified about American society and culture, they had at least one suggestion about what might be done to prevent to some degree at least recurrences of the grisly disaster.

1. Make it more difficult, if not impossible, for below-age young people to get or buy guns.

2. Metal detectors should be employed at the schools' entrance.

3. Parents who possess firearms should keep them under lock and key.

4. Parents should know what their children are thinking, doing, reading, or watching on TV and the internet. Better communication between parents and children is needed.

5. School personnel should be far more sensitive to and knowledgeable about student cliques, the way others perceive and judge them, and, where indicated, school personnel should take preventive or corrective action. Students know well who are the marginal, frowned-upon, alienated individuals, the potential "troublemakers."

6. Ours is a society in which violence, shootings, killings are daily fare on movie and TV screens. Film makers and network officials should be discouraged or in some way punished for making such violent fare.

7. We are paying the price for a historic transformation in the stability and overseeing functions of the nuclear family. Youth are increasingly on their own, and their parents have little idea what their children are doing, thinking, and planning.

I said earlier that no one blames the medical and public health communities for initially being mystified, even confused, about HIV and AIDS. In regard to violent and criminal behavior, however, Littleton is not a new social phenomenon. School violence has dramatically increased in the post World War II era. However narrowly you may define psychology, you will not say that the definition is irrelevant to comprehending the Littleton series of events (and its immediate aftermath). Indeed, school psychologists, whether connected to Columbine High School or not, volunteered or were asked to be available and helpful to students, families, and school personnel; psychology has something to contribute in terms of therapeutic procedure and knowledge. If that is the case, you are justified in asking: What can psychology tell us about the sources of increase in school violence in the post World War II era? Repair is one thing, prevention is another.

As prologue to answering that question, let me very briefly discuss an instance or series of problems in which psychologists (and similar types of professionals) have played an important role based on their rather clear comprehension of why these problems occurred and would increase. That comprehension went as follows:

1. World War I changed everyone and everything and so did World War II.

2. Too many people who entered the armed services were personally and intellectually vulnerable to or disabled by their experiences.

3. Marriages and families during the war were subject to near intolerable strain either because of sheer worry about possible injury or death of their loved ones in the war. It was a long war.

4. Veterans would find returning to a normal civilian role difficult either because they had changed or the country had changed or, far more likely than not, both had discernibly changed.

5. Existing facilities for helping the returning veterans were totally inadequate, and the existing medical-mental health system would literally have to be scrapped and a new one created.

What has been called the Age of Mental Health had its infancy during World War II; several years after the war's end saw the creation of National Institute of Mental Health, the Kinsey report on male sexuality, Leonard Bernstein's Age of Anxiety concerto, and the new and dramatic influence of psychoanalysis in universities where heretofore that theory and therapy had been given little serious attention. The Age of Mental Health was at the time characterized in the title of an article by a leading psychiatrist in a national magazine: "What This Country Needs are Good Five Dollars an Hour Psychotherapists." The upward climb of the divorce rate began soon after World War II.

In contrast, there were other significant developments that received far less attention by the mental health communities: the rise of juvenile gangs and delinquency, and associated with that were over-crowded, educationally inadequate, understaffed schools. Only one agency saw the seriousness of the situation and that was the Ford Foundation which supported action programs in several cities. It was that Ford Foundation initiative that later was the basis of the federal war on poverty programs. At the same time, but unconnected to that initiative, American schools became objects of scathing criticisms for their perceived anti-educational, non-intellectually stimulating features, their watered down curricula, their least common denominator approach to standards, their inability and resistance to change. And then, of course, the Supreme Court's 1954 desegregation decision and the violence, verbal and physical, that soon erupted in, to name but two, Louisiana parishes and Little Rock—viewed by millions on TV—escalated the frequency and strength of the violence that was on or just below the surface of many of those students and adults who got caught up in the bitter conflicts.

There is a myth that the 1950s were "silent" and conformist. It is a myth with no historical justification. Whatever became clear in the 1960s was evident in a muted way in the earlier decade. And that was no less true in schools, especially high schools, than elsewhere in the society. Yes, it showed up differently in urban and suburban schools, but it showed up in both. From 1945 until today, violence of one kind or another has been a feature in and around schools. It is true that the shootings in Columbine High School and several other schools in the 6-week period beginning April 20, 1999, have no match in the previous years following the end of World War II, but it is very misleading to conclude that violence in and around schools is a recent development. Shootings, of course, are contained in any taxonomy of violence. Actions intended to be harmful take many forms in schools and related sites. You do not have to be a perceptive observer to see such forms in hallways crowded with students, in lunch rooms, on school buses, on playgrounds, in boy-boy, boy-girl interactions, and in school sports. It was when I was on my school football team that I learned that some of our opponents took obvious satisfaction in using their arms and legs in ways that were illegal and harmful if they thought the umpire would not detect them. And that was no less true for some members of my team.

Over the centuries our legal system has developed a taxonomy for violence and the punishments that go with its different offenses. It is interesting that the taxonomy and especially the punishments are not applied to minors except under very special conditions (which are increasing in number). No one has seen fit to develop a taxonomy for violence in and around schools, and there are, as a consequence, no barometers by which to know whether the incidence of this or that form of violence is rising, declining, or hardly varies. Given the ahistorical stance, the absence of such barometers make it too easy to say that there was a time before the sizzling 1960s when school violence was rare—maybe not in urban schools but certainly in suburban ones. Twenty-five years ago the superintendent of the most affluent Connecticut community in what may be the most affluent county in America called me to say there had been a stabbing and would I come down and try to be helpful. I said yes. I never heard from him again. Beginning 10 years ago several other high schools in that county asked to have a police officer assigned to their schools. Violence in schools has long been a topic school administrators do not like to become an item for public discussion. Littleton has changed that; in the weeks after Littleton, school systems around the country have organized task forces to come up with ways to prevent school violence. And by violence they mean what happened in Littleton. If that is understandable, it is also a case of missing the forest for the trees. One reason for this is that the imagery associated with Littleton is of the most extreme and rare form of violence, a form as shocking, as impossible to ignore, as it is puzzling. Of course, it is puzzling, but so is the fact that the presence of a policeman at the high school before the shootings was not uncommon in Columbine. Are there features of the culture of schools, especially high schools, which stimulate and sustain a variety of forms of violence? On what theoretical, let alone empirical, grounds should one be puzzled by the incidence of these forms of violence? *Granted that it would be an egregious mistake to explain these forms only in terms of the culture of schools, are we not obligated to try to fathom what it is about that culture that sets the stage, so to speak, for the appearance and incidence of such forms?* If we seek to decrease the incidence of such forms—there is no way one can totally prevent their occurrence—should we not understand better than we do why these forms of unacceptable behavior occur in schools? Not only in its most extreme form but in its less lethal forms as well? If you want to prevent shootings, that goal might be achieved, as some have suggested, by putting metal detectors at the entrance of every school. Is that suggestion, or ones similar to it, the "lesson" we are to draw from Littleton? Or is the lesson far more complicated, far more nuanced, far more serious in its educational implications, far more fateful in some ultimate sense for the society?

So let me (at last) come back to the question I raised at the outset: What does psychology have to contribute to our understanding of Columbine as a school, as a complicated place? That is the specific and timely question, but it would be a form of tunnel vision to see that question apart from the more general question: What has psychology contributed to our understanding of the school culture and to efforts to improve educational outcomes? The general question implies that any effort to change and improve schools—such as reduction in the different forms in which violence is manifested in and around schools—should take into account how and when the school culture responds to other efforts at desired change. To offer any explanation of Littleton and of similar but less horrendous happenings as if they are unrelated to other types of happenings in the school culture is at best myopic, theoretically indefensible, and at worst a source of disillusionment and failure.

I shall begin with the man from Mars fantasy I employed in earlier books (1971, 1996b). For my present purposes, imagine that the man from Mars is parked in his spaceship above the sites where the American Psychological Association is having its annual meeting. And my man from Mars, who cannot understand English, can see all that goes on, besides which he has the most avant garde computers which allows him to note and categorize only what he sees. He has no way of comprehending what is going on inside what we call heads. What are some of the regularities he would note?

1. His computers tell him that over a period of 5 days 15,000 humanoids were observed. On any one day the number was less because some humanoids left the site after 2 or 3 days and were replaced by new humanoids. During each day a small number of humanoids spent approximately 1–2 hours sitting in rooms of varying sizes watching someone on a raised podium, his lips moving at the same time he looked intently at white papers he was holding.

2. Aside from those couple or so hours, the humanoids spent the rest of their time eating, drinking, walking with or talking to each other, or strolling in a large, cavernous room containing open cubicles each of which had on its back wall an indecipherable inscription and in front of which was a table containing objects which the stroller picked up, opened, and looked at.

3. At any one time there were upwards of 50 rooms in which there was someone on a podium and those who listened to him or her. The number of viewers varied dramatically, ranging from 15 or so to a much larger number. Strangely (to the man from Mars) there would come a time when everyone got up and left and would or would not go to another room, but those who went to another room seemed to move unaccountably as a group. They infrequently went to a new room in which no one else from the previous room appeared.

These regularities (and others) mystify the man from Mars. So, to continue the fantasy, this superhuman spaceman does three things: He learns English, takes several humanoids hostage, and plies them with questions. He learns about annual conventions in general and the American Psychological Association in particular. Two questions preoccupy him. The first is where do these psychologists go after the convention is over? The second is what do they do there? He is given a very long list of places and activities. He finds the answers overwhelming and unrevealing. He returns to Mars, ruminates for a year, and decides to gather an army of spaceships, and park them over the next convention for the purpose of being able to follow each psychologist and see where they go after the convention and what they do there.

My Martian would have found a number of things. For starters, he would have found that of those who attend the annual convention—approximately 10% of the total membership—no more than 2% spend time in schools. That approximation is misleading, however, because relatively few of them work full time in schools. Some of them are in colleges and universities and do their research projects in schools. Some may consult every now and then to this or that part of a school, on this or that specific issue. They do not, except for the very few, "live" in schools.

Two interrelated conclusions are warranted. The first is that a minuscule number of psychologists have or take the opportunity to experience the culture of schools: their traditions, organizational structure and dynamics, the nature and extent of their commerce with their community surround, the ways they define problems, their prepotent attitudes to change and criticism, and the ways in which the creation and sustaining of contexts of learning are consistent or inconsistent with what is thought to be known or previously demonstrated in research. The second conclusion, of course, is that for all practical purposes *there is no relationship—let alone a symbiotic one—between those psychologists who consider themselves as "basic" researchers and the people in schools who have problems. It is the absence of that kind of symbiotic relationship that Garner (see Chapter 2) so incisively critiqued. To expect, therefore, that American psychology has much of significance to contribute to changing and improving our educational system is illusory.* I am not asserting that American psychology has contributed nothing to understanding the inadequacies of schools but rather that it is contributing very little to our understanding and how that understanding provides direction for effective actions, not for tinkering or cosmetic actions. Organizational theory, learning theory, intervention theory—these are what have to be interlaced when school change is conceived as it should be: a systems problem.

An instructive example: A number of years ago I received a call from a Dr. Kenneth Wilson, professor of physics at Ohio State University. He said he was involved in a statewide effort to change and im-

prove the teaching of physics in high schools that required long summer institutes for the retraining of teachers. He also told me that he was
a close observer of Reading Recovery (housed at the university), a very
successful program for first graders who seemed at risk to become non-
or poor readers. Reading Recovery had spread at the time to hundreds
of schools around the country. (It is several thousand today.) Dr. Wilson had read several of my books, and he wanted to visit and talk with
me. I was hesitant to say yes because of prior knowledge of and experience with "hard" basic scientists who indulged their rescue fantasies
in regard to schools. But I said yes because of my practice to see any-
body who wants to see me, a practice which has paid off handsomely.
By the end of a long visit I had come to several conclusions. First, he
had made it his business to become more than knowledgeable about
the history of education in general and school reform in particular.
Second, he was not one of those hard scientists who believed that if educators could learn to think like scientists, and do rigorous, focused research, the major educational issues would soon be clarified and could
be appropriately remedied. Indeed—and to me, wonder of wonders—
he had concluded like me that reforming education would take many
decades and that the time perspective which current reformers had was
self-defeating, if not ridiculous. Third, our educational system was a
non-self-correcting, non-self-improving one and that there were other
areas of organized human activity from which school reformers had
much to learn. In a truly basic way our major educational problems
were systemic, not in terms of a school or school system but in terms of
all those parts (for example, the university) who had and exercised a
vested interest in what goes on in schools. For him, the words *system* or
systemic were not buzz words which had no concrete referents and their
interactions. As he did in physics, he took the concept of system seriously. That is why he was so impressed with Reading Recovery; it was
very deliberately set up in ways that could change the relationship between the university and schools, and to do so in data-collecting, self-
correcting ways.[1]

Wilson's book (with B. Daviss) *Redesigning Education* (1996) and his
article (with Barsky) in a special issue of *Daedalus* (1998) are in striking
contrast, conceptually speaking, to that which has typified the reform
movement. I have in several books described and lauded the fact that
he has taken the concept of a system seriously, which is why in the past

---

1. It was several weeks after Wilson's initial visit that I learned that he was a Nobel laureate
in physics.

several years he has taken the difficult steps required to mount a be-ginning effort for action. His task is extraordinarily difficult precisely because the concept of system is the opposite of second nature either to psychologists or any other education-related professionals. Ironi-cally, although the concept of system may be second nature to physi-cists and other types of hard scientists, those who, like Wilson, got in-terested in education were unable to transfer to their new endeavors a complex conception of system as Wilson has done. My personal expe-rience may be helpful here.

In 1971 I wrote *The Culture of the School and the Problem of Change*. It was a book rather widely read in the educational community, not in the psychological one. It was not until 1990, after it was obvious (to me) that the goals of the educational reform movement could and would not be attained that I realized that whatever the virtues of that earlier book its title well reflected its major blindspot: I was focusing on *the* school in the same way American psychology riveted on *the* indi-vidual. I had not seen—my education in psychology and previous pro-fessional experiences was a hindrance rather than a help—that the school was part of a local system which in turn was part of a larger sys-tem of parts (for example, parents, colleges and universities, state de-partments of education, and the local, state, and federal branches of government). If it was a system, it was not a coordinated one; its parts were far more often than not in an adversarial relationship, and it con-tained no self-correcting, self-improving ethos or mechanisms. I then wrote a series of books the most relevant here are *The Case for Change: Rethinking the Preparation of Educators* (1993), *Parental Involvement and the Political Principle: Why the Existing Governance Structure of Schools Should be Abolished* (1995), and *Political Leadership and Educational Fail-ure* (1998).

The fact is that before writing these books I had concluded that our educational system was fatally flawed, but I had a lot of internal resist-ance accepting that conclusion for two reasons: It was a radical and clearly pessimistic conclusion, and I was insecure about how I should conceptualize the system qua system so that it would lead to construc-tive action. Wilson had much less to unlearn than I did. However, if I have learned from our continuing relationship, it has not changed at all my assumption that however you change the educational system, its ultimate consequences will be determined by how seriously and consistently the evolving system is informed and directed by the dif-ferences between contexts of productive and unproductive learning. Potentially psychology has much to contribute here. If you go back to William James' *Talks to Teachers and to Students* in 1900 and to John

Dewey's (1978) presidential address to the American Psychological Association in 1899, you will see that they were talking about the differences between contexts of productive and unproductive learning. Although Jean Piaget's writings have been very influential in psychological and educational circles, he was the opposite of pleased at how his ideas were being interpreted and applied in education. Only once did he agree to write an introduction to a book on educational practice and that was for a book by Kamii and DeVries (1978/1993), a book that explicitly dealt with the differences between contexts of productive and unproductive learning; it is a book that would have warmed the cockles of James' and Dewey's hearts. For most of the twentieth century what passed for learning theory in American psychology was and is a trivialization of a problem and process central to human existence. Psychology had other fish to fry.

Let me now try to explain how I responded to what happened at Columbine High School. Like everybody else my initial response was one of horror and puzzlement. I had no way of comprehending or identifying with the minds and actions of two troubled, disaffected, mammothly alienated, strange boys who would commit murder and suicide. I may be a psychologist presumably sophisticated about human thinking and behavior, but I cannot kid myself that I had anything to offer about why these boys thought and did what they did other than to pin labels on them or, worse yet, to indulge hell diving into their psychological interiors, or to play the blame assignment game: A dysfunctional family? A violent society in which getting guns is no big deal? Violence on the movie screen and TV? Unperceptive or insensitive school personnel? Genes that predisposed the two boys to be vulnerable to psychological pathology? We will never be able to answer the why questions because the two boys are dead. But what if we learn more, even much more, about the psychological history and makeup of these two individuals? Not one person, professional or otherwise, who was interviewed by or quoted in the mass media was in any doubt that learning more about the two individuals would only confirm the obvious: Why these individuals were what they were and did what they did was not explainable by one type of experience or one source of stimulation—for example, family, school, movies, TV—but by several factors reflecting American society, culture, and history. However, that glimpse of the obvious is overwhelming in regard to *action* if only because you cannot deal with all causes at the same time. Understandably, some people emphasized the role of the family, or TV and films, or peer groups, or easy access to guns, or schools. Regardless of emphasis the intended goal was *preventive* action, in some way to change those sources external to the individual that engendered violent thought or action. In what follows I restrict myself to schools, a restriction which we shall see later we will be required to give up.

Prevent what? The murder of students and faculty by other students? As a member of one TV panel said, "Is that all we want to avoid or is that the tip of an iceberg? Murders in school are, thank God, truly small in number, less than a handful in any one year. Does anyone really believe that any person, student, or adult, who sets his or her mind to murder someone can be prevented from doing so? When President Kennedy, and then Martin Luther King Jr., and then Robert Kennedy Jr. were murdered, did anyone say that we will prevent such things from happening in the future, that we know how to prevent such things?" In all that I saw, heard, and read in the mass media in regard to schools, the following were by far the most frequent and to which agreement was unanimous.

1. There are far more troubled, disaffected, and educationally directionless students in high school than students who physically harm other students, even taking into account the increase in school violence in recent decades.

2. Many of these students are "diagnosed" or known to other students far better and validly than school personnel.

3. Lines of open and safe communication between students and school personnel are both few and inadequate.

4. High schools are comprised of many informal groupings or cliques each of which has a hierarchy of values such as: who or what is desirable or undesirable, attractive or unattractive, worthy or unworthy, popular-fashionable or not, sociable or reclusive. Without question, athletes (especially "stars") have the most cachet. Sometimes a group has a visual logo that identifies them, like the "Trench Coat Mafia" at Columbine. (No one who commented on the ways students group or judge themselves and others mentioned or alluded to informal groupings based on intellectual-educational values or accomplishments.)

None of this was new. None of this was stated polemically. None of this contained anything resembling initial, concrete actions, either from professionals or others. Psychologists, as individuals, or representatives of psychological associations, had nothing distinctive to say, then or in the ensuing weeks and months.

There are two ways in which you can think about prevention. The first is the prevention of some pathological or deviant condition or behavior, such as violence in its different forms and degrees; this is what commentators meant when they would say that ways must be found to avoid repetition not only of the Columbine disaster but of all forms of school violence. The other way is to think of prevention as the promotion of attitudes, values, and intellectual and social skills that make it likely that individuals will be able to withstand the stresses and strains, the traumas that life predictably brings. Put more positively, it promotes the acquiring of psychological assets that make it likely that interests, talents, and goals will be productively utilized.[2]

So how to think about what happened in Littleton? What guidelines does psychology provide? As I said earlier, psychologists are trained to think about individuals, not about institutions or organizations (for profit or not). And although psychologists are conversant with the different types of and rationales for prevention, the emphasis in research and practice is on individuals. In regard to schools I had a lot to unlearn. More correctly, I had to learn that the problematic behavior of *any* individual in an individual school almost always said something about the school as an organization and its reciprocal relationships in the local school system as well as to one or another part of a larger state administered system. But that conclusion is also arrived at by people with little or no experience in schools. When they read in the newspapers that the test scores in a school system are well below what they should be—or that school attendance has declined, or the dropout rate or suspensions have increased—they conclude that something is amiss in the system qua system. However, as in the case of Littleton, "only" two boys committed murders, the searching spotlight is put on two individuals and the system qua system is hardly questioned except to suggest that the system has to become more sensitive to other students at risk for becoming violent. That is the first type of preventive approach I mentioned above: targeting a specific, circumscribed form of untoward behavior. However, more than a few commentators described the school's student culture in ways suggesting that violence

---

2. Parents are relieved and grateful that vaccines exist to prevent their children from getting certain diseases like polio, small pox, and more, an example of targeting a particular pathology. But there is no vaccine parents can employ to prevent their children from developing outlooks, behavior styles, social deficits, and the like, that are not maladaptive, that make for wasted abilities and lives, for unhappiness. Parents have the responsibility of promoting in their children a "healthy" sense of self that enable the child to react to, without debilitating consequences, the problems or challenges that inevitably arise in an unpredictable world children and their parents do not control. That responsibility goes a long way to explaining why books on how to rear children are avidly read by parents. *Promoting* health is not synonymous with preventing this or that disease.

was not the only problematic student behavior at Columbine, and allows one to raise the question: Does the school deliberately, adequately, and effectively seek to promote a constellation of attitudes, motivations, and relationships which one might call socially desirable and intellectually enhancing? I have never been to Columbine High School, but over the course of decades I have been in many high schools including many which, like Columbine, were in relatively affluent communities. I would bet and give handsome odds that Columbine is in all major respects similar to what I observed or read about. Those high schools have been described in the literature by many investigators. If I had to pick one such publication it would be that by Aiken (1942), the beginning chapters of which are as searing and knowledgeable critique of the modal American high school as has ever been written. He then describes a program which involved changing a large number of schools informed by a "promotion of health" rationale. It has been deservedly regarded as a pioneering study (over 8 years) of heroic proportions. Its subsequent impact on the field has ranged from minimal to zero.

I was shocked by the shootings, but I was not surprised. If my lack of surprise mystifies the reader, let me at this point just say that high schools breed and sustain untoward attitudes and motivations in many, certainly not all, of its students. Nothing that I shall say should be interpreted as suggesting that Columbine in any way "caused" the shootings, a degree of violence I could never have predicted. Once the sense of shock wore off, however, I had to conclude that this type of extreme and infrequent behavior had to be seen in terms of the culture of high schools, and when seen in that way the actions of the two boys remain shocking but not surprising.

Let me start with the fact that Columbine had 1,800 students, and when you add to that teachers and administrative and support staff (secretarial-clerical, cafeteria, janitorial), it is likely that the number of people in the school probably is near 2,100. Now, you do not have to be a sophisticated thinker, let alone a trained psychologist, to conclude that such a large number is conducive to a variety of problems, probable or actual; let us not gloss over that the number refers to people varying in age, function, power-authority, personality, competence, family and socioeconomic background, personal goals, and commitment to the stated purposes of the schools. If you observe, study, or have reason to work with families, however small or large, variation among members of a family is impossible to ignore. What we have at Columbine, which is typical, is an exponentially greater number and degree of sources and sites of variation. Not long after he became president of France, General De Gaulle plaintively asked, "How can you rule a country that makes 500 different cheeses?" That question is no less applicable to a high school in which its population breaks down into many groups varying in the ways I have indicated, not including, as I should have, the wondrous complications of gender in interpersonal relationships.

About all this, psychological theory has little or nothing to say. It is as if it is, so to speak, a nonproblem, an unpsychological problem, in that one is trying to conceptualize organizational structure and not the minds of individuals in that structure. Of course, psychological theory recognizes that structure impacts on individuals and that individuals impact upon and transform structure, as, for example, in the arena of perception, but even there the focus is on the individual response: its speed, accuracy, and personal meaning. The focus is on what the individual mind does in its transactions with structure, and for many problems in perception that focus on the individual cannot be faulted. But once one goes beyond the field of perception to the significance of the structure of complicated human organizations on mind and behavior—especially schools which no psychologist denies is societally crucial, not just important, but crucial—American psychology has shown little interest and has little to say. There is one notable and instructive example.

It is one to which I earlier alluded and in earlier decades was called industrial psychology, and today tends to be called organizational behavior or some other rubric intended to emphasize organizational structure and dynamics (when, why changes do or do not occur and with what consequences). Those in this field represent a minuscule percentage of the membership of the American Psychological Association, and most of them do not find the association a congenial home but nevertheless identify themselves as psychologists. It is a field represented not at all (the usual exceptions aside) in undergraduate psychology programs and hardly in doctoral programs. Today it is probably the case that there are many more theorists, researchers, and practitioners of organizational behavior in business schools than in departments of psychology. In psychology, organizational behavior is very marginal and for two reasons. First it smacks of the applied. Second, its subject matter is regarded as crassly materialistic, raising questions and engendering imagery about the ethos and values of corporate American and its inhabitants. And partial proof of this is the perception that people in this field have discernibly larger incomes than those in the more traditional fields in psychology; from all this one should expect no contribution to a basic psychology. Ironically, this negative judgment exists side by side with the acknowledgment that most of the working adult population spends a significant portion of their lives in complicated organizations, one of the most mysteriously complicated of which is the university, which someone once said was the least studied organization of all. (If you read Thostein Veblen's *The Higher Learning in America,* published in 1957 but written much earlier, you will begin to understand why university faculty are by no means disposed to study their "home" in a searching way. Veblen was an economist by training—he became the persona non grata type—but in his writings he was as much the psychologist and sociologist as he was the economist. He ran against the tide of what in his day was an emerging, balkanized social science.)

I do not feel called upon here to pass judgment on the field of organizational behavior (another time in another life!) except to say that it is asking the right questions, important questions with significances, theoretical and practical, for other fields of psychology. For example, the conceptualizations and types of interventions are clearly relevant to educational institutions but only a handful of its members have more than a passing interest in schools. That is disappointing but not surprising because it reflects the balkanization of the university in general and psychology in particular. The university is comprised of schools, departments, institutes, each of which has fiefdoms zealously guarding its boundaries. The university is not a community of scholars or researchers if by community you mean that its members seek seriously to forge intellectual and interpersonal relationships with those in other fields or in a neighboring one for the purpose of building bridges that lead to more encompassing explanations to what seem to be discrete problems. *Not so incidently, what I have just said is true in spades of high schools.* Schools are not unique organizations. They are different, to be sure, but in no way is the adjective *unique* appropriate or valid. In all that I saw, read, or heard about Littleton the unverbalized assumption seemed to be that high schools had no organizational-behavioral similarities to corporations or any other complicated, non-educational institutions. If there is one conclusion the field of organizational behavior has illuminated and buttressed, it is that any effort to change an organization—even if that effort is sought and welcomed—will be minimally successful, if at all, unless it is based on first-hand knowledge of how the history and rationale for the organization's structure are both cause and effect of the differential behavior of its people. That conclusion goes a long way to explaining why the educational reform movement in the post World War II era has been (generally speaking) a failure and will continue to be a source of puzzled disillusionment, and that will be the case of any reforms stimulated by Littleton.

In being critical of American psychology and the university, I am not assigning them the role of villain. Villains are immoral; psychology and the university are not. We know how to deal with villains, at least we think we do. In the case of the university and organized psychology, the core issue is one of values which determine who is more or less worthy, which problems are more important than others, how resources are allocated, and how the public good is best served. Changing values, even recognizing and confronting the basic role of values, is no easy task because it can and usually does engender the possibility of change, the need to change, and that is something we as individuals or collectivities resist. We are all familiar with the quip that the two things we can count on are death and taxes. Resistance to change is third. Because I consider values so bedrock in the change process, and in an effort to concretize the issue, I trust I will be pardoned if I recount some personal and institutional experience. I will try to be commendably brief.

1. I received my doctorate in 1942 from Clark University. After 3 and a half years working as a clinical psychologist in a state institution, I became a member of Yale's department of psychology. For someone with my background coming to Yale was, had to be, an intimidating experience. As Churchill said about the Soviet Union, Yale was for me a puzzle, embedded in an enigma, wrapped in mystery. Churchill, of course, literally knew more about the Soviet Union than I knew about Yale and any other university. Believe it or not, I did not know what tenure was; that revelation came 2 or 3 years later.

2. The psychology department occupied most of the center three stories of the Institute of Human Relations. On one side of the department was Gesell's Institute of Child Development, and on the other side the department of psychiatry. The doors between the department and its two neighbors were locked physically, psychologically, and socially. They remained locked for several years until Gesell retired and a palace revolution in psychiatry forced the early retirement of its chairman. I was mystified by all this, but as an anxious, professionally self-absorbed assistant professor posing as a mature adult, my concerns were elsewhere.

3. On the third floor of the institute were the offices of what was called the labor-management unit consisting of three or four people only one of whom had a faculty appointment (in economics). For all practical purposes the unit could have been on the moon, it was related to nothing else going on in the institute. One member of the unit was a psychologist whose name was identical to that of an outstanding

Newark (New Jersey) high school football star who was one of my boyhood heros. (From age 5 to 18 I lived in Newark.) So I introduced myself to Chris Argyris and asked if he was related to my boyhood hero. The answer was not only yes, but he and his older cousin were part of an extended family long ensconced in Newark. I may have talked with Chris several times over the next few years, but they were superficial, largely nostalgic discussions. I have to confess that I felt both superior to and sorry for him in that I was a member of a prestigious department and he was an apparently insignificant member of an isolated unit. Besides, what conceivable connections could there be between my research program on test anxiety and the work place? If asked at the time if Chris would over the decades make stellar contributions to conceptualizing and understanding organizational behavior and interventions, I would have answered no and would have said that with certainty. If asked if our department would or should have a place for someone like Chris, I would have said the chances were as good as those of the Pope inviting me to join the College of Cardinals. Needless to say, I had already and quickly absorbed a view of what a psychology department should contain and the high walls that contained it.

4. Several years later Yale created the department of administrative sciences of which Chris became a member. In addition to him the department consisted largely of several psychologists at least two of whom had national reputations, and some younger psychologists who later achieved academic prominence. Now, it is by no means unusual in the university that when department X adds to its staff an individual who department Y considers as having expertise the latter respects and has something to contribute to its teaching, scholarly, or research programs, that department Y will seek to give that individual a courtesy appointment. That never happened in the case of the departments of psychology and administrative sciences except in two instances: One was a psychologist (Richard Hackman) accurately perceived as having unusual talents in conceptualizing, research design, and data analysis; the substance and direction of his research was a secondary factor, if it was a factor at all. The second instance was an individual (Donald Taylor) who came from a department and university no less prestigious than Yale. He became chairman of the new department. He was personal friends of several professors in the Yale psychology department. I have good reason to believe that our department did not initiate the offer of a joint appointment but rather that it was a precondition of Don for coming to Yale and also that the dean of Yale's graduate school very much pressured for it. Even so, when the tenured professors were asked to approve the joint appointment, several said they would reluc-

tantly vote in the affirmative; they would never vote affirmatively—more correctly, never seek him out—for a full-time appointment in our department. Ironically, and because no professor wanted to assume the burdens of the chairmanship of our department, Don became chairman of our department and later dean of the graduate school. In all the years he was chairman and dean, he studiously avoided even raising the possibility of joint appointments for several of his former colleagues who he rightly respected for their accomplishments at the same time he, again rightly, knew had substantive interests uncongenial to what our department considered substantively worthy and far too applied, far too directed to the business world. Why was the new department given the name Administrative Sciences? That was not happenstance. In the university, especially in its arts and sciences departments, the established departments do not have to be concerned with explaining what their title signifies. Departments exist to promote scholarly and research activities which contribute to our basic fund of knowledge, not transient knowledge of no general significance. So what should the new department be titled given the fact that it was to be part of arts and sciences? To fit the existing ethos and its values, to make it academically kosher, so to speak, "Administrative Sciences" was far better, safer, and palatable than any title suggesting the business world even though those who joined that department had a much broader view of the matter. The word *administrative* has some of the qualities of an inkblot, but the word *sciences* conjures up imagery of an individual who spends his or her days and frequently nights in a building on campus, isolated from the "real" world, intent on discovering new knowledge, upsetting old laws, always questioning the conventional wisdom.

I am not being critical but rather descriptive for the sole purpose of indicating, in this case in psychology, how treasured values which have more than a kernel of truth (let there be no doubt about that) but which have their downside in that they unwittingly, and it usually is unwitting, can foster a parochialism that robs the field of new ideas and experiences which have the potential of dramatically widening the range and even the substance of its generalization. That has been the case of American psychology in its distancing itself from the field of education. The example I have just given was about psychology and the field of organizational structure and behavior. It is to me no end ironic that the field of organizational behavior has always distanced itself from study of schools as organizations.

Writing a book is like studying lives, or an organization, or the brain, or damned near anything else of obvious importance. You start with some knowledge, you obsess about a starting point, you ruminate, and by the time you begin you have some idea or outline of what you want to do and what its implications are for going down the road you have chosen. That sounds relatively linear and rational, but it is a myth you cling to even if your past experience has disconfirmed that myth time and again. The fact is that as soon as you begin to write ideas come up you had not thought about, you see connections that had escaped you, your need for desired linearity has to adapt to curvilinearity. Should you *really* include this, exclude that, put this chapter here, that one there? This is by way of saying that when I started this chapter on Littleton I did not expect that it would include what it has, that I would be discussing to the extent that I have the field of organizational behavior as well as the university, with the consequence that Littleton was not, as I had expected, always in the center stage of the chapter. So in the next chapter I shall try to be more linear about the significances of Littleton.

CHAPTER 5

Columbine High School and Contexts of Productive Learning

It is impossible for me to discuss Columbine or any other school without asking and at least trying to answer the question: What is the purpose of schooling? I say purpose rather than purposes because I assume that the reader, like me, knows that there are many purposes to schooling and they are not of equal importance (to me or the reader). Even if unanimous agreement could be reached on a short list of major purposes, it is most unlikely that each of us would consider each purpose on the list of equal importance. It is a basic axiom in economics that resources are inevitably limited and we have to make choices in allocating resources: This purpose is important, that purpose is important, and there are other important purposes, but precisely because resources are finite, however we wish it otherwise, we have to decide by some criterion (or criteria) where each purpose should be on our priority list. That does not mean that any one purpose on our short list receives no resources but that it should not receive as much as another purpose. Agreeing on a short list is one thing, agreeing on prioritizing the list is quite another thing. That has been the case in regard to schooling as is all too clear when you read or observe the deliberations of boards of education and local, state, national political officialdom as they decide on how to allocate resources to education. We expect disagreements, they are inevitable, they can be productive, but in regard to schooling they have not been productive. Practically no one experiences anything resembling satisfaction with the outcomes of the educational reform movement in the post World War II era, and, yet, however dissatisfied people and the policy makers are, they direct their criticisms to this or that group or practice and never ask the question: Is it possible that our short list of purposes is faulty, wrong, incomplete, self-defeating? Is it possible that what we say are the sources of our dissatisfactions is confirmation of Mencken's caveat that for every important problem there is a simple solution that is wrong? Should we examine and challenge our short list of purposes? Can it be that our short list of purposes and even the ways we prioritize it is on target, but we have not taken its practical implications seriously? That there is a difference between rhetoric and decisions consistent with it?

The two most frequently stated top purposes of schooling are:

1. To aid each child's actualization of his or her potential; the assets of each child should be identified and developed.

2. To insure the learning of subject matter and those cognitive skills which together prepare the student for a productive adulthood.

In practice, of course, the two purposes are seamlessly intertwined; they can be considered two sides of the same coin. The first purpose emphasizes the importance of respect for *individuality;* the second reflects or implies or assumes a *societal* consensus about what a student should learn over the school years about human knowledge, experience, and accomplishments. The store of human knowledge is vast and (again) choices have to be made in selecting from that store what is deemed essential. So, for example, music and art are considered important but not essential and, therefore, are allocated fewer resources, if any, compared to "basic" ones: literature, science, history, math, social studies, and a foreign language (not always). In times of financial crises no one suggests that any of the basics be eliminated, but that is what is done in the case of those subjects and activities which are judged as less important, or as a luxury, or as a frill. Prioritization comes with two obligations: to create the conditions which are consistent with priorities and then to test for the outcomes.

How does a high school containing somewhat more than 2,000 people achieve the two purposes to which practically everybody pledges allegiance? So let us go back to our Martian, who now is fluent in English, and ask him to direct his x-ray-like technology to provide us with "data" relevant to several questions:

1. How many times in the course of a month do students talk *alone* with a teacher or any other adult in the school? How many of those times are during the school day or after school?

2. How many times and with what durations do teachers or other adults talk with each other during or after the school day?

3. For any one teacher, with how many of the other teachers does he or she *never* interact?

4. During whatever is the classroom period, how much of the time

does the teacher talk? The student? How many students never talk to or with the teacher or do so one, two, or x times?

5. How often do two or more teachers meet, and for how long, to talk about individual students?

6. Because the number of school personnel is not small, how often are there general faculty meetings? Where are they held? How many times does a teacher raise a question or issue? What is the total time teachers talk? The principal and/or some other administrator?

7. After the school day how many students stay to engage in a teacher led or supervised, school-related activity? How many teachers perform in such a role? (Athletics requiring being outside the school building are not included.)

8. How many times does a teacher phone or write a parent asking for a meeting? How many times, invited or not, does a parent come to school?

9. At the end of the school year several hundred students are graduated; they never return. They are replaced two months later by several hundred younger students. Are the data we request from the Martian in any way different for these replacements compared to the older cohorts who are still in the school?

There are no existing data relevant to the overt behavioral regularities for which we seek the help of our Martian friend. But does anyone doubt that regularities the Martian would provide us are relevant to the two most frequently stated purposes of schooling? I did not dream up the nine questions out of whole cloth. They do not derive solely from my personal observations, although they are far from small in number. They derive from talking to scores of parents, teachers, and students. I never asked any one of them in a direct, explicit way these questions: How well do you think your child is known to and understood by his or her teachers? How well do you know and think you understand the 100–125 (or more) students you teach each day, divided as they are into four or five non-overlapping classes or sections? How well do you feel your teachers know you? Would you say you have a personal relationship with most, if not all, of your teachers? With some exceptions, I did not "confront" those with whom I talked. On several occasions when I was meeting with a small group of teachers whom I had gotten to know well—who did not see me as an intrusive professor foraying into matters about which he knew little—I asked: "Given the number of students you teach, how long does it take you to associate names with faces?" That always drew a laugh. By far the most frequent answer went like this: "By the end of the first month I could associate correctly the names and faces of the 20% or so of the dumbest, brightest, and misbehaving students. Even at the end of the semester I would still have to consult my seating chart like the law professor in the TV series *The Paper Chase.*"

The second exception was when I was asked to evaluate three high schools participating in a school reform project. The schools were in different parts of the country. In each school I met with several small groups of students. The purpose of the meetings was to determine if the juniors or seniors in the school had noted any changes in their school. Without exception the answer was no, even when I pressed in regard to several changes which had been initiated. At the end of each meeting I asked, "How do you like school?" The only way I can describe their reactions was their facial reactions. It was as if I had asked a stupid question in that it assumed that one should like school. One or two in each group finally said, "It's O.K.," the socially desirable response to a stranger whom the principal had obviously invited to the school. No student ever said they found school interesting, quite the contrary. They were never vehement and certainly not expansively critical; they simply did not see the point of my questions. School was not a place you were supposed to enjoy. After one of the groups left, I remained in the room to jot down some notes. There was a knock on the door, and two students entered to tell me that they had not wanted to convey to me the impression that they disliked the school as if there was nothing good that could be said about it. It was, they said, "an O.K. school but it could be better." Beyond that they had nothing more to add.

There are high schools with significantly more students than Columbine. They are bureaucratic in that, like the university, those in one department know very little about those in other departments, and there are no incentives to change this. In addition, the layers of administration are not small and their contacts with and relationships to teachers are indirect, relatively infrequent, and more often than not take the form of written (or Xeroxed) messages concerning procedures, information, record keeping, and the like. It is understandable if many teachers regard themselves as workers at the bottom of a mountain on top of which is Kafka's castle from which emanate policies and directives; there is not a safe and effective way for messages from below to reach the top or if there is a way, it has no consequences.

You do not have to be a sage to conclude that "helping each student to realize his or her potential" is empty rhetoric of the emptiest kind. To achieve that purpose implies that students are known and feel known, that relationships with teachers and other personnel are not fleeting and superficial, not as strangers passing in the night, not as people assigned narrow roles with rigid boundaries not to be crossed. I should hasten to add that I have no doubt that my Martian friend's data would identify exceptions in any high school, including Columbine, to what I have said. But they would be, as my personal experience attests, just that: exceptions.

My master's thesis required me to give the 1937 Binet test of intelligence to students in two schools. One of those schools was for gifted children. If I remember correctly their chronological age averaged 11–12 years. So I am testing Robert Wald (I never forgot his name), and it was obvious that I would have to go through with him to items of the highest difficulty. One of those items required that one explain the meaning of proverbs, one of which was "You cannot make a silk purse out of a sow's ear." To which he replied, "Oh yes, you can. They did it at MIT." High schools are sows' ears. Once you accept the overarching purpose above, their size, and the way they are organized, high schools will remain sows' ears. That does not mean they cannot be improved in this or that respect but rather that they will continue to sustain empty rhetoric. You can, of course, change your priorities, but if you do so, you should acknowledge that helping each child realize his or her potential is low on the short list of priorities, if it remains on the list at all.

Most school personnel will be unfamiliar with the name and work of Roger Barker (1968). He was a psychologist who almost single-handedly created the field of ecological psychology. Except for a small group of community psychologists—a very marginal area in American psychology—recent generations of graduate students hardly know who he was and pitifully few have read his work. Today, ecology is a buzz word untied in psychology to theory or research, except for a few, like me, who were much influenced by him. The one of his books directly relevant to what I have said in this chapter is *Big School, Small School,* written in 1964 with his colleague, P. V. Gump. The differences in size of school make enormous differences in the quantity and quality of relationships among students and between students and school personnel. You will find the concepts of undermanned and overmanned settings both illuminating and provocative. If it is the case that ecological psychology has hardly had an influence on American psychology, in the case of the educational community it has had no influence whatsoever. And that includes educational policy makers (local, state, national) whose intentions are honorable and serious but whose ignorance is bottomless.

The size and organizational structure of a school in determining the frequency and quality of interpersonal relationships are obviously important, but the significances we attach to or deduce from them depend on organizational purposes which always reflect a time perspective.

That is to say, an organizational purpose explicitly or implicitly says, so to speak, that to achieve the goals of that purpose you must judge how much time to allocate to that purpose. Time is a finite, precious commodity to be judicially allocated in accord with the priorities of stated purposes. Time is not democratically allocated as if all purposes are of equal importance. For example, the federal Senate has one fifth the number of members compared to the House of Representatives. (This disparity is not happenstance. It is in accord with the stated purposes of the Founding Fathers, but that is another story, a most fascinating and instructive one.) With its 500 plus members, and its changing composition every 2 years, the House is a place where a small number of people make the most important decisions, not every member knows everybody else in a meaningful way, "freshman" members experience an unwanted anonymity, and the time a member has to address the house is severely limited. With its 50 members the Senate has been described as a "club" in which its members know each other, each is elected for 6 years, a freshman senator does not remain anonymous for very long, and each senator has more than ample time to address his or her colleagues—in the case of filibusters "time" can be many hours, even days. Practically all members of the House—not including its small number of party power brokers—would rather be in the Senate. What is most relevant for my present purposes has to do with time. Although both have the same stated, overarching purpose to legislate for the public welfare—to debate, pass, or reject—each allocates time to the purpose in very different ways. To achieve their identical purpose, the Senate allocates time to its members which the House realistically does not and cannot do. It is understandable if the general public has a higher opinion of the Senate than of the House, a judgment with which the Senate, of course, concurs.

The above was prologue to how the time perspective enters the educational picture. I have over the decades had discussions with individual teachers, or small groups of them, about their reactions to what I have said as an invited speaker at their professional meetings and conventions. Since I am a Johnny-One-Note about understanding the learner as an individual, it is rare that I do not sermonize about it. I cannot do better than to paraphrase what teachers have said regardless of whether they were elementary, middle, or high school teachers, although the intensity of feeling in the latter two is always dramatically higher than in the first one. "You talk as if teachers are not interested in students as individuals. If that is what you are implying, you are being both unfair and wrong. For example, students are in school for about 6 hours a day, but when you deduct settling down time in the morning, lunch time, gymnasium, only about 4 and a half hours are left for basic subject matter and instruction. It is not really different in middle and high schools, maybe it is worse. There is limited time and don't ever forget that. Given limited time is one thing, but you have to see that in terms of a curriculum we must cover because we are under a gun: At the end of the school year we as teachers will be evaluated by standardized tests to see how well we covered and taught the curriculum. The pressures from administrators and parents are real and enormous. Keep on track with the curriculum, everything else is secondary. Of course, each student is a unique person and learner. Do we ever know that! But there is precious little time to fathom and adapt to individuality. If teachers suffer from anything, it is guilt that we know there are kids who need more help than we have the time to give them. We have to teach by the clock and the calendar because there are deadlines and consequences. Of course, we are in favor of individuality, however you define it, but for all practical purposes we have very little time to take it into account. And please don't forget that if you have one or two troubled disruptive kids in your class, you cannot ignore them and the extra time you are forced to give them takes time away from teaching the curriculum and from the very small amount of time, if that, we can give in a one-on-one to the other students."

My response had several parts. The first was that they were largely correct; I agreed with them but had to say that there are teachers, a small minority, who deal with the issue of individuality better than others. The second was that in agreeing with them we were both conceding that "helping each child realize his or her full potential" was empty rhetoric. The third part was in the form of a question: Why are you telling me this in the confines of a professional interchange, while as individuals and the formal organizations of which you are a part you monotonously repeat the rhetoric to the public? Does this not border on hypocrisy?

In response to Littleton, I zealously read what psychologists were saying on TV, what they were quoted as saying in newspapers and national magazines, and letters to editors and op-ed columns. In all that I read, saw, and heard, there was only one time that someone mentioned size of school. That exception was in a three-sentence letter to the editor of the *New York Times* where the writer, Dr. Sidney Trubowitz, a professor of education, plaintively wondered why no one was discussing the implications of size of school. The psychologists were not hypocrites, they simply do not know any better because neither their training nor accustomed professional role gives them an understanding of the school culture or brings them into meaningful contact with school personnel. Their relationship to the school setting is the opposite of what Garner (see Chapter 2) called a symbiotic one. That, I should hasten to add, does not mean that school personnel are the experts. As I learned and pointed out decades ago, it is the rare educator whose socialization into the school culture has not dramatically narrowed the direction and range of their comprehension of the school culture. I say this sympathetically because as a psychologist, an academic one to boot, I had to struggle to unlearn what I thought I knew about the school culture. Psychology prides itself, as it should, on the emphasis given in training to the difference between opinion and conventional wisdom, on the one hand, and demonstrated and tested truths, on the other hand. It is because of psychology's emphasis on the individual, its neglect of organizational tradition, structure, and dynamics, that the response of psychology to Columbine was so conventional, superficial, and an unwitting reinforcement of oversimplifications, if not irrelevancies. Psychology rightly reveres the role of the experimental method which, to state it succinctly, derives from the axiom: If you want to test your understanding of an existing state of affairs, do nothing with one group and try to change it in a comparable group. The experimental method requires action and some understanding of that state of affairs before you go into action. You do not fly into action. You act on the basis of personal experience and available or existing knowledge.

I am in no way suggesting or advocating that the experimental method is the best answer to understanding and improving schools at the present time. I brought up the experimental method as a way of underlining the importance—*importance* is too weak a word—of gaining a secure familiarity with the state of affairs you seek to understand, evaluate, and change. The experimental method is not inherently virtuous; it has its time and place, and in regard to the major problems of schools, its present virtues are few and obstacles to applying it are many and gargantuan. What I do consider inherently virtuous, especially at this time, is the effort to describe, clarify, and conceptualize what we think is the state of affairs in what Goodlad called and described as *A Place Called School* (1984). But if American psychology continues to train psychologists, the large bulk of whom have had no experience in schools and there is no desire or incentive to gain such experience, American psychology is manifesting, in my opinion, social irresponsibility. That is why Chapter 3 was devoted to the Boulder conference which created and set standards for modern clinical psychology. Psychology was responsive then to a clear social need. Responding to that need should not have meant that there was no other equally important social need which psychology should do *something* about.

In creating the field of modern clinical psychology, aside from quantitative methods and research design, American psychology had little of a substantive or theoretical nature to provide the new field. (The one exception, and that came later, was to base therapeutic interventions on psychology's long interest in conditioning, an interest that goes back to Pavlov, Watson, and then Skinner.) In terms of theory and practice, modern clinical psychology was shaped by developments beyond the formal boundaries of academic psychology. But there was one major focus in psychology that was tailor made for the educational setting, that provided an unexcelled "laboratory" in which to test, illuminate, and revise what had been conceptualized, done, and written in and around that focus. I refer, of course, to the learning process. The motivation and incentives for learning, the interpersonal and social contexts in which learning occurs, the influence of varying types of positive or negative reinforcement, how long what is learned is remembered, the whys and wherefores of the relationship between IQ and the speed and level of learning, how attitudinal and personality affect learning, if and how genetic factors set limits to what can be learned—these and more long occupied a prominent place in psychology's research and theoretical literature.

In commentary on this literature, I shall say little about the thousands of studies of the individual rat in a maze. However you define human learning, it always is in a context in which there is at least one other human and more frequently far more than one. Even when we are alone and trying to learn something, our thoughts, feelings, attitudes, and fantasies include others. From the time we are born, learning is an interpersonal-social affair. Children frequently learn significant things when they are alone, but it is totally unwarranted to confuse physical isolation with psychological aloneness. The one indisputable contribution of the rat studies is to have demonstrated the importance of motivation, usually measured by food deprivation in learning to reach a goal that is rewarding. Put in human terms: How much you want to learn mightily influences what and how you learn; *wanting to learn is not synonymous with the need to learn;* a distinction the rat studies did not have to confront in whatever generalizations they offered about human learning. As parents and teachers well know, what they think a child needs to learn is not necessarily what he or she wants to learn.

What has happened when a relatively small group of theorists and researchers—most of whom were not psychologists—studied gorillas and chimpanzees? The most stirring example of what can be learned is a video I saw on PBS showing how Jane Goodall got gorillas to learn that she could be trusted, they could approach her, they could accept food from her, they could eat with her. Goodall was learning and so was the gorilla; they were changing in relationship to each other. The gorilla had no need for Goodall; it was her goal to make it safe for the gorilla so that he would want to approach her. If I may put it in my own words: Goodall started where the gorilla was psychologically and that required a time perspective that would test the patience and equanimity of most humans. What Goodall demonstrated is more relevant to schooling and pedagogy than the entire corpus of studies of learning in the rat. In recent decades psychologists who were much influenced by her work have studied similar animals in similar ways in regard to learning, concept formation, and perception. In fact, "Do these primates think?" has become a focus of discussion and controversy among primatologists. That does not mean that those who answer the question in the affirmative are claiming that these primates think, the way we conventionally mean when we say humans think, but rather that the way they learn is not explainable without implicating some mental processes that are strikingly human-like.[1] In addition, in a recent report some of the most renowned primatologists (including Goodall) agree that chimpanzees have a culture they transmit to others, a transmission not explainable by genetics (Angier, 1999).

In a commentary that accompanies the new report, Frans B. M. de Waal of the Yerkes Regional Primate Research Center in Atlanta points out that some hard-core anthropologists and psychologists have sought for years to keep the "culture" tag unique to human beings, an exclusionary desire that has demanded increasingly elaborate definitions of the term.

The latest record of chimpanzee inventiveness and diversity, Mr. De Waal writes, "is so impressive that it will be hard to keep these apes out of the cultural domain without once again moving the goal posts."

In the new report, Dr. Whiten and his colleagues make their case for ape culture by citing 39 behaviors that vary in prevalence and style among the seven chimpanzee communities. He and eight other primatologists, including renowned figures like Jane Goodall of the Gombe Stream Research Center, Richard Wrangham of Harvard University and Toshisada Nishida of Kyoto University, set aside their often competitive ways to pool their years of painstaking observations from field studies that ranged from 8 to 38 years.

The researchers first compiled a list of 65 candidate behaviors that

---

1. This issue was raised by the gestalt psychologist Köhler during World War I and described in his book *The Mentality of Apes* in 1925. He describes learning in problem-solving contexts, best explainable by a process of insight that the behavior seemed to reveal.

they suspected might be specific to different chimpanzee communities. Some of the proposed behaviors turned out not to be unique at all, but rather nearly universal, while others varied for reasons easily explained by the local ecology. For example, the decision about where to build a sleeping nest appeared to depend more on local predators than on prevailing community taste.

Finally, the researchers came up with 39 behavior patterns that fit their definition of cultural variation, meaning they were customary in some communities and absent in others, for reasons that could only be explained by learning or imitation.

I brought this article of primates into this discussion to underline the point that for a good part of this century American learning theorists and researchers stayed in their laboratories instead of going to the natural settings in which, and only in which, the purport of their narrow, laboratory-based conclusions could be tested, revised, and enlarged in scope and utility. By ignoring the classroom—the one place all children are required to learn diverse skills and subject matter—American psychology impoverished, if not unwittingly subverted, its own agenda.

Let me give you an example of what I mean. Some time in the sixties, some of us in the Yale Psycho-Educational Clinic were intrigued by three papers written by Dr. Jacob Kounin and colleagues of the department of psychology of Wayne State University (Kounin, 1967; Kounin, Friesen, & Norton, 1966; Kounin, Gump, & Ryan, 1961). The studies were about classroom management. We invited Dr. Kounin to give a talk at the clinic. He brought with him a film of two teachers in the same school with comparable children in terms of age, social class, and IQ. You did not have to be an astute psychologist or observer to conclude that the students were in dramatically different learning contexts. What the reader needs to know is that Dr. Kounin was much influenced by the German gestalt psychologists (he may have been a student of Kurt Lewin, who before fleeing Nazi Germany had been a rising star in the gestalt firmament illuminated by the three senior stars: Kohler, Kofka, and Wertheimer). It is not happenstance, therefore, that Kounin was interested in contexts of learning and how to account for differences among them. In all respects that film was consistent with what we observed, experienced, and had to deal with in our work with teachers whose implicit theories of learning were as oversimple and self-defeating as the academic theories to which they were exposed in their preparatory programs. If you make the assumption, as we had already been driven to make, that what Kounin was showing us was the opposite of atypical, you could have predicted as we did, some of the major reasons why learning in schools would remain a sometime thing. And if you have lingering doubts on that score, you should read Wertheimer's *Productive Thinking* (1945). And, if you have time, play (or replay) the video of the film *Mr. Holland's Opus*. It is really two films: In the first half Mr. Holland proceeds with a conception of learning that produces disinterested, sullen, semi-somnolent students. In the second half he has an epiphany, he sees the invalidity of his theory and his students become alive and want to learn. I have never met an educator who said the film was a distortion of the existing realities of schools. But I have never met an educator who had ever heard about Kounin, and my guess is that if I surveyed the membership of the American Psychological Association, a truly minuscule number of older psychologists (like very senior citizen me) would even recognize the name and an even more minuscule number would be familiar with his work. For American psychology schools are not where the action and the rewards are; it is content to let schools be the responsibility of schools of education. Having done that, however, they do not inhibit expressions of disdain for the students, standards, and the quality of theorizing and research of the faculty of schools of education.

Neither I nor anyone else has any empirical basis for judging whether Columbine High School provided contexts of productive learning. However, nothing I have read about the school disconfirms my experience and assumption that it is not an atypical high school. But what are the major features of contexts of productive learning? Before answering that question—which in its own right deserves a book—let me discuss a *New York Times* article by Wendy Wasserstein (1999), a very well-known playwright, who was seeking ways to make the theater accessible and relevant to high school students who could not afford the high cost of tickets to the Broadway and Off-Broadway theater.

The eight students, all of non-White minority families, with whom Ms. Wasserstein worked, had never been to a New York theater which, as several said, was for old, white, middle-class people, not accessible or relevant to the likes of them. On Saturdays over a period of several months Ms. Wasserstein and the students went to a Broadway production: a play, or a musical, the ballet, and so forth. Following the theater they would go to a pizza parlor to discuss the production and the reactions of the students, each of whom kept a journal which would be the basis of a term report which would be judged and graded by one of their teachers. To get a sense of the experiences of these students and how it shaped their attitudes and perspectives, the reader should read Ms. Wasserstein's long article in the Arts and Leisure section of the newspaper. It was not only a transforming experience for the students but for Ms. Wasserstein herself.

Ms. Wasserstein is well aware that she was reared in a financially secure family and that her parents had interests they wanted her to assimilate. She also knows there are many parents, poor or not, who have no interest in the theater or the other arts and, therefore, never spoke to their children about them. She also knows that in most communities there are no theaters at all, that New York has theaters galore. Finally, she knew, or she assumed, that if she could have these students under appropriate conditions, they would experience what she had experienced when she was their age, and perhaps with similar consequences. That she was not a teacher did not occur to her. She knew the theater, she knew where the students were coming from, but she did not know if their curiosity had been aroused because they had been encouraged to apply. So now let me briefly answer the question: What are the major features of a context of productive learning? Then we will return to Ms. Wasserstein.

1. From our earliest days we are curious, question-asking organisms. Differing as we do in temperament (and more), our curiosity may attach to very different things. In order for curiosity to be manifest it must be reflected in some form of overt action.

2. Curiosity is not necessarily motivating. Whether curiosity becomes motivating depends on the response it elicits in adults (in some cases from a cat or dog or other pet).

3. Curiosity and question asking occur before a child can talk. The facial expressions we associate with the two—attentiveness, puzzlement—which parents and other adults may or may not perceive and respond to are early manifestations of curiosity and non-verbal question asking. Around 9 months of age many children display what is called stranger anxiety: a reaction of staring, puzzlement, frowning, and then a turning away and/or a clinging to the parent. Again the consequences of this reaction depends on how the parent understands and responds to the child.

4. From the time the child begins to talk, the rate of question asking steadily mounts to the point where some parents become annoyed and give an answer which to the child is unrevealing and unsatisfactory. The answer of the parent or other adult plays an important role in determining how curiosity and question asking play a role in the child's exploration of self, others, and the world. Parents differ widely in how they regard or value or support the role of curiosity and question asking in cognitive and personal development.

5. When children come to school for the first time, they come with loads of questions about what their experience will be. If asked, they

will say they will learn to read, write, and so forth. But they hope and expect more which they do not or cannot verbalize. Will *I* like or be liked by the other children? Will *I* like or be liked by *my* teacher? What will she ask *me?* What will *I* be able to ask her? What if *I* do not understand what she says? Will *I*, should *I*, tell her *I* do not understand? Will she think *I* am dumb? The questions are legion. The pronoun *I* is italicized as a way of suggesting the obvious: The child is self-absorbed, the self is the center of the child's world. That, so to speak, is where the child is coming from.

6. How well and how much of the substance of that self is recognized and exploited for intellectual and personal development depends on the teacher's conception of individuality: what obligations this requires of her, how and to what extent she can adapt to a child's individuality, how to allocate precious time so that her response is not interpreted by the child as insensitive or a brush off. Time, no less than the conception of individuality is always part of the context if only because the context includes other children. (In our schools time is the major enemy of innovation, individuality, and creativity for students and teachers.)

7. Students know the difference between needing or being required to learn and wanting to learn. They may not object to the former, but they want to feel that what they are required to learn has some personal significance for the questions they have about the world they see and experience, for the roles and places they have or may have in that world. Subject matter matters, but so does the relationship between subject matter and the world they experience matter. They want to experience the sense of cognitive and personal growth, the sense that one is changing, horizons are enlarging, that the more one learns the more one wants to learn.[2]

Ms. Wasserstein knew in a general way where her students were coming from: struggling, minority families, no exposure to the theater, considered bright and achievers by their school, no less curious than Ms. Wasserstein about how they will react to their new experience. Her "pedagogy" and its purpose were not to expose them to live theater, period. And it certainly was not to provide them with preorga-

---

2. These seven points, I must emphasize, are less than the bare bones of the features of a context of productive learning. But, I hope, it gives the reader some basis for distinguishing between contexts of productive and unproductive learning. If I have emphasized the universal human features of curiosity and question asking, it is because their manifestations in classrooms are truly rare, less than frequent (much less).

nized information in any form resembling lecturing or handouts. What her article makes clear is that she knew she had to be vigilant during a performance about how and when they responded in their individual ways; that was what she could capitalize on in later discussions, that would give them the sense that she understood them and their world. Indeed, her choice of productions obviously was influenced by what she intuitively knew would be of personal significance to them. She did not tell them what to look for in a play, and in post-theater discussion she did not cross examine or "test" them. She gives several examples how in these discussions students were challenging and learning from each other. Although she does not give us an explanation, I assume that her decision to conduct these discussions while eating pizza (rather than in a conventional restaurant) was not happenstance. If they had never been to a Broadway theater, it is very likely they had never eaten in any restaurant in the area. Pizza and relaxed informality go together. Also, Ms. Wasserstein was prepared to do something she hoped the students would be able to do: to talk about themselves, their hopes, dreams, ambitions. They did and so did Ms. Wasserstein tell them about herself. Finally, time was not the implacable enemy it is in schools. Her allocation of time did justice to the goals of her "curriculum." The dog of learning was not being wagged by its tail of time.

In the millions of words written about the Columbine tragedy, the focus has been solely on the causes of violence in young people: absence of more stringent gun-control legislation, TV Hollywood movies, and a society historically noted for the frequency of displays of violence. In invoking these as precipitating causes, no one was suggesting that schools could do much about them. As more than one person said, "Schools are for the purposes of learning, not for the purpose of lobbying to change this or that in the society." But there were things schools could and should do better. And one of those things derived from the fact that other students in the school were aware of something of which school personnel apparently were not: The two boys were part of a small group who dressed in a strikingly flamboyant, attention-getting manner, who often were heard in and out of the classroom to express hostile thoughts and intentions, and were loners. If no student thought they were dangerous, they saw them as relatively asocial and different. But what was apparent to some students was not known to school personnel who, even if they knew, took no action of any kind; we can say that no teacher or administrator was quoted as saying that they had concerns about the boys.

What could and should schools do? To that question countless commentators, including psychologists, offered the same bromide they gave to parents: to be more knowledgeable about, sensitive to, and vigilant about what children are thinking, feeling, and doing. I label it a bromide because it will do no good (or harm) because it bypasses the question: What is there about a school as densely populated as Columbine that fosters and sustains a psychological cleavage between students and teachers? You do not have to do more studies to confirm again that students and teachers inhabit different worlds and that each of their worlds—in this case the school world—is comprised of many groups which vary in numerous ways: transiency, fluidity, boundaries, composition, degree of gender mix, and hierarchy. Those factors are more pronounced for student than for teacher groupings, if only because the number of students is so large and one of the purposes of their groupings is to give and receive personal and social support, a kind of safe haven that dilutes the sense of unwanted privacy and allows for some degree of intimacy. It is the rare student who begins high school who is not from day one scanning the surround to determine with whom he or she will feel comfortable and safe. That scanning frequently has the quality of desperation; the need to belong can be as pressuring as the need to eat. The strength of their need to belong, to be accepted, to be understood, cannot be overestimated.

In their groups the students talk about many things and that includes teachers and administrators: their personalities, their quirks, whether they are likeable or not, whether they are good or bad teachers, fair markers, and what the gossip in the rumor mill tells them about the lives, families, the outside-of-school activities of this or that teacher, as well as relationships among school personnel which are in one or another way "juicy." These groupings reinforce and sustain a "we-they" dichotomy in the world of the school, and it is frequently a dichotomy which has an adversarial flavor.

In a general way school personnel know, feel, experience that cleavage. They regard it as going, so to speak, with the territory called generational gap. There are individual teachers, albeit few in number, who try to bridge that gap with this or that student, especially if this student seeks out the teacher. Students are well aware of who these unusual teachers are even though most students do not feel personally secure or safe enough to approach them. Most teachers regard the cleavage as one that students "cause" and is desired by them. In the dynamics of the self-fulfilling prophecy, teachers react in ways that sustain the cleavage.

We say—we certainly are told ad nauseam—that teachers are role models for students. But the concept of teacher as role model clearly implies that teachers create and foster a social-interpersonal context in which the learner regards the social and intellectual life of school as stimulating, interesting, mind expanding; that one is changing as a thinker, that the more you know the more you need to know, that what you are learning has a personally meaningtul direction you willingly take. For students in middle and high school the school is frequently *socially* interesting, and even enjoyable, because that is where they have friends whom they feel understand, accept, and support them. *That interest does not extend to the classroom,* a point that is confirmed in studies and readily acknowledged by teachers. As one teacher said to me, "Trying to get students interested in what I teach them is like pulling teeth. Their minds are elsewhere. They dutifully show up and go through the motions." Scores of teachers have said versions of that to me literally scores of times. There are, I hasten to add, exceptions but they are just that, exceptions, which is to say exceptional teachers.

Why is it that in the hundreds of interviews reported on TV, radio, and other mass media of Columbine students, school personnel, parents, and assorted others, nothing was ever said about the classroom context of learning? There is more than one reason, but there is one I have to mention, and that is because in an affluent Denver suburb test scores of the students were at, and probably above, national norms. So what is there to say about the context of the classroom that has bearing on cleavages, reduced interest, values and goals, the sense of apartness or alienation or adversarialism? No one, including so-called expert psychologists, counselors, educators, seemed to know what has long been reported, studied, known: as students go from elementary to middle to high school their interest in and their motivation for learning, for intellectual inquiry, steadily decreases. Why is it that no one mentioned that even in our most respected colleges and universities faculty bemoan the fact that entering students too frequently cannot write clear sentences, paragraphs, and essays, and that they do not know "how to think." This, I should emphasize, is never said with the intention of tarnishing all entering students but rather to indicate that a number of them have educational deficits that were unexpected given their test scores. And in some, perhaps all, of these esteemed institutions, they offer remedial programs. In other colleges and universities whose standards for admission are discernibly less stringent, faculty complaints are louder and more poignant and remedial programs are elective standard fare, sometimes required fare.

For students, especially those in middle and high school, the classroom is an uninteresting, unstimulating, boring place where you do what you are told or expected to do, you answer questions, you do not ask questions, and only when you leave the classroom can you do, think, and talk about what "really" interests you with other students whom you understand and they understand you. Such relationships with and feelings toward teachers is the exception not the rule.

The classroom is not (again the usual exceptions aside) a context of productive learning. It has few, if any, of its features. That students learn subject matter and pass tests is not to be sneezed at, but neither should it be judged as proof that what has been learned has been absorbed in ways that are personally and intellectually meaningful, a goad to want to learn more and give direction and shape to emerging interests and goals, to visions of a career. As I have said elsewhere (Sarason, 1996a, 1998a, 1998b), there is one overarching criterion by which schools should be judged: If when a student is graduated from high school, that student wants to continue to learn more about self, others, and the past and present world, that school has done a good job. At the present time that criterion is very infrequently met.

If your doctor tells you that you have normal body temperature, he or she will not say that you are well and healthy because he knows that in fact the symptoms you report may indicate you are not all "well." Body temperature is by no means a totally valid indicator of health: the physician goes beyond that single indicator. Similarly, passing tests does not mean that the student is intellectually "healthy," that the student has assimilated knowledge, attitudes, and a style of thinking that have sustaining, productive consequences.

It is totally understandable that the nation riveted on the Columbine tragedy and in unusually muted, non-polemical way agreed, on among other things, that school personnel should be more sensitive to and vigilant about what students are doing, talking, and thinking. In focusing only on violence, the nation ignored a critical question: Is there something about the size of high schools, the way they are organized, the way time is perceived and allocated, and the selection and preparation of educators that should caution us to look beyond extreme violence, that may suggest a preventive approach rather than an exclusive dependence on repair, the track record of which is by no means significantly effective?

One of the distinctive contributions of American psychology has been devising and applying statistical techniques to determine the degree to which psychological characteristics and performances cluster within individuals and within and among groups of individuals. Which characteristics to study as well as which tests to be used to measure them are determined by theoretical considerations, the previous findings of others, and what may be called hunches. It is an approach that takes the obvious very seriously: No single psychological characteristic is comprehensible apart from its degree of relationship to other characteristics of an individual.

What would it mean if we were to take seriously what is obvious in that approach for the purpose not of understanding one school (like Columbine) alone but rather to pursue this question: In order to evaluate what we think we know about Columbine, as well as the appropriateness of our suggestions about changing and improving it, should we not determine whether there are trends or developments *in schools generally* which may confirm or disconfirm what we think we know and recommend for Columbine? Columbine is not an individual human being but rather an organized collection of individuals who vary in many ways. The question we are now asking is not about discrete individuals but about discrete schools. Let me put it more concretely and personally: Is my analysis of Columbine illuminated by developments in other schools where violence has not been an issue? When the unit of analysis is not an individual person but individual organizations, American psychology is of no help even though potentially it has much to offer. The interest is simply not there.

What is a charter school? Why have a large majority of states enacted legislation creating charter schools? Why did President Clinton ask for and receive congressional funding to create 3,000 new charter schools? A charter school is one that is created and administered by a small group—teachers, parents, and other community individuals—based on what has been considered to be an innovative plan that gives promise to increase and/or enlarge what students experience and learn. Crucially, the charter school is exempt from the usual rules and regulations of the existing school system; the charter is permitted to go its own unfettered way to achieve its stated goals. They are "free" of the existing system.

Although it is rarely stated explicitly, the justification for charter schools derives from a conclusion: If you want to innovate in order to demonstrate a more productive context of learning, you have to be free of the stifling rules and regulations of the existing school system whose capacity to change, let alone innovate, is not far above zero. That conclusion can be put more succinctly: For all practical purposes the existing system is unrescuable if the goal is to change and improve it.

I have read scores of applications submitted for approval of a charter school. I have talked to many individuals starting or planning to start a charter school. For my present purposes here, there are characteristics the creators of charter schools state without exception.

1. The school will be small. It will start with a truly small cohort of students, that number will increase in subsequent years but not to the point where size defeats the innovative purposes of the school.

2. Students will be known, treated, and respected as distinctive individuals, not as part of a homogeneous group in which individual differences are ignored, or glossed over, or not capitalized on.

3. The collegial relationship among teachers will be close, even intense, in order to insure that their knowledge of and experience with students are shared, discussed, and utilized in ways appropriate to the needs and characteristics of individual students.

4. The relationship between teachers and parents will not be a superficial or transient one. Parents should and will have a responsible voice and role not only in regard to their child but to the overall, innovative purposes of the school. The usual gulf between parents and school, community and school, will be bridged.

Even if these purposes were recognized at Columbine and similar high schools (and middle schools), they could not be realized. Their size and the balkanization of subject matter in unconnected departments make it impossible. It is understandable if those who commented on the Columbine tragedy said that teachers should be more vigilant about and sensitive to what students are thinking and doing. If it is understandable, it also exposes an appalling degree of ignorance—more charitably, a total unfamiliarity—of the size and organizational features of these schools. What should be the frequency and quality of the relationship between Columbine parents and teachers? What roles and responsibilities should parents assume? Neither question got raised or discussed in all that was said about that school. Is it that parents are uninterested? They feel strange and unwelcomed in the school? No one has ever said that they have a crucial role to play? Or is it that in subtle and non-subtle ways the message has been conveyed that parents should do only what the educators ask them to do, that all other matters are the exclusive preserve of the educators? The charter school movement, in addition to the growing support of parents for vouchers, plus the dramatic rise of the number of parents who opt for home schooling are symptoms both of parental interest and dissatisfaction with schools as they are.

Why is it that the overwhelming number of charter schools are elementary schools? Why is it that the educational reform movement in the post World War II era was, on the level of action and practice, also concentrated on elementary schools? How does one explain this selective emphasis? There are several important reasons but two I will briefly mention here, although the answers the question deserves would require a book.

The first is, again, the size and organizational balkanization of middle and high schools. Assuming that you are not a proponent of change by dictate, where do you start? And "you," far more often than not, is external to the school, although in every such instance someone in that school or in a higher echelon seeks your help. We have learned by bitter experience that seeking to bring about institutional change has to ask and answer this question: Do the minimal conditions exist which suggests you stand a fair chance of achieving change and below which you should say, "no, thank you"? For example, is one of your minimal criteria—and I consider this a very important criterion, if not the crucial one—that after the goals, the nuts and bolts, and the commitments that will be required are fully explained to the educational staff, at least 80–90% in secret ballot agree to proceed; otherwise, the change process is aborted? What is a realistic time perspective? What resources of time, people, and money will be required? By what criteria will the effort be evaluated?

The questions are many. That is, or should be, obvious, especially as the number of targeted participants is large and the organizational structure is complicated and bureaucratic. That is why educational reformers steer clear of middle and high schools.

The second reason is more subtle, almost always undiscussed or even formulated. Only one educational reformer put it in clear language to me: She said "Middle and high schools are modeled after colleges and universities in their organizational structure. These schools are less byzantine but nevertheless byzantine. Many educational reformers have been academics, and every one can give you gory accounts of efforts meaningfully to change this or that part of the college or university. Frankly, when my interests turned to educational reform, I knew enough about middle and high schools and decided to focus on elementary schools."

I should emphasize that I have not been comparing high schools and charter schools but rather indicating that the forces, ideas, and experiences which gave rise to the charter school movement are highly similar and relevant to middle and high schools generally. That is to say, once you understand when and why charter schools appeared on the educational horizon, you look at middle and high schools and the proffered solutions to their problems in a way different from your accustomed one. High schools do not exist in a societal vacuum; they are institutions part of an educational system which serves students, parents, and community. When something new and very different appears in the system (like charter schools), it is very likely an implied criticism of all other schools in the system. When we rivet on one type of school, which is what happened in commentary about Columbine, we cannot derive the potential clarifications from asking: What else is happening in the larger system we should know about, however different on the surface those happenings are from the type of school we seek to understand and improve?

Let us look at one other happening in the world of schooling. It is a happening with a long controversial history, but it is one that in the last decade has picked up steam. It is a happening which was feebly alluded to in the case of Columbine: Teachers and administrators should be more sensitive to what students are thinking and doing. The happening I refer to is the frequency and force of criticisms about teacher competence, psychological sophistication, pedagogical creativity, and preparatory programs. Within the past year a number of states have adopted a "shape-up-or-ship-out" policy putting preparatory programs on notice that unless they improve the quality of performance of those they select and train they will be terminated. Aside from increasing the timing and number of postgraduate requirements for teachers, many states have sought to change the length of the interval between finishing a preparatory program and being granted tenure. Back in 1962 I, Kenneth Davidson, and Burton Blatt published *The Preparation of Teachers: An Unstudied Problem in Education.* That book went nowhere, which did not surprise me. But as the years went by and my 1965 prediction (Sarason, 1965) that the education reform would go nowhere was being proved correct, I wrote in 1993 a related book, *The Case for Change: Rethinking the Preparation of Educators.* That book had much more of an impact, not on the level of action but in terms of the number of educators who wrote to me to express approval of what the book contained. And then in 1996 appeared the report of the National Commission on Teaching and America's Future, written by Dr. Linda Darling-Hammond who was the commission's executive director. It is a damning report, and it seemed obvious, at least to me, that Dr. Darling-Hammond had to exercise a good deal of self-control to avoid demonstrating the depth of her feelings.

But none of this was even alluded to by those Columbine commentators who said that teachers should be more vigilant about and sensitive to what students assimilate, value, and utilize in the subject matters they are learning. What these commentators said was not intended to be applicable only to Columbine but to schools generally, but they gave no indication that they were aware of two things: the inadequacies of teacher preparatory programs and the failure of past efforts to change and improve them.

The substance of this and the previous chapter, and in keeping with the aim of this book, requires that we return to my discussion in Chapter 3 of American psychology's decision to make clinical psychology a new and major field in graduate education. The reader will recall that two factors in the World War II years and their immediate aftermath were decisive in the adoption of that policy. The first was the sense of obligation to the millions of war veterans who would require clinical psychological services. The second was the recognition that problems of living, of personal misery and unhappiness, of wasted potential, and of extreme disabling disorders of thinking, feeling, and personal-social competence were frequent in the society generally. In brief, American psychology was responding to a perceived and very important societal problem which if not confronted could or would over time affect the society in untoward ways. As a participant at the Boulder Conference I did not quarrel with that assessment or the decision that it made, I did quarrel with that part of the decision which in effect maintains the gulf between psychology and education to the detriment of both as well as the larger society. By riveting on the clinical and repair approach, psychology would be short-changing the potential contribution it could make to the preventive orientation. My thinking and experience at the time were far from comprehensive, but sufficient to have engendered in me the intuition that over the long term psychology potentially had more to "give and get" from an alliance with education than with the medical-psychiatric community. I did not at the time foresee what was going to happen in American schools, but within a few years what had been an intuition became an explicit conviction. Why? Primarily because my research program required that I begin to live, so to speak, in schools, many schools; the word *school* no longer signified a place but rather a diversity of relationships, practices, values, and purposes. And I quickly learned that there was a world of difference between what people said formally and informally and what they would say on and off the record.

I had done clinical work with troubled people. I marveled at how the picture of the client that formed in my mind after, say, the first two sessions differed dramatically from that I arrived at in the final two sessions. Although I had been trained to expect that, I had difficulty taking distance from the picture that had formed after the first two sessions. There was, for me, a compelling concreteness to that initial picture. I recount those experiences here because they are in principle why American psychology has contributed so little to our understanding of schools. What they know about schools comes from memories of their school days, or what their children tell them, a place that houses few adults and many children and where learning occurs, and learning means for them what students do or do not learn; it does not mean what teachers do not learn. Learning is a one way street!

The reader will recall that in Chapter 2 I presented part of Wendell Garner's account of when and how certain theories of perception had to be corrected, or changed. It is not happenstance that his accounts occurred during World War II when perceptual theorists were presented with "real life" practical problems of great importance to the military. It was not only a sobering experience for them, it became a creative experience because it improved the scope and validity of their theories. That is why Garner concluded that the snobbery implied (and often explicitly expressed) by the basic-applied research dichotomy was unjustified, ill advised, and impoverishing for the basic researcher. And that is why those who consider themselves the protectors of the ethos of basic research in American psychology look upon schools as places teeming with practical problems from which they will derive nothing that would cause them to change their theories. Practical problems are for lesser folk! Besides, they would say, the practical problems in our schools are messy and complicated and schools are not places designed or organized to permit rigorous and systematic research. With that point I am in total agreement. But is it the aim of a scientific human psychology to develop theories and knowledge only for behavior in unmessy settings? Is it inconceivable that what appears to be messy is highly ordered to those in it and that it is a type of order that generates practical problems but that the relationship between that order and those problems is incorrectly understood or not at all perceived by those in that ordered setting?

Must we be content to await the time when events in the society are of such gravity and magnitude that it will force psychology to see fit to bridge the chasm between it and schooling? And when and if such events develop, will psychology opt for the repair, as it did in regard to clinical psychology, or preventive orientation?

In concluding this chapter I feel obliged to make clear that I did not emphasize size of school because reducing size is sufficient basis for expecting that it would have robust consequences. Such an expectation will lead only to disappointment. For me, size is a telltale sign of how as a society we understand and take seriously the features and requirements of a context of productive learning. Why are our middle and high schools as large as they are? They were not built over the opposition of our communities. They were built because they were deemed a fiscally efficient way of providing an effective, productive education, places in which students could grow and flourish. I daresay that few if any member of any community took other than pride in supporting the construction of these schools; they had no doubt they were doing the right thing for the right educational values and outcomes. And, it should be noted, the educational community led the way. And through it all, there was no challenge to a conceptual orthodoxy in which the requirements of contexts of productive learning never were articulated or discussed. It could be argued that such a challenge would have been fruitless because of fiscal restraints, that building more and smaller schools would never have been approved. So why pose a challenge that you know will fall on deaf ears? But that argument concedes the point: These schools were not built because there was clarity about the contextual requirements for productive learning. Productive learning was not on the agenda except in the form of hope and empty rhetoric. We have paid a very high price for very disappointing (but predictable) outcomes. And the price we have paid and will continue to pay has been for repair, and the history of the educational reform movement is a history of the more things change the more they have remained the same. We will be fortunate if things *only* remain the same. My fear and prediction are they will get worse.

Today we are witness to the clamor for smaller class size. That is an encouraging sign if only because *finally* the issue of size of learning contexts has been raised and in some states being implemented. But here again the rationale is grievously incomplete because it is based on an unarticulated assumption for which there is not a shred of evidence. The assumption is: A teacher who is inadequate or mediocre with a class of 25–30 students will become adequate with a class of 15–20 students. And by inadequate and mediocre I mean the degree to which a teacher creates and sustains a context of productive learning. Over the decades I have observed, truly observed, upwards of 500 teachers. Perhaps 10% met *some* of my criteria of creating and sustaining a context of productive learning. Perhaps 2% met them all. I am by no means the only one who has come to that conclusion. I have discussed this in some detail in my 1999 *Teaching as a Performing Art.* Wrapped up in the size variable are all the important issues in education. Realistically, we cannot deal with all issues at the same time. But one thing is for sure: If you go the route of smaller contexts and at the same time do not change the way teachers are selected and trained, the desired outcomes will fall very short of the mark.

CHAPTER 6

Contexts of Testing
and Contexts of Learning

To write about psychology in a meaningful and comprehensive or semi-comprehensive way is a daunting task. Even when the effort is restricted to one of psychology's major foci, the task is daunting, especially if that specialty is put in a historical context. But if, as I have chosen to do in this book, the task is to write about *American* psychology and schools, it is impossible for one person. By italicizing *American* I obviously am suggesting that the relationship between psychology and schools has to be seen in terms of a particular society and culture, and that goes beyond the capabilities and knowledge of one person (let alone an aged one!). History and culture are omnipresent variables, but what makes them so fascinating, complex, and even confusing as variables is that different historians "read" history in different ways with different emphases. History is always a continuous account marked by new data, values, and purposes; it has no single beginning and end points, it is always being added to and revised, it seeks to understand a perceived present by a perceived past at the same time that it is acknowledged that an inscrutable future will illuminate where we were incomplete, or wrong, or misguided.

That is why I resisted for so long writing this book. I knew that American psychology—more than that of any other country—is, organizationally speaking, a very large affair which was what it was and became what it is because of sea-swell changes in America and the world. American psychology did not have a socially virginal birth and development. And that is certainly the case in regard to the origins and development of our schools. If they are both creatures of the same society and its culture, two questions have to be asked. The first is: Why did American psychology come to play such an influential role in schools through the development of intelligence and achievement tests? The second question is: Why has American psychology shown such little interest in how schools have used psychological tests and how in the culture of the school tests are among the most crucial factors in determining the lives of students and teachers?

Let me make my point by analogy. We are all familiar with the functions of the federal Food and Drug Administration. Briefly, the FDA exists to prevent the sale and distribution of drugs-medications which have harmful short- or long-term consequences or do not have the effects their makers claim. And to prevent such occurrences developers are required to go through a step-by-step, costly, time-consuming process that provides scientifically convincing evidence that the drug is effective for the humans for whom it is appropriate and that untoward side effects are absent or minimal. One thing is crucial in the process: The drug is used in the same kind of clinical setting, with the same kind of patients, and administered and supervised by the same kind of physicians as would be the case if and when the drug is finally approved. In short, there is no professional gulf between those who employ the drug in the clinical trials and those who will be using it after it has been approved. In fact, if approved, the drug is accompanied by written materials, which can be lengthy, that advise physicians about how and when the drug should be employed, what to be alert to, when use of the drug should be terminated, and with what other medications it can or should not be used.

In contrast, there exists a wide gulf between the psychologists who developed intelligence tests and those who gave the tests in schools. And, for all practical purposes, that was also the case with achievement tests. The tests were developed and sold much the same way as the over-the-counter pharmaceuticals. The conditions in which the tests were being given in schools, how the test results were being interpreted, how frequently the results were being interpreted inappropriately—in those matters the test developers were in no position to judge. It may sound strange and unfair, but they were not knowledgeable about the organization and culture of the school. From the standpoint of the use of tests in schools there was no quality control. Developing and selling intelligence tests in this country is big business. One of the biggest corporations in this arena is the Psychological Corporation, which was created by James McKeen Cattell, one of the founders of the American Psychological Association. The important point is that tests developed for the purposes of the education of children are produced by psychologists who have spent little or no time in schools. Given the extent to which psychological tests can affect the lives of students, I find it both strange and inexcusable that an agency like the FDA has been neither created nor called for by the psychological community.

The history of psychological testing is the history of controversy having many sources which go beyond the narrow confines of American psychology. Indeed, the origins of the testing movement and its controversies were in France. Alfred Binet started it all, so to speak, shortly before the turn of the twentieth century. That history contains all of the theoretical and practical issues with which we continue to deal. Tests are not "things" independent of national history and traditions, the form and strength of its social problems, what kinds of individuals develop tests and why, and why their use and their results become a passionate concern far beyond their academic origins. Tests are—and I would argue they inevitably are—social lightening rods because different people and groups have conflicting views about how to explain differences in human performance. In a country like ours where it is rhetorically axiomatic that "all men are created equal," it should occasion no surprise that when test results appear to contradict the rhetoric, controversy comes on to the societal stage. Let me begin by very briefly presenting three of the major sources of controversy.

1. There is the definitional-conceptual problem. So, for example, intelligence is not a concrete thing or object which you can see, feel, or touch, let alone taste or hear. Intelligence is a concept invented by a conceiver and different conceivers come up with different "inventions." There are psychologists who believe that intelligence is a general factor that plays a role in all areas of cognitive development and performance; some people have more and others have less of the general factor. This is disputed by other psychologists who believe there is no general factor but rather several relatively discrete factors and no single test or single number (IQ) can give you a picture of the presence and strength of those factors. For example, an individual may be low on the memory factor and high in matters of spatial relationships. The practical import of the dispute is of obvious importance because it raises this question: What should we want or need to know about a student's cognitive ability or abilities if we are to help a student play to his or her strengths and cognitive style? How do you go from test scores to an appropriate pedagogy?

2. Within any group of students of a particular age, there are individual differences in test performance, and that is also the case in regard to differences between groups who differ in ethnicity, color, social class, or religious affiliation. How does one explain these differences which have persisted over time and in some instances have resisted efforts to change them? Early in the twentieth century eminent psychologists were not in doubt that these differences were largely due to genetic factors. Then came psychologists who believed that a genetic

explanation was far too simple and unjustified; they emphasized environmental factors. In almost every decade of the past century the heredity vs. environment, nature vs. nurture controversy would erupt and opposing explanations were passionately expressed. When and why they erupted when they did are complex stories reflective of a distinctive American society. Although the country welcomed immigrants because of its economic needs, there was fear that the millions of immigrants arriving in waves would weaken the social fabric; the facts are that they did contribute to a rising crime rate in addition to performing poorly on the early intelligence tests and in school performance. And, no less important, the immigrant parents were perceived as unintelligent and passed on their poor genes to the many children they had. The eugenics movement, state laws permitting sterilization, the rise in the number and size of state institutions to house wayward or mentally defective individuals (the term mentally retarded came much later)—this and more were seen as confirmatory of a genetic explanation. And when the test results of the recruits for World War I were analyzed and published and the low test scores of Blacks and the offspring of immigrants were at or near the low end of the distribution of scores, the nature-nurture controversy took on new dimensions. And, closer to our time, when beginning in the late fifties the federal government began to spend billions upon billions of dollars to improve schools and raise achievement test scores, and those efforts did not meet with success, it was predictable that controversy would erupt again, and it did. The controversy continues, and at its core are the questions: What do we mean by intelligence? Are our tests (unwittingly) biased in favor of some groups and biased against others? Are schools organized in ways that make for contexts of productive learning? Is it, as many have said, that preparatory programs for teachers are major obstacles to school change and increased learning?

3. What is the controversy today? It is not about theories of intelligence or the sources of bias in tests or the nature-nurture issue. It is about standards for educational performance: raising standards, employing achievements tests which reflect the substance of those standards, not promoting or graduating any student who is below a set standard, and giving students the opportunity to spend summer in school in order to meet the standards, and if he or she never meets the standard, so be it. It is a shape-up or ship-out policy. In addition, if after a few years some schools continue to have a significant number of failing students, the school will be closed. It is a policy that sends a warning message both to students and teachers. In the state of New York the Regents changed the substance and format of the achieve-

ment tests in ways they considered reflective of higher standards. And when in 1999 the tests were administered to all students in certain grades, the media duly noted that parents and their students approached the day of testing with anxiety and resentment. But apparently no one was prepared for the finding that suburban schools had a surprising number of students who did not meet the new standards and that the gap between urban and suburban schools was less than it had ever been. New York City is spending millions of dollars for summer schools for students whose schools were below the standard. It is surprising that there has been very little public criticism of the newly developed tests, but there have been individuals who interpreted the results as further proof that the decline or watering down of standards in urban schools had also occurred in suburban schools.

And there are more than a few people who regard our schools as intractable messes. I should also note that not only have teachers been silent on these findings but beginning a decade or so ago the late Albert Shanker was one of the most articulate proponents of raising standards. I assume that readers of this book are well aware that on achievement tests given to students in different countries but in the same grade, the United States did not come up smelling roses, a fact that was experienced in the United States as a narcissistic wound similar to that experienced after the then Soviet Union was the first country to put a satellite into orbit. As today, when that happened in 1956, it sparked—coming as it did after the 1954 Supreme Court desegregation decision—a heated controversy which became an explosive one.

When you review the history of psychological testing, two questions can be asked; the answer to the first will seem obvious, and the answer to the second is a can of theoretical and practical worms. The second question is one American psychology ignored.

The first question is, Why did American psychology concentrate on the development of tests of school-related import which had several features? The tests would be given in schools in formally structured situations over which, from the standpoint of the student, he or she has no control or a say. Students do not ask to take the tests, they are required to do so regardless of the student's feelings, maturation, opinions. In this sense the test situation is one contrived by others for their purposes. And it is contrived in the sense that the test items bear little resemblance to the substance or content of problems with which the students deal outside of school. The psychologist's answer was that the litmus test of the efficiency of the psychological test is whether it predicts well the student's academic level and performance and/or what

the student has learned in school. The fact that the substance and format of this test may on the surface appear to be very different from the
problem-solving situations students confront outside of school is beside
the point, which is that the tests do reasonably well what they purport
to do: provide valid and useful information about the ability of students
to learn what they are asked or what the test results indicate they
should be able to learn. That is the kind of information schools need
and want, and American psychology should be given credit for providing that kind of information which allows educators to be helpful to
students. Absent that information, the teacher is very likely to make
the error of expecting too much or too little of students, expectations
which can be damaging to their personal and intellectual development.

The second question is, What is the relationship between the kind
of information provided by school tests in the school situation and the
kind of information that would be provided by observing problem-
solving behavior in naturally occurring situations outside of school? No
one would deny that outside of school students confront problems,
they are asking questions to which they seek answers, they are motivated to become to feel competent and to enlarge their sense of understanding of themselves and their social world. Only in one respect did
psychologists take that glimpse of the obvious seriously and that was in
their developmental theories, as in case of Binet. Then and now no theorist would say that how, what, and why students learn in school is
highly correlated with the whys, whats, and hows of learning outside
of school. The fact is there are no existing systematic data to determine
the correlation. We have stories, anecdotes, and opinions, but those are
bases for raising questions; they are not the substances of briefs prepared for the court of evidence. Single cases can be important and conceptually important as long as you keep in mind that they are just that:
single cases.

The correlational issue I am raising was not in my head when I took
my first professional job in 1942 as a psychologist in the Southbury
Training School. The facility could be described as an encapsulated "village" in which approximately 2,500 people lived and worked. Because
of its geographical isolation there were living quarters for personnel.
There was a large school building, sites for work-training purposes, a
well-equipped hospital, a similarly equipped farm, a barbershop, a shoe
repair shop, and more. I note these features because the Southbury
Training School, which covered hundreds of acres, should be described
as a total community rather than a village. Except for a small number
of employees, *everyone else worked and/or lived there.* The significance of
what I am describing is in the fact that I lived and worked there. *I had*

the opportunity to observe the residents I saw in the testing situation in many other non-testing situations. And it was by no means rare that I was surprised by the discrepancies I noted between their behavior and quality of problem solving in the two situations. I can sum up my experience in Southbury by saying that by the time I left there to go to Yale, I was convinced that the behavior, quality, and level of an individual in the testing situation was not *highly* correlated with those same features outside the testing situation. I italicize "highly" because I do not want to be interpreted as suggesting that there is no or a very low correlation. What I am saying is that if the conclusions you draw about an individual's behavior and intellectual-conceptual performance derive only from the testing situation, you will be wrong or misled in an undetermined number of instances. Somewhere in the corpus of Erik Erickson's writing he says something relevant here: before seeing a child in therapy he would have dinner and spend the evening with the child and his or her family. That is a way of saying that absent that kind of experience he might be misled in interpreting the child's behavior in the one-on-one situation in Erickson's office.

The issue here is not the psychologist, the test, or the test situation, but rather the obvious fact that these tests were developed to understand and predict behavior and performance in one or more nontesting situations. Even when these test are used to predict classroom and school performance, the underlying assumption is that these tests say something important about the child's ability and learning outside of that situation. If a child scores low on an intelligence test or on a reading or arithmetic test, we do *not* say that those results have no bearing on that child's style and level of learning outside of school. We unreflectively assume it has a bearing. And that is the issue because we do not have a "test" by which to evaluate learning and performance outside of school. We have two kinds of contexts of learning. The first is the "naturally occurring" one outside of school, and the second is a formally organized, highly structured, calendar driven, adult-determined context. I am not passing judgment here. I am belaboring the obvious. They are different kinds of contexts.

But why in regard to tests and schools did American psychology ignore the obvious? Why did they want and hope that their tests would be used by school personnel as one of the most important bases for judgment and action in regard to pedagogy and education policy? The answer is complex, and I restrict myself to several of its features.

The first feature returns us to the massive immigrations of the nineteenth and the early decades of the twentieth century because the new arrivals were perceived as, among other things, unintelligent. Just as immigration authorities sought to keep out those with serious physical disease or mental derangements, they also sought to keep out obviously unintelligent individuals. For the former they could use physicians who had ways of identifying serious illness (like tuberculosis), but they had no way to identify different levels of intelligence of people who did not speak English, and looked, acted, and dressed in strange ways. What has to be emphasized is that we are talking about an era when the political, social, and intellectual American establishment was mightily concerned with consequences of immigration for American society and for sustaining and improving the "genetic stock" which had catapulted the country into international power; Good stock = good intelligence, bad stock = poor intelligence. Darwinian theory with its theme of the survival of the fittest, Galton's studies and explanation of genius, as well as studies of one generation passing on inferior gene pools to subsequent generations stirred public interest, anxiety, and movements to devise ways to identify different levels of intelligence. American psychology was born, so to speak, during that era, and a number of psychologists—almost all of them holding views identical to those of the "native" establishment—seized the opportunity to demonstrate the potential contribution the young field of psychology could make to the American society. They devised a variety of tests with different content and format purporting to measure intelligence, including tests which did not require spoken language by the testee. When Binet's writings appeared, they were much taken by his methods, his use of age scaling, and his way of relating mental to chronological age to arrive at a number, the IQ. Binet's methods were tailor made for an American psychology eager to appear quantitative and therefore scientific. Intelligence was a thing or power, and they wanted to quantify, to measure it.

What is the imagery ordinarily conjured up by the word *measure?* The imagery involves an agreed-upon, calibrated, or standardized instrument or mechanism or process used to describe attributes of objects or people at a particular time in a particular place for particular purposes. And when those attributes change over time, we expect that the measuring instrument will tell us how much they have changed. And, more important, the measuring rod should not be influenced either in its application or calculation of results by personal characteristics of the user. The imagery associated with science always contains something about measurement.

It is to the credit of American psychology that it early on began to confront the problem of measurement of psychological attributes including, of course, intelligence and school performance, for both of which there was good reason to believe that personal judgments by teachers were unreliable. What was needed were psychological measures that gave unbiased results. Developing such tests, psychologists found, was no easy matter because the process is beset by thorny problems of item and population sampling, scaling of item difficulty, test and retest reliability, and choosing external criteria by which it can be determined whether the tests predict what they are supposed to predict. It is a very time-consuming task which requires resources of personnel and money. That is why among the many thousands of tests psychologists have developed so few of them have passed the tests of scrutiny and time. That is certainly the case in regard to tests of intelligence and school performance.

I deliberately left out one feature of the imagery associated with measurement, and it is one I consider most influential in that it riveted the psychologists' attention on the relationship between test scores and school performance, almost totally ignoring the relationship of test scores to level and quality of problem solving behavior outside of school.

Imagine that we can interview the dozen or so psychologists who played a major role in the development of tests of intelligence and school performance. We ask them four questions:

1. *Do your tests rest on a conception or theory about the components of intellectual functioning and how they relate to each other?* The answer would have been; of course, my theory determined the substance or content of the items of my test.

2. *Why is it that you almost exclusively relied on criteria of school performance to demonstrate that your test was a valid measure of an individual's ability to learn?* The answer would have been that schooling shapes lives, that it is our obligation to provide information that gives a valid measure of the student's ability that the school needs if schooling is to be of maximal benefit to that child. An appropriate pedagogy depends on valid assessment of ability to learn. You cannot and should not try to make a silk purse out of a sow's ear. Similarly, you should not be ignorant of when you are teaching the equivalent of a silk purse.

3. *Do you assume that the abilities your tests measure and predict rather well as to the level of quality of school learning would be highly correlated with level of quality of those abilities outside of school?* The answer would have been that they would be highly correlated, but we cannot say how high the correlation would be. We recognize that abilities salient for school learning will not be called for in environments different than those in schools. Nevertheless, those abilities are needed and present in and out

of school environments, and we assume that the levels in quality of those abilities would not differ from the display of those abilities in school.

4. *Should not that assumption be tested? Why has it not been?* In asking those questions we are not suggesting the correlation would be low, let alone zero, but rather that as long as we do not know that correlation we may—and we emphasize may—be overlooking data of theoretical and practical import in regard to our tests, learning contexts, and the determinants of learning. The answer would be that the scientific and methodological requirements to which one must adhere in developing reliable and valid tests must be carried out in *controlled* conditions and that clearly would not be possible in out-of-school contexts over which we have no *control*. Out-of-school contexts are too complicated, varied, incomparable, and unreplicable to be rigorously and systemically observed and measured. We did our best to approximate a laboratory in which we would exercise *control* over the relevant variables in as objective a way as possible. If we had done what you are suggesting, control goes by the boards, and we are back to personal opinion, anecdote, and methodological and conceptual messiness.

I italicized the word *control* because it illuminates the importance those psychologists attached to obtaining data in situations they developed and controlled, ignoring the possibility that the behavior and cognitive attributes they observed and measured were by no means representative of those attributes and behavior; that is, they look somewhat different in what I call noncontrived, naturally occurring contexts.

I am not saying that these psychologists should not have proceeded as they did. I am saying that they never considered, let alone took seriously, what they or any other person knew either from personal experience or observation: learning looks different in different contexts, a statement for which there is a good deal of case literature. Admittedly, reports of single cases are frail reeds of evidence. But some studies go beyond single case reports. For example, in 1953 Ginzberg and Bray published a book *The Uneducated,* a book that never received the recognition it deserves. That book is a comprehensive analysis of inductees in World War II who had IQs in the retarded range or who were for all practical purposes illiterate or both. It turned out that several of these people had been awarded the Silver Medal of Honor, which is one notch below the Congressional Medal of Honor. Now, in order to receive such an award some superior officer has to write a detailed description of the battle situation in which the individual displayed a most unusual combination of problem solving, motivation, and courage. What they did and accomplished was not explainable by their test scores or low level of literacy. You do not get the Silver Medal of Honor on the sole basis of courage. You were faced with a problem which if not "solved" meant that other soldiers would be killed or taken prisoner or more likely overrun or killed.

Ginzberg and Bray report data directly relevant to tests and schooling. As in World War I, in World War II the military faced manpower shortages because of the large number of people who had been rejected for service on intellectual, educational, psychiatric, or medical grounds. Also, a large number had been accepted who were retarded and/or illiterate and unable, therefore, to read and follow instructions at a fourth-grade level, the level deemed minimally necessary to be competent in various work sites. If those below the minimum were terminated and returned to civilian life, the existing shortage would be more than troublesome. In one army installation they came up with a plan that might reduce the number of soldiers who would have to be terminated: They would be given the opportunity over a period of 120 days to meet the minimal requirement of literacy and if at the end of that period they were unsuccessful, they would have to be released from service. And the opportunity required that they live in small groups with someone (not specified) who would be their "teacher." With few exceptions they met the criterion within somewhat more than 90 days.

One more example from my experience at the Southbury Training School. In my first year there I did psychological test workups on at least two hundred of the retarded residents. One of the tests I administered was the Porteus mazes each of which is printed on one page and the individual is asked to use a pencil and trace a path from a central starting point to the exit point without going into blind alleys or crossing lines. The series of mazes go from very simple to the complex. The series is considered a test of planning and foresight. Now, in that first year, approximately 25 residents ran away from this isolated, highly supervised setting. Several were never apprehended, but most were, usually because they ended up back at their homes, which were many miles away. Probably because by the end of my first year there I was puzzled by the number of discrepancies between test scores and behavior I was able to observe outside the testing situation since I lived in that total community, I decided to look at the scores of those who had been runaways. What relationship, if any, was there between planning and foresight on the Porteus and the planning and foresight required to successfully run away from such an isolated, highly supervised, "total institution"? There was a relationship but it certainly was not high.

I would not argue with anyone who considers such (and many more) instances as no basis from which secure conclusions are justified. But I would argue with anyone who would contend that the issue I am raising is neither important, perhaps crucial, or deserving of study.

I may have created the impression that test developers, then and now, made a conscious choice about how to proceed. There is no evidence that they were aware that they had choice. They were so invested in what they considered to be a scientific approach, with its emphasis on measurement, that they were unable even to think about the issue I have raised, because it would mean proceeding in two parallel ways one of which would be amenable to a rigorous scientific approach and the other not. That is a strange way of reading the history of science. Science starts with a formulated problem or question for which existing knowledge cannot provide a ready answer, or frequently, the problem suggests that existing knowledge gives a misleading or wrong answer. The next step is to devise ways that would confirm or disconfirm your view of the problem or question. I say "step" but it can be the most time consuming of steps because it may force you to reformulate the problem and refine or change your methodology. Now, it is a glimpse of the obvious that the issue I have raised is a can of methodological worms because identifying, describing, and "measuring" problem-solving behavior in naturally occurring contexts is messy. Of course, it will be messy, frustrating, demanding of imagination and persistence, with many false starts. But when did science say that you should not study problems unless you already possess tried and true methodologies to deal with them? Because an approach to a problem will have to deal with a lot of messy issues is no excuse to ignore the problem, or if studied, to judge the value of the research by watered-down criteria.

If anything can be said about American psychology in the past 100 years, it is that, as a group, psychologists are very bright, creative, and ingenious. But I have to add—and this is one man's opinion—that those sterling characteristics have been too frequently manifested in relation to trivial problems or important ones which are studied in ways that are so overlearned, conventional, and traditional as to render psychologists incapable of challenging the undergirding rationale and axioms by which they formulated the problem. The issue I have raised is a challenge to the ways in which (and sites in which) tests of intellectual and educational performance are interpreted to say something about the ability to learn.

I have asserted that psychologists should not have unreflectively or automatically assumed that what is observed and measured in their standardized, contrived testing situations is in principle what would be found in naturally occurring situations. A variant of that issue is implied by the question: How and why are these tests used in schools? One can put the question in another way: How did (and do) psychologists want their tests to be interpreted and used by schools? Psychologists do not develop their tests in a random manner. They have some kind of theory about the cognitive attributes and/or of the substance and structure of the subject matter they seek to measure. It goes without saying that they seek to meet the expressed needs of schools in making judgments about the students' ability to learn or as a measure of how much they have learned. From whatever vantage point you approach schools, the nature, process, and levels of learning become central issues.

There are two major ways schools use psychological tests. The first is for administrative purposes. By that I mean test scores are a basis for placement of students in what is deemed an appropriate grade or program, for determining class or group achievement over the year, for comparing schools within the system, for comparing teachers within a school, for presenting and explaining the results to the board of education, and, depending on the results, for purposes of planning in regard to program, curriculum, and personnel changes. This is an *impersonal* process in that there is no intention to focus on *individual* students. In fact, it is almost always the case that these are the purposes of administrators and boards of education who have little or no contact with students, teachers, or classrooms. They are policy makers and shapers, and as Pauly (1991) has convincingly argued, the relationship between a policy's intent and what happens in classrooms is slight indeed, which is to say that its effects on learning are hardly discernible. Long before Pauly's book I heard that argument from countless teachers who would say, as one did, "They mean well when they dream up and proclaim policy, but they seem not to have the faintest idea what a classroom is like and what problems and obstacles teachers are faced with." Another teacher put it more humorously, "They are like parents who tell their child that from now on he is to act in this or that way, and the child, who sees no sense in what he was told, decides to play the game of *appearing* to comply"; the italics reflect her emphasis.

Should test developers know this? Should they at the very least be troubled by the fact that their tests, when used for administrative purposes, will have little consequence for classroom learning which one has to assume is why they developed their tests in the first place? Or are they justified in saying "Our specific obligation is to develop valid tests, and it is not our job to tell the administrators that the policies they adopt on the basis of group tests are not likely to have the desired effect. We are a certain kind of psychologist, we are not reformers or policy makers." That answer contains a kernel of truth and would be semi-acceptable were it not for several facts. First, we are living in an era in which tests, standards, school learning, and the fecklessness of school reform are front-page news in mass media, controversial in state and federal politics, and indirectly a source for voucher and charter school legislation. I should remind the reader that unlike the every-10-years controversies about schooling in the first half of the twentieth century, in the second half, far from being occasional, they were omnipresent and have been picking up steam in the twenty-first century. The questions that have to be asked of the test developers are, "Is it possible that the tests you have developed, however evaluated by your scientific-statistical criteria, are being used, interpreted, and *acted upon* in ways that do not influence classroom learning and may in fact explain why the more things change, the more they remain the same? If that is true, or even partially true, is it not your *professional* obligation to examine why tests designed to improve student learning do not accomplish that purpose at all well? After all, if tests were designed as a basis for improving school learning but in the culture of schools that hardly happens, are you not subject to the criticism that your tests do not meet the criterion of practical or social utility?"

Please note that I am not asking the test developers to become educational reformers or educational do-gooders, or to develop a social conscience that requires them to be social activists. What I am saying is that they have a professional, scientific obligation to determine why the administrative policies based on test results have so little impact on classroom learning (Pauly, 1991).

The second major use of tests is for the purpose of obtaining information considered necessary for altering in some way a student's educational status. Is the student gifted, or retarded, or disabled in some way? These are some of the questions which require a one-on-one testing situation. Unlike the use of group tests for determining administrative policies, here the individual is front and center stage. Up to 1975 the decision to employ tests for individual purposes was made by a teacher or principal who requested a psychological examination. Only rarely was permission of the parents sought; they would be informed later, although it was by no means rare that they were never informed even if the child's placement had already occurred. That may sound strange to the modern ear, but I can attest from personal experience and observation that it was far from unusual. Just as the test developers saw their mission as providing tests schools said they needed and were little concerned about how the tests were interpreted and used, the school saw its responsibility to test, diagnose, and take action *on its own* about the individual. Parents were not in the picture. They were not consulted; they were told what the decision was. What it meant for parents, even how it would be interpreted by the child, got short shrift. Just as test developers wanted to help schools, schools wanted to help students, and each rendered help in terms of a very restricted sense of responsibility. Individual tests are administered in an interpersonal context: one student, one psychologist. But that context reflects and impinges upon larger social, familial contexts; it takes place in and/or has ramifications for other contexts every one of which is concerned with the student's learning.

I feel compelled to emphasize that my criticism of test developers does not rest on moral grounds but rather on scientific grounds in that they have the obligation to improve their tests in terms of both their contexts and the ways they should be used and interpreted. The self-correcting stance is a cardinal feature of the scientific enterprise. That means the developers have to know if their tests are used in ways that conform to or violate the maxim "Do no harm" to those who have an obvious, vested interest in the testing and its consequences. The fact that the test users *say* the tests serve *their* purposes is not sufficient. What are needed are independent studies on the basis of which changes in substance, procedure, and manuals can be made. As best I can determine, the major producers of tests used in schools have never conducted such studies. I truly cannot believe that test developers do not have serious reservations about how tests are used and interpreted by school personnel. Can it be that they have done little about these reservations because they fear that the hand that feeds them is the hand that can starve them? Testing is big business. Business or not, the basic question is, how frequently are tests used and interpreted by school personnel in ways inconsistent with the purposes for which the tests were developed, and what should be the relationship between how the tests are used and interpreted and classroom contexts of productive learning? I am not directing that question only to test developers but rather to American psychology generally because American psychology has long taken pride in its contributions to the development of tests and to the nature, contexts, development, and vicissitudes of human learning. Those two arenas of study have become inextricably interrelated in our schools, an obvious fact that American psychology has not taken seriously. And if the reader doubts that assertion I suggest that he or she peruse the 452-page program of the 1999 convention of the American Psychological Association held in

Boston over 5 days. I am not letting the test developers off the hook when I say that the question I have raised goes beyond the purview of the test developers.

Why is the tobacco industry so embattled, so disdained? The answer is that for years they knew but deliberately ignored the research evidence that their products had untoward effects on health, not of everyone who smoked but a sizeable number. Their initial stance was to criticize the research and then to support research in the hope that it would produce counterfindings. Even when the research evidence on smoking as a health hazard continued to pile up, they lobbied against laws requiring warning labels on their products. Obviously, the story would have been different if there had been no credible research evidence. The question I raised above about tests and learning in schools was my way of indicating that we possess no credible research evidence to support the conclusion that the use and interpretation of tests in schools, and the actions taken based on them, have no untoward psychological effects on those tested, their families, and classroom learning. That conclusion can only be held by adults, psychologists or otherwise, who have had little or no experience in schools. That my personal experience in many scores of schools indicates that the frequency of untoward effects would certainly not be miniscule is not the issue; you can dismiss it by putting it in the category of opinion. If I understand that dismissal, I do not understand how you can dismiss the fact that we have no credible basis for saying that the question I have raised is an instance of raising a problem where in reality no problem exists. The problem is a very complicated one—one of the understatements of the century—and researching it will be beset by many issues among which the most thorny are: agreement on what will constitute relevant data, how the data will be obtained and analyzed, and definitional-theoretical problems in regard to such concepts as learning, contexts of learning, and "untoward effects." It will be a case of the more you learn, the more you need to learn. And, let us not forget, that with each passing year the general public cannot think of schools without thinking about standardized tests. And that twinning is suffused with anxiety both in students and parents. I and my colleagues spent 15 years studying test anxiety in school children (Sarason, Davidson, Lighthall, Waite, & Ruebush, 1960), and we were able to demonstrate that level of test anxiety was a difference that made a difference in classroom learning. Our results were replicated by other psychologists. These findings are relevant here. The first is that although high test anxiety was found at all levels of IQ, it was significantly more frequent among those of average ability, and more so among Black students. Second, school personnel were at least mildly interested in the overall findings, and they never indicated that *perhaps* they should consider using our or any similar measure in conjunction with the usual standardized tests of achievement and intelligence.[1] Third, the judgment of school personnel of the internal state and attitudes of students is far from accurate, a finding that confirmed what other researchers had reported years before we did.

Let us take a more recent study involving psychological variables for which teacher judgment is fairly accurate. If, as I have, you have had an opportunity to talk with high school, middle school, and elementary school teachers and other personnel, you will find that high school teachers will tell you that arousing and sustaining in students motivation to learn is like pulling teeth. The usual exceptions aside, middle school personnel will say the same thing. Far fewer elementary teachers will say that. Steinberg's study is confirmatory in spades (Steinberg, with Brown & Dornbusch, 1996). As students go from elementary to middle to high school, their interest in and motivation for school learning noticeably decreases. That is true both for urban and suburban schools.

Are these two examples irrelevant to the use and interpretation of tests of intelligence and school achievement as well as to the actions to which they lead? Are they irrelevant to how we interpret school learning as measured by achievement tests? Is it unjustified to say to test developers that as researchers and scientists who never deny that they always seek to improve the *practical utility* of their tests *for purposes of school learning,* they should start finding out how variables not measured by their tests may affect how these tests are used and interpreted? I ask the reader to ponder these questions because if he or she concludes (as I do, obviously) that they are legitimate questions, the reader will not view current practice as before. The first step is to recognize there is a problem in current thinking and practice. It is a problem test developers have not only ignored but helped to create. And it is also a problem exacerbated by educators who are so schooled to regard tests as possessing an unusual degree of practical validity, that it can never occur to them to ask if perhaps the emperor is naked. And that is also precisely the case for a general public who has bought the same message. I recently had the opportunity to discuss these matters with a group of school administrators. They listened respectfully to me. When I was done, I asked for questions and comments. There was a

---

1. Our test anxiety scales were never copyrighted. Copies were available without cost.

long silence. Finally, thank God, it was broken by an individual who said, "I think you made some good points, but are you aware of the can of worms you are opening?" As soon as he said that, almost everyone else agreed, emphasizing that the changes that would be required would confront mammoth obstacles from parents, boards of education, and political leaders who have long had the quick-fix virus, and the testing establishment within and beyond the school. I replied that I appreciated that they recognized that the implications of what I had said were many, and went on to say that it was probably the case that I saw it as more complicated than they did. I was tempted, but refrained, from saying that if they had read the umpteen books I have written on educational reform and the culture of the school, they would understand why the problem was more complicated than they thought. I did not want to make the mistake of the test developers: making self-serving statements intended to convince consumers that their products are like manna from heaven, or particles of truth and enlightenment, all in the service of improving school learning.

Let me now turn to the relationship between testing and helping students learn, and I shall do this by using those tests (e.g., intelligence tests) administered to single individuals, although we shall see later that the issues I will raise are no less salient for school achievement tests administered to groups of students.

As I have said earlier, American psychology has long been interested in the nature and dynamics of learning. I deliberately did not say human learning because, as I have pointed out previously, up to two decades or so after World War II the volumous research literature was about animal learning, the most used animal being the Norway rat. This is not to suggest that that literature should be judged as without merit, let alone worthless, because a case can be made that some of the findings would have theoretical and practical relevance for human learning. The fact is that such theorizing never occurred; the arena of research on learning was an encapsulated one and came to be seen by the rest of psychology as a field with no future. That is why in the last 30 years the field dramatically became much smaller, leading one highly regarded experimental psychologist to say that for all practical purposes the field was moribund; the death rattle, he said, was audible. But there were two other interrelated reasons. One was the dramatic growth in membership of the American Psychological Association. The other was the interest of these younger entrants in clinical psychology; social issues; gender differences; equity, gay and lesbian issues; child development; and more. All this was taking place at a time when to be "relevant" meant to be engaged, individually and professionally, in the major problems of the society. Research on learning in the Norway rat obviously did not meet the criterion of social relevance. What about schooling and learning? The fact is that more than a few psychologists became interested in schools from the stand point, for example, of the consequences for students of bussing to achieve integration, gender discrimination in the classroom (and in the contents of textbooks), racial discrimination, and selective placement of minorities in lower academic tracks and special classes. These were, and still are, legitimate and important problems for research, and psychologists contributed to illuminating them. That is certainly to their credit; their findings gave ammunition to others seeking to change schools. Those findings indicated, albeit indirectly, the importance of the contexts of learning in classrooms. I say indirectly because with very few exceptions the researchers were interested in classrooms and learning but from a narrow albeit important perspective. Granted the importance of perspective, it is fair to say they were not interested in how the classroom context has the features it has and how they affect for good or for bad the learning of subject matter. It is one thing (and a very good thing) to demonstrate that in the conventional classroom boys and girls are reacted to differently and they "learn" to regard themselves in ways that can influence performance differentially in different subjects as well as in career choice. To me at least, such findings should have (or could have) brought to center stage several questions: What do we know or should we know about the relationship between classroom contexts and student learning in regard to subject matter? If we studied that question, what light would it shed on our understanding of why in the post World War II era, the benefits of the educational reform movement have been so minimal? What has American psychology contributed to understanding the differences between contexts of productive and unproductive learning, and how frequently and to what extent are those contributions in evidence in classrooms? Has American psychology missed the boat, so to speak, in not seeing that what happens in classrooms is fateful both for students and the society, just as it decided during and immediately after World War II that it had to take an active part in the effort to deal with mental health problems?

I am not in any way denigrating the work of those psychologists— a truly miniscule percentage of the membership of the very large American Psychological Association—who in recent decades have done research in schools on gender and social issues and published their findings with the expectation (I have to assume) that their work will somehow, sometime, some where, have an effect on school practice. But why have they little or no understanding of the educational arena, not only in regard to the culture of schools but also of the educational *system?* The single school is one thing, the system is quite another matter. Who has a vested, formal role in the system? The single school is a complicated subsystem, embedded in an even more complicated local subsystem, each of these related directly or indirectly to colleges and universities as well as to a state board of education, all of the foregoing related directly or indirectly to the federal department of education, which means, of course, that the system is related to the local, state, and federal political system. And then, of course, there are parents and teacher unions. Most people tend to think of a system as comprised of cooperating parts. The educational system is one in which adversarialism is a distinguishing feature. You cannot *see* the system, you have to conceptualize it. I emphasize that because what you observe in a single classroom or a single school, however valid your observations and interpretation, will be incomplete, sometimes egregiously so, if you do not understand that what you observed bears in large and small ways the imprimatur of other parts of a larger system. And what I have just said goes a long way to explaining why most educational reformers suffer from burnout: they did not know schools well enough to comprehend them as part of a troubled, uncoordinated, change-resistant, system. If it is absolutely crucial for a reformer to know the culture of schools comprehensively and well, it is no less crucial for that reformer to know and deal with the system in which it is embedded. Very few psychologists have an experiential basis to deal with one, let alone both.

As luck would have it, on the very day I was writing these words (September 2, 1999), George W. Bush addressed the California Latino Business Organization as part of his campaign for the Republican nomination for President; his address was about education reform and policy. The address was carried on C-Span, and the next day it was given a place on the first page of the *New York Times* as well as a full inside page. The address is very directly relevant to what I have already said in this chapter and will say in later pages. Measurement, meaning "tests," is uppermost in Mr. Bush's mind. If the government is to hand out bucks, he wants the bang to be audible and measured. Here are his major points:

1. Every child can and should be expected to learn.
2. These expectations should be reflected in high standards which should not be lowered because of unjustified stereotypes about race, ethnicity, or social class.
3. Head Start programs will be altered so that learning to read begins at age 3.

4. There is no doubt that teaching reading by phonics is the best of all methods.

5. Charter schools and vouchers are crucial as means for enlarging parental choice for their child's schooling, and that is why he is also in favor of home schooling.

6. The federal government will support no school (Head Start, Title 1) which cannot demonstrate measured and expected educational development. Meeting standards by measurement will be federal policy.

7. One of the fateful consequences of the fact that the federal government became part of the educational system is the paperwork it requires of states and schools.

It is beyond my purposes to discuss each of Mr. Bush's major points.[2] I use his address to suggest that if we are currently the most psychologically tested population in the world, we should not fear that we are in danger of losing that number one position. And I also have used his address to illustrate the point that what takes place in a single classroom in a single school reflects directly or indirectly, in small or large ways the part that the federal government plays in the educational system (for example, every school and school system is governed by and must conform to federal legislation about students with disabilities).

With those remarks as background, let us return to the use and interpretation of individual tests and their relation to learning. I start with the question: Why do schools administer these tests? The conventional answer is that the test provides information about ability that allows the school to alter or not to alter a child's placement in the school. A student is referred for testing because someone in the school, usually the teacher, or the parent has raised a question about whether the classroom he or she is presently in is appropriate for that student's ability level. Or it may be that the student's behavior in the classroom is indicative of the possibility of some form of brain dysfunction. In any event, there is a question about the student's rate and quality of learning. It should not be glossed over that referrals are rarely made because someone thinks a student is gifted or just smarter than records indicate. Referrals for individual testing are couched in clinical language suggesting dysfunction in ability and learning.

Let us begin with the obvious: Individual tests are the basis for judgments about the ability to learn. *But those judgments are not based on*

---

2. For how I would react to his address I refer the reader to my 1998 books *Political Leadership and Educational Failure* and *Charter Schools: Another Flawed Educational Reform?*

observing the student learning. The judgment is based on scores which the test developers have statistically demonstrated are significantly correlated with rate and level of school learning as measured by achievement tests. Note, however, that neither type of test is based on observing the student learning but rather on test items which are scored according to right-wrong, pass-fail, criteria. In the case of achievement tests, it is *assumed* that the scores tell us not only *how much* the student has learned in the classroom but *his or her ability* to learn that subject matter. Let me illustrate with an item in an individual test of intelligence which is a discriminating item because approximately 50% of an age cohort do not pass it. The item requires the child to reproduce a diamond displayed on a card.

The test manual contains examples of reproductions that should or should not be credited. Having earlier in my career administered hundreds of times the test (1937 Stanford-Binet) containing that item, I can assure the reader that scoring the item involves little judgment on the part of the psychologist. Early in my clinical days I asked myself a question in regard to an 8-year-old child whose reproduction of the diamond was demonstrably poorer in quality than her answers to other types of items: Could I right then and there help the child learn to reproduce an acceptable diamond? To do that was a no-no; the psychologist was expected to administer the test precisely as the manual prescribed and to avoid doing anything that would affect the reliability and validity of the test. But I went ahead. It took me no more than 12–15 minutes to get her consistently to reproduce the diamond and meet the criterion for getting credit. I then asked her to reproduce another geometrical form involving diagonal lines, and she had only a little difficulty reproducing it; I provided no direct aid.

Several questions arise about this 8-year-old child's inability to reproduce an acceptable diamond, which approximately 50% of 7-year-olds can do. All one could say is that she could not do it. You could say that 6 months or 1 year later she *might* be able to do it. But what do we mean or imply when we say that the girl had an *inability* to reproduce the diamond? We could say that she is physically or neurologically immature. We might also say she may have some kind of brain deficit because there is a long line of research indicating that reproducing diagonal lines is difficult for people with a known brain-deficit injury. But we would not imply that she had the ability to reproduce the diamond within a period of minutes following instruction right then and there in the testing situation. The testing situation is not structured or intended to be a learning situation. The testee either passes or fails an item and that's that. You are not observing a learning process.

The objections to what I did are not to be taken lightly. I employed the example to make the point that although an individual test is used to say something important about the level and quality of classroom learning, the test situation provides no sample of the learning process. What about the achievement tests mandated by the state, sent and scored by it, the results tabulated for each local school system and required in some states to be published school by school? The students, let alone the teachers, never see the test after they have taken it, only the numerical scores. Like the individual intelligence test, the group-administered achievement test tells us whether a student knew something or not, or possessed a certain computational skill or not; in no direct way does it tell us whether or not the student has learned what he or she was expected to learn in the ways intended. The undergirding assumption is that the scores tell us something important about students, their teachers, *and the contexts of classroom learning.* I italicized those words because scores have meaning only in the context of a learning process defined by the reciprocal relationships between students and teacher. Student learning is not independent of the teacher, and teacher pedagogy and style are not independent of who the student is. Achievement and intelligence test scores tell us nothing about the context of classroom learning. It is *presumed* that they tell us something important for and about classroom learning, but they do not or cannot because the scores from the two types of tests are used to make decisions that hardly, if at all, are determined by recognition and substantive clarity of what should be the most important question of all: How do we distinguish between classroom contexts of productive and unproductive learning? That is a question that has had little or no interest for American psychology which has long acknowledged that what and how one learns over the life span is embedded in contexts fateful for one's state of being, attitudes, and accomplishments. Take, for example, the field of child development which in the post World War II era experienced a dramatic increase in the number of psychologists engaged in research on how infants and preschoolers learn what they do and the way they do it in diverse contexts (natural and contrived). They have learned a great deal, from how an infant, a week or so old, learns to make a discriminating response to a presented picture of a human face, to how and when the growing preschooler learns this or that in the context of interactions with parents, siblings, or strangers. Learning is not conceptualized as a process within the child, and it is not conceptualized as a process that exists within the parent. *Learning is conceptualized in terms of relational dynamics in a context.* But very few developmental psychologists have shown an interest in contexts of classroom learning even though none of them would deny its importance for cognitive, interpersonal, and social learning (as well as self-attitudes). Are their conceptions and findings applicable to classroom learning? How do contexts of classroom learning differ from other learning contexts previously encountered by the child? What would constitute a systematic and comprehensive theory of human learning, or are we to remain, as we now are, with a "theory" of this aspect and that aspect, pieces of a puzzle seemingly incapable of integration? Young people spend a very large amount of hours in a context of formal learning. How can one justify that only a small number of psychologists study classroom learning?

It is hard for people to take contexts seriously. We literally do not *see* contexts, we have to *conceive* how their components are in relation to each other. Lacking that conception can make for mischievous, untoward consequences. Let me illustrate the point by discussing the school reform program of one of the few psychologists who has taken context seriously. I refer to Dr. Robert Slavin whose Success for All program has a more solid research base than any other reform program (Slavin, Madden, Dolan, & Wasik, 1996).[3] As a result, his findings and work have received much play in newspapers and other mass media whose obsession with why reading scores in urban schools are so poor is, to indulge in understatement, a source of anxiety and a basis for their criticisms of schools. That they should be anxious and critical I understand and applaud. But in their enthusiasm for Dr. Slavin's demonstration that reading scores can be, have been, significantly improved they ignore the significance of context, thereby misleading, albeit unintentionally, the general public. Here are the major features of his work and program:

1. It took years to develop the program. It required the opposite of the quick-fix way of approaching educational problems.

2. The school not only accepts the program, but budgets for its costs.

3. The program is described in detail to all school personnel, which means that they know what changes will be required in classroom pedagogy and ambiance. The program is not an add on; it is intended to

---

3. This is also true for Reading Recovery, a more narrow approach than Slavin's but which has a solid research base. It is more narrow in that it is not geared to reform of the school, but rather focuses on those children in the first grade who appear to be at risk of becoming a reading problem.

change how things are done and why in the classroom and school. This also includes the support services which will be available to them.

4. Unless 80% of school personnel agree in secret ballot to participate, the program will not be made available.

5. Each school is provided with a coordinator whose responsibilities are several among which is to engender and sustain parent interest and involvement.

6. Data are systematically collected to monitor student progress and teacher effectiveness.

The program is clearly more than about reading, although at present the development of literacy is the major criterion by which the program is judged. The program takes place in a context in which school personnel have committed themselves to change, there is parental support and involvement, outside support services are provided, and the collegial relationships among teachers are changed. So, when one of the mass media headlines an article on Dr. Slavin's work with "Now Johnny Can Read If Teacher Just Keeps Doing What He Has Been Told" the message conveyed implies two things: The teacher had been the culprit in why Johnny had not learned to read, and Johnny was now learning to read because the teacher was now adhering to what the newspaper called a "rigid reading program." By ignoring or downplaying context, by vastly underestimating the role of the different aspects of a changed school culture, the quick-fix, shape-up-or-ship-out mentality gains strength. And so does the tendency to rivet on and interpret test scores as if literacy is primarily a function of teacher and student. That teacher and student are major actors goes without saying, but they are acting in a context and a system which is never zero in its influence. Rivet on the child and teacher, and you are not only missing seeing the trees for the forest but, worse yet, you see neither forest nor trees.

So, when I say that the most basic question is distinguishing between contexts of productive and unproductive learning, I am asking for clarity and agreement about learning in general. Can you have a productive American psychology which has so little to contribute to a beginning answer? Should not psychology examine its history to find out why its earlier, deep interest in learning petered out? Was it a case of throwing the baby out with the bath water? What will it take to reinvigorate that interest?

I shall offer an answer to the last question by way of a scientific achievement that altered the world as we know it; it happened early in World War II.

1. It was demonstrated that the atom could be split and its energy released.

2. That achievement raised the possibility that the energy released by the splitting of one atom could cause other atoms to split, thus increasing exponentially the energies released.

3. The crucial and practical question was, Could that release of energies be harnessed, controlled?

Years before the atom was split (point 1 above) theorizing about splitting atoms clearly indicated that it should be possible and, if so, point 2 above was very likely to be accomplished. But that same early theorizing indicated that it could only be done if the society was willing to commit huge sums of money to support such a research effort, and those early theorists could not even imagine that happening in their near- and long-term future; that was pie in the sky. They did not foresee World War II. When the war started, physicists quickly recognized two frightening things. First, physicists in Nazi Germany, like those in Allied Countries, would grasp the potentials of the new knowledge for military purposes. Second, if Nazi Germany developed an atomic bomb first, the war would be over, and the world as we knew it would be changed in the most negative ways. President Franklin Roosevelt followed the advice of his scientific advisors to spend whatever resources were necessary to develop an atomic bomb. The Manhattan Project was born, scores of decades earlier than physicists ever imagined.

Reform of our schools will not be achieved unless and until political leaders gain a better grasp of how and why our ineffective educational system is setting drastic limits to achieving this country's stated purposes. And by better grasp I mean recognizing that what we have done and are doing will only confirm the adage that the more things change, the more they remain the same. Unlike the story of atomic energy, where it was demonstrated that the atom could be split, we have nothing comparable in the case of educational reform. There is nothing resembling agreement on what should be done. But that is the point, what do we need to demonstrate that will convince people— make it difficult for people to deny—that something important has been achieved. One thing is for sure: to support such demonstrations will cost a lot money and will require a quality of research and researchers that is now in very short supply in the educational community. It is not in such short supply in the psychological community but the interest in education is. It is the case, fortunately and unfortunately, that the substance and direction of research in a field is mightily determined by what funding agencies are prepared to support. If the kind of support I am suggesting is made available, I have no doubt that many psychologists will become interested in schools and the differences between contexts of productive and unproductive learning. After World War II this country's political leadership made a convincing case for why problems of mental health needed to be addressed and why funding for better research and services was necessary and would not come cheap. It was that kind of message and funding that made it possible for American psychology to depart from its past traditions and to create the field of modern clinical psychology. That is one of the major reasons I wrote Chapter 3 in this book.

Splitting the atom was a piece of cake compared to providing a credible research basis for educational reform. It is not that we are at ground zero, as if nothing has been learned by past efforts. But, to give but one example, we have hardly recognized, let alone addressed, the fact that the single classroom and the single school bear the imprimatur of a system of parts: colleges and universities, the political system, state department of education, local boards, parents, and I would add test developers and textbook publishers. It is not only an uncoordinated system but one containing adversarial parts.

I did not write this chapter to pillory test developers and publishers. I am not opposed to tests and standards. I wrote this chapter to indicate that there is a disconnect between how tests are used and interpreted, on the one hand, and theory and research about learning, on the other hand. Schooling serves many purposes, but regardless of how you prioritize those purposes, you are obliged to have a credible basis for answering what I consider to be the most important of all: How do you create a context of learning in which students want to learn? There is a world of difference between feeling you want to learn something and feeling that you need to learn it to satisfy external agents. In my experience students understand the difference better than anyone else. At least that is what students have told me. Classrooms are not places where students feel safe to raise such questions. Their role is to learn what they are told they need to learn, and I have never met a person, lay or professional, who disagreed with my assertion that asking substantive questions was or should be important in the learning process. When I would then tell that person that in modal classes of 50 minutes the average number of questions students ask—and in some instances it is one student asking the questions—was two, and no one said that that is the way it should be (Susskind, 1969). You can change a lot of things in schools, but if you have done little or nothing in regard to creating and sustaining contexts of productive learning, do not have high hopes that your efforts will be rewarded by improvement in test scores. It has not been in the past and will not be in the future. I know that in some quarters I am regarded as a kind of wet blanket, a Henny Penny predicting doom and gloom. All I can say in response is that what I say in this book I began to say, orally and in print, in 1965 after I had immersed myself in the problem of describing and understanding the culture of school. What I then did not comprehend was the nature of the educational system.

Experience dictates that I say something here to counter the criticism that I am advocating that it is the student who should determine what should be learned, and that such advocacy is implied by saying the teacher should know and start "where the student is coming from." That starting point I consider absolutely crucial. But the goal and artistry of teaching inheres in using that starting point as a way by which the student learns other things or subject matter we consider educationally and intellectually vital, that we as adults have cause to believe is developmentally important. That is why I reacted so favorably and strongly to the movie *Mr. Holland's Opus.* When Mr. Holland began where *he* was coming from, it was a disaster. When he began to understand where the students were coming from, it was another story.

CHAPTER 7

Standards, Tests, and the Current School Scene

I did not expect to write this chapter, but in September 1999—a time when I thought I was finishing this book—two things happened directly relevant to Chapter 6. Each in its own way speaks to the question, In using psychological tests and making decisions on the basis of the scores derived from them, what other kinds of data should be used to determine a student's ability to learn and meet standards?

In the spring of 1999 the Chancellor and Board of Education of New York City adopted the policy that students who were discernibly below grade level, according to an achievement test that would be given to all children in some of the early grades, would not be promoted, which meant that some students would not be graduated to the middle school. Failing students would have the option either to repeat the grade or go to summer school, take the test again, and hope their scores would justify promotion. That policy affected at least 300,000 students. Only a small percentage of these students chose to go to summer school. Of those who attended summer schools, a small percentage were promoted. (At one point the Chancellor's office seemed daily to present new numbers, usually worsening an already grim picture.)

Then in mid September it was made public that the test developers had wrongly scored the test, not only in the case of New York City, but in other school systems as well. On September 16, 1999, the *New York Times* reported:

> There was confusion yesterday among administrators and parents about what the revised scores may mean. Yesterday, board officials said that of the 8,668 students who were assigned to summer-school in error—4,460 third graders and 4,208 sixth graders—5,176 went to summer school and passed a second test. But 3,492, the board said, either never showed up for summer school or failed the second test by scoring below the 15th percentile on a national curve.

Those 3,492—regardless of their absence from summer school or failing the test—will be promoted unless their parents request they not be, Dr. Crew said.

The mistake occurred through a miscalculation of the percentile score that showed how the students compared with a national sample.

The uproar that followed has to be seen in light of an earlier report in the *New York Times,* well before the uproar. The headline of the article was "Schools Taking Tougher Stand with Standards: New Emphasis on Tests, Standards, and New Penalties."

No more fun and games: As children across the nation head back to school this fall, many are encountering a *harsher atmosphere* in which states set specific academic standards and impose *real penalties* on those who do not meet them.

"We are clearly moving into the phase of the standards-based school reform movement where the rubber hits the road," said Robert Schwartz, president of Achieve Inc., a nonprofit school-reform group in Cambridge, Mass., that is made up of governors and corporate executives. "Kids and schools know there are consequences looming on the horizon if they don't do well, and that gives this school season a different kind of edge in New York, Massachusetts, Virginia and a bunch of states where this is just beginning."

Much of the no-nonsense, no-excuses mood springs from an intensifying emphasis on the results of *high stakes assessment tests,* whose results determine whether students will be held back a grade, stopped from graduating or sent to tutoring sessions, Saturday classes or summer school.

Just last week in New York City, the schools chancellor announced that the city would hold back more than 21,000 third, sixth and eighth graders who, because they did badly on standardized tests in the spring, were assigned to summer school and either failed the summer school tests or did not take them.

The article goes on to describe why such states as New York, Massachusetts, and Virginia (among many others) have increased their emphasis on tests and adherence to standards. No nonsense is no nonsense!

I was "introduced" to what was coming by a telephone call in June from a neighbor of mine here in Connecticut. She was quite upset and near tears. Her grandson in Brooklyn, she said, had been told the day before that he had done poorly on the achievement test, especially reading, and that he would not be graduated to a middle school. What should the family do, I was asked. Naturally, I indulged my rescue fantasy tendency. I know Rudy Crew and I have respect for him even though I question the sanity of anyone who seeks to become Chancellor of New York's 1,100 schools system. I also know his right-hand associate, Judith Rizzo, whose level of street smarts had few peers in the educational community, although, again, I question her sanity. I got through to Dr. Rizzo's office, she was not in, but I was assured that she might be of help. I told her assistant what the grandmother had told me, saying that I was only requesting that someone look into the matter. She said two things: the matter would be looked into, and that similar cases had already been brought to the attention of central office. As it turned out, my call very likely played no role in the reversal of the decision because the day after the grandmother called me the mother, a highly educated professional, had gone into action. Here is a letter the mother felt constrained to write a month later to the district superintendent. The italics are mine.

Mr. John _____
Superintendent, District _____

I am writing to express my dismay at Ms. X's approach to my son, John. Ms. X was the teacher of his *fifth grade gifted Eagle class* at P.S. _____ in District _____. I have written letters to this office before in praise of two exceptional teachers. I regret that this letter does not follow form.

At the end of the school day on June 9th, 1999 Ms. X informed my son that he was not eligible to graduate to Junior High School. She gave him several papers requiring his attendance in summer school to bring home to me. Nothing in these papers offers an explanation for this, although John said she told him that he scored too low on his state-wide reading test.

John came home emotionally shattered and was able to contact me immediately at work. I attempted to phone the school, but the office was already closed. The following day was a school holiday. I phoned Ms. X that night at home, but was unable to confer with her until the next afternoon when I phoned her again.

Our conversation was pointed and brief. Ms. X confirmed that John was not graduating from 5th grade because his reading score was below the cut off for promotion. She did not acknowledge that there might be a mistake and recoiled from questions for an explanation. She denied assistance in addressing his spurious failure. She offered doubt that John could master Junior High School work given the result of this testing even though she acknowledged that she had expressed confidence in his abilities on numerous occasions throughout the year. She said that she was told to give John this letter and was surprised that I considered her at all responsible for John's devastated reaction.

John's score on this examination is an anomaly from his previous performance, of which Ms. X is aware:

This year John scored 62 percentage points below his 4th grade reading score and 71 percentage points below his 3rd grade reading score on the achievement test.

A multi-disciplinary team evaluated John this past October and determined that his reading ability was "at or above the 5th grade level"

She and I had at least five formal communications throughout the school year that had confirmed John on-grade level performance as well as confirmed that John was competitive *within his gifted class*

Throughout every school year John's performance was consistently evaluated on his report card as "satisfactory," "good," or "excellent" and Ms. X had evaluated John this highly, as well.

Clearly, Ms. X failed to act as an advocate for her student. In this situation, Ms. X failed to make a reasonable effort to protect my son from conditions harmful to his learning as outlined in the National Education Association's Code of Ethics of the Education Profession. I am outraged at her inability to recognize factors that would facilitate or impede communication as well as her lack of initiating effective communication between us as mandated in the framework for New York State Teacher Certification.

I am grateful for the support and attention given John, my husband and me by the principal, Mr. Z. As was appropriate, John graduated with his class and felt a real part of all the festivities and celebrations. However, he continues to feel betrayed by his teacher.

Please look into how this matter was mishandled at the classroom level. No child should be treated with such disesteem.

Regretfully,

John's Parents

Cc: Ms. X
    Mr. Y

The following letter to me (personally) accompanied the copy of the first letter written to the district superintendent. The italics are mine.

After much deliberation and discussion, I decided to send my letter to the District _____ Superintendent. I sent copies to the principal of John's elementary school and to his 5th grade teacher. I am very glad I expressed my outrage, but *I'm not sure I would have sent the letters if John were not graduating to a new school this coming year.*

Interesting article in today's *NY Times* about a group that calls themselves Advocates for Children. They are a grass roots group that are equally outraged over how their children have been treated. They are trying to overturn the decision to bar promotion of children who failed the state reading test on grounds that the new mandate disregards established protocol to alert parents of failing students prior to holding them back. I can relate to that.

Also I have heard of an organization that is advocating for parents that refuse to have their children tested. They base their protest on the private school model where most schools opt out of the standardized testing method to evaluate academic achievement. I am very close to choosing such a school for John, but my belief in the public school system—that mirrors my long-standing principles of social and economic justice and the need to expose my children to the realities of this complicated city and this discordant society—hold me back.

I'm dancing as fast as I can. Feel free to use these letters in your writings.

All of this well before it was learned that the tests were wrongly scored by the company who developed the tests. This case is illustrative of many points but for my present purposes I will discuss only a few.

It is mind boggling that a teacher who over a period of a year has judged a child's learning ability very favorably should on the basis of one test score change her mind and conclude that he is not ready for the next grade. It is no less incomprehensible that she refused to serve as an advocate for the child. A test score is a test score, rules are rules, and that's that; the test is a better indicator of learning ability than direct observation over a year. You could say this is an unfair judgment of the teacher, that so much prior emphasis in and outside the school system to prevent promotion on social or age grounds, to go only by independent test scores in order to maintain standards, intimidated this teacher; she did not want to do battle. Perhaps yes, but perhaps no. We simply do not know, and we never will know how atypical this teacher is. All that can be said on the basis of the mother's letter to me and, more important, accounts in the city's press, is that this teacher is not in a category containing one person.

We all make mistakes. The test developers made a mistake. So what lessons did they learn? What they did was to put a message on their web site proclaiming the dangers of using one test score. But that was not a message they previously proclaimed in anything resembling bold letters. They are sophisticated people, they know the dangers of making a decision on the basis of one score. The tobacco industry was forced to put on a pack of cigarettes the sentence, "Smoking may be dangerous to your health." The developers of tests should put on their test manuals the sentence (in a very bold type) "Making a decision on the basis of a single achievement score may be injurious to the health of students." The point is that test developers have always known that the users of tests can make egregious mistakes in going by test scores. I may be wrong in saying that because test developers have *never* seriously studied how school personnel actually use and interpret tests. Besides, their experience in schools and knowledge of the school culture are minimal. They, like the tobacco companies, are in business to sell their products and they accept the caveat "let the buyer beware."

I have to assume that the test developers have been no end pleased in recent years by the emphasis put on tests and standards, witness the number of states that have mandated the use of the test developers' products. They do know what their bottom line is. And boards of education and school administrators, as in New York City and elsewhere, have heard and implemented the message. If over the last 2 years you collected editorials in newspapers and magazines calling for the use of tests as the way to judge how well standards were being met, you could fill a very large file cabinet. So it comes with ill grace that the *New York Times*, which had been highly critical of the school system's generally low test scores and the dumbing down of standards in the city's schools, says in a September 17 editorial after the fiasco:

> This page has supported tougher standards and higher expectations for New York City's children. But the error by CTB/McGraw-Hill has thrown a Klieg light on what happens when a system bases momentous decisions on a single, standardized test. This problem vindicates the Board of Education's recent decision to move toward multiple criteria that include not only tests but also grades, student portfolios and the teacher's sense of whether or not the student has mastered the material.
>
> Such systems require more work to develop and maintain, but they also minimize the system's vulnerability to statistical errors like this one— and protect children from judgements based on a single bad day at school.

But those children and parents also need to be protected from sloppy management.

Finally, the newspaper which has the largest education staff in the country, and, more important, has never in my experience reviewed a book on the use of tests (one child, one test) recognizes that the emperor may be semi-nude. They applaud the board's move to explore multiple criteria, but, I suppose, it is asking too much to expect it to recognize what will be required because what it will require is a difficult, complicated, costly, long-term research program for which no school system has the personnel and fiscal resources. An item for systematic research, short or long term, is unheard of in school budgets. The problem is as thorny as it is not only because of methodological considerations (sampling, statistical design, specification of criteria, and so forth) but because it requires clarity and agreement about what is meant by learning as a developmental process. And what about the editorial's singling out "the teacher's sense of whether or not the student has mastered the material"? As I have indicated elsewhere (1999), teachers are ill prepared (an understatement) to understand both learning and students. Indeed, there is general recognition that no educational reform will have more than minimal effect, if that, unless preparatory programs are radically changed. Teachers are not experts, they are victims, both of their preparation and the systems in which they work. In the 1992 presidential campaign the chant of the Democratic party was, "It's the economy, Stupid." In regard to our schools one could say, "It's the system, Stupid." That is not a message people want to hear or believe. I can understand that reaction. It took me decades to realize that I had been stupid.

And where has American psychology been in all of this—matters so central, so crucial, for one of society's pivotal institutions? The American Psychological Association has not been silent, quite the opposite, in advocating and lobbying for more recognition and support for more and better programs serving the needs of children. Indeed, it was a small group of developmental psychologists who played a key role in the initial enactment of the Head Start legislation. And it has been chiefly Dr. Edward Zigler who devoted a heroic expenditure of time, energy, and political sophistication to protect that program from mindless budget cutting. The Head Start legislation, as it's name indicates, had clear and legitimate purposes. But there was one that was not publicly stated and without which Head Start made no sense to me. Briefly, Head Start was based on the medical rationale for inoculation against disease. That is to say, Head Start was an inoculation so that when poor children started school they would not catch the disease of lack of motivation, reduced interest in learning, and school failure. That is why, in a public lecture I gave at Boston University when Head Start was enacted, I said two things. First, I predicted that the culture of the school would drastically limit the degree of school achievement of these children. Second, if I were a member of Congress, I would enthusiastically vote for passage. The degree of success of the program has been less than was hoped, and that limited success was not only expected by Dr. Zigler but increased his efforts to improve the program, which, let us remember, was despite his many caveats begun as a 6-week summer program. As he ruefully recounted to me, "I couldn't go before congressional committees and say we needed more support to feed kids. I had to say that the program would increase IQ, as I knew better then and I know a helluva lot better today."

Why "only" limited success? That question and its implications did not stimulate other than minimal interest among developmental psychologists in schooling. Developmental psychology is a large, important, and productive field. If you peruse texts in that field, you find the concept of learning very frequently and legitimately employed. But if you go from the indexes of these texts to the body of them, you find very little about classrooms, schools, classroom learning, and the culture of the school, and next to nothing about the nature of the system.

The second thing that happened directly relevant to Chapter 6 was publication of an article by Jacques Steinberg in the *New York Times* of September 15, 1999, smack in the middle of the New York City uproar about tests. The headline of the article read "Idea of Rewarding 'Strivers' is Opposed by College Board." It is an accurate but misleading headline because it neglects to emphasize the significance of the fact that for the first time a test developer, on its own initiative, was conducting a research project to develop indices which users of its test could employ in interpreting and making decisions based on a single score of its test. The test developer was the Educational Testing Service, and the test was the SAT, the most widely used test for college admissions. In the excerpt below the italics are mine:

> According to descriptions of the research provided by the testing service, a student would be identified as a striver with a score of at least 1,000 on the test, out of a possible 1,600, and a performance at least 200 points better than expected. The expected score would be calculated by assigning values to *dozens of factors in the student's life and background,* including how many books and appliances are in the home, how many years of school

the student's parents attended, and the total of advanced placement tests taken in the student's school.

The formula would permit universities, which would be responsible for analyzing the scores, to factor in the student's race or disregard it. *Though their scores would not change, the students would, in effect, be credited with doing better than they actually had.*

I do not know what "dozens" refers to, but I consider it very significant, and very refreshing, that the Educational Testing Service is taking seriously that a single test score is just that: a score is by no means a perfect indicator of whatever may be meant by the ability to learn, that ability is not a Platonic essence, and that its manifestations can vary on a host of factors that have been overlooked or unstudied, that the concepts of ability and learning are more fuzzy than we like to believe, that if the proof is in the pudding, these concepts may be no more edible than the millennial-old concept of women's ability to learn. And for millennia it was considered self-evident, if not divinely sanctioned, that the mass of a country's people *obviously* did not have the ability to learn to govern themselves, power had to be wielded by a self-proclaimed elite. Concepts of ability and learning have not and never will be completely independent of time, era, and opportunity. If we look back over the ages and smugly indulge feelings of superiority, the odds are overwhelming that posterity will similarly view us in today's world. (Let us not gloss over that the twentieth century has been the most bloody in human history.)[1]

Now to the public criticism of the research:

> Among the criticisms of the "striver" research, most of them raised since the *Wall Street Journal* first reported on the project late last month, has been that it represents an affirmative action effort in disguise. Critics fear that the formula might hurt more affluent students by setting the bar of expectation higher than that for strivers.
>
> "I think it's too simplistic and, in a way, demeaning," said Karl Furstenberg, the dean of admissions and financial aid at Dartmouth Col-

---

1. In the late nineteen seventies the National Research Council appointed a Committee on Ability Testing, chaired by Wendell Garner. This was as sober, competent, interdisciplinary group as we could wish. The first of two reports was published in 1982 with the title *Ability Testing*, edited by Wigdor and Garner (1982). Nothing I say in this and the previous chapter is contradicted by the contents of that book, although the criticisms and conclusions it contains are written in a style less heated than mine. As I expected, that report has had no discernible effect on educational practice, educational policy makers, or on the direction of psychological research. My guess is that few psychologists read the book. Ability testing is a minor tributary in the mainstream of American psychology.

lege. "I worry about a program like this stigmatizing people, and in effect saying 'just because you come from background x-y-z, you are not expected to do well, and if you do well, you get this gold star of being a striver.'"

In the wake of the *Journal* article, which suggested that admission officers would be able to start using the formula this fall, the testing service has taken great pains to say that its research is continuing and that it has yet to decide whether to disseminate the formula to colleges.

In previous pages I said that as a group (and not the only professional one), few psychologists in the American Psychological Association have had any sustained experience in schools. (That is not true for members of the National Association of School Psychologists, many members of which are ineligible to join the APA because they lack a doctoral degree, which aside from not being wanted was the reason why the NASP was formed.) But in regard to how colleges and universities select students, undergraduates and graduates, many psychologists are very knowledgeable because they have served on admissions committees in diverse capacities. For example, I served on the graduate admissions committee of Yale's department of psychology for 17 years and for 45 years participated in departmental meetings where acceptance or rejection of a committee's recommendations was voted on, candidate by candidate. There have been thousands of psychologists with similar experience; I am by no means atypical. So what? The answer is in two parts. First, none of them—except those who are unfortunately mentally deranged—would ever describe these meetings as cool, linear, rational, or objective, by which I mean that one could count on controversy about several, sometimes more, candidates. Almost all departments require the SAT or the GRE (graduate admissions test), previous school transcript, letters of recommendation, and a statement by the candidate explaining why he or she should be admitted. Before the anti-discrimination laws of the 1960s most colleges and universities also required a photograph, and it was not because they were conducting a beauty contest. Scores on the admissions test were heavily influential, of course, but in a number of cases questions were raised based on information other than test scores or grades. The questions can best be characterized as intuitions, personal interpretation: "This candidate strikes me as a grind, not capable of creativity." "The letters of recommendation unequivocally say the student is decent, likeable, and a school leader, but they don't say very much about how well he uses his head." "I know one of the recommenders, and I wouldn't trust what he says because he can't say anything bad about anyone." "His personal statement strikes me as if someone told him to say what he knew we wanted to hear." "His test is barely above our cut-off point, and there is nothing in the application to suggest he will be able to meet the competition he will encounter here." "She strikes me as a social butterfly." "I don't care what his high score is, there is nothing in the application to suggest he is high on anything else." A colleague of mine who had served on these committees in two colleges and one other university remarked that "applications are regarded as Rorschachs scrutinized and judged as if all of the faculty were experienced clinicians."

I intend neither criticism nor satire. These psychologists know that they are engaged in a game of high stakes both for the individual candidate and for the colleges and universities. And, perhaps more important, they know from past experience that if they judged only by test scores they will admit a small but significant number of students who will drop out, be terminated, or simply not fulfill expectations. They look to non-test data for signs that confirm or disconfirm judgments based on test scores. And few such signs are as important to them as signs of the degree of maturation, the degree of "striving."

What I am saying, of course, is that the criticism being directed at the research on "strivers" by the Educational Testing Service is also applicable to the process that today characterizes how judgments are made by college and university admissions committees. Critics betray, wittingly or unwittingly, their ignorance of the psychological dynamics operative in these committees, dynamics which are predictable and even praiseworthy in that they know well that test scores are just that: numbers that can be as misleading as they can be revealing. I am not privy to the details of the research being conducted by the Educational Testing Service and therefore, can not judge in terms of substance, scope, and method. But I give them credit for recognizing and trying to address a crucial problem. And the problem is not one of how to eliminate personal judgment but rather how to provide explicit data or indices which may make for more reliable and valid judgments and predictions about ability and learning. Judgment is and should be part of the process, and anything that gives promise of providing basis for improving judgment is, as I have said, both necessary and praiseworthy.

Theories of human behavior and ability *always* reflect personal attitudes toward and experience with tests, an assertion made more generally a hundred years ago by William James and illustrated in countless biographies and autobiographies before and since. So let me in conclusion relate two experiences which shaped the view informing this. I could fill a modest sized book with similar instances but it would be boringly repetitious. Besides, I am quite aware that the personal experience of one person, however numerous and even interesting, is still but one person's experience. The view shaped by those experiences may turn out to be totally or partially right or wrong. That is besides the present point.

I was a psychology major in college. In a psychology course in my junior year Professor Fred Gaudet wanted to demonstrate different tests of intelligence. One was the Kohs Block Designs, consisting of painted wooden cubes each of which has the same colors and geometric configuration. The testee is shown a card and has to organize the cubes to match the pattern of the card. The card went from the simple to the complex. Professor Gaudet asked me to take the test while the rest of the class watched; he liked me a good deal and assumed I would have no difficulty. I froze. I could not do the designs except for the relatively simple ones. Elsewhere I have described why high school geometry was the only course I almost flunked. I was crushed, to say the least, to have done miserably before my classmates and professor who was as puzzled as I was embarrassed. My college grades were excellent, I had a good opinion of my ability, but essentially failing a test that correlated with IQ was traumatic. Matters were not helped any when several days later he had the class take the paper and pencil Henmon-Nelson test of mental ability. My score put me in the seventy-fifth percentile, certainly no great shakes of a score. That really shook me. Maybe I was not as smart as I like to believe. Besides being physically handicapped from polio, maybe I had an intellectual handicap. It took me several years before I concluded my scores had been "flukes." (These two experiences explain why I initiated and directed a 15-year research program on test anxiety, the findings of which have stood the test of time.) I was and remain an ambitious person, a quintessential striver, characteristics that permitted me, forced me, to continue to believe that I could succeed: go to graduate school, get my Ph.D., and then prove to the world that I was an unusual psychologist despite my poor showing on the only two tests of mental ability I had ever taken. Professor Gaudet urged me to apply to graduate school, and I applied to at least 12, including Yale. I received 11 consecutive rejections. Again I was crushed and demoralized. But it was not a complete surprise to me; more correctly, I could point to reasons which did not require me to reassess my ability. The first was I was Jewish, and in 1939 that was strike one. The second reason was the University of Newark in New Jersey was a small, struggling, commuter institution which had newly been accredited to give degrees; that was strike two. Even though my college grades were excellent, they would not be judged highly by the very well-known, distinguished universities to which I had applied. But hope does spring eternal and hopes had been high. About 3 weeks after the accept-reject deadline a letter of acceptance came from Clark University, one of the fountainheads of American psychology. Why did they accept me? When I got there I learned that the luminaries in the department had left *en masse* because of a dispute with the president who I learned and later observed had cornered the market both on parochialism and ignorance. As a result, the number and quality of students who applied and were accepted had discernibly plummeted. I was the beneficiary of a departmental upheaval.

The second experience occurred in the late 1950s. One of the applicants to the graduate psychology program at Yale was from Brooklyn College. His score on the Graduate Record Examination was not much above our cutoff point. His grades and supporting letters were good, and he had done a research project for his senior thesis. Our department was very eager to admit Blacks who we felt would not embarrass us or the applicant, but the handful that applied after World War II contained no such individuals; none had scores at or above the cutoff point. After a few minutes of discussion, it appeared as if the Brooklyn student would be rejected because there was a surfeit of applicants who on the surface had far more impressive credentials. "But wait," one faculty member said, "I wondered if he was Black and for obvious reasons would not mention it and neither would his recommenders." He went on to point out that the applicant's research project was on attitudes and race relations and, in addition, Brooklyn College had more than a few Black students. "After all," he ended, "he is above our minimal criteria and his personal statement certainly bespeaks of enormous motivation for a research career." The tenor of the meeting changed dramatically. Every faculty member wanted to reread the application right then and there. Before a vote was taken, a colleague asked what we would do if the applicant experienced trouble in coping with our demanding courses. Were we being fair to him? To which several members replied, "If he needs extra help, we'll find a way to get it for him." He was admitted. When he showed up at Yale, we found he was white and Italian, not the Jamaican one colleague thought his name suggested. The applicant's name was Philip Zimbardo who became a deservedly eminent psychologist. He needed extra help the way Bill Gates needs food stamps. That Phil is a striver goes without saying, but he is also a very creative psychologist.

As used in the newspaper article, the concept and indices of striving are considered as important for decisions in cases where test scores are not impressive or slightly above a cutoff point. That is justified, but it is a misleadingly narrow view because it begs the question: Are not those indices also important for decisions about individuals whose test scores are highly impressive? There are two ways I answer that question. The first is that in my 45 years at Yale I know of no colleagues who were completely satisfied with how well we chose high-scoring people who were also strivers. The department held assessment meetings twice a year to review the performance of all students; one at mid year and one at the end of it. It was at those meetings that most of the discussion centered on students whose level of striving and motivation was either low, or unacceptable, or down right puzzling. I do not want to convey the impression that the number of such students was large, although the number was not insignificant, approximately 10–15% of all students in the department. That does not include students who were strivers but whose performance in courses and research were acceptable but unimpressive: they passed their courses, carried out their research projects at levels and in ways that indicated they were the kinds of students who might confirm the expectation that they would make contributions to psychology as a science and field of practice, the sole basis for having a graduate program at Yale.

The second part of the answer is that in my discussions with colleagues in the medical and law schools, they expressed the same opinions. (We are talking about opinions, there are no other "data.") And those same opinions were voiced by psychologists in other institutions. The critics of the research that the Educational Testing Service is conducting seem unaware that the assessment process for entrance to colleges and universities is not a basis for self-serving congratulations or smug satisfaction.

Let me in the next chapter continue my discussion by focusing on the derogation of the field of education by American psychology.

CHAPTER 8

Schools, and the Values and Culture of Higher Education

On reading this book I assume that readers have asked themselves this question: "You talk about and judge American psychology as if it were an individual. Isn't that a gross oversimplification, and an unfair one to boot? It is as if you expect that if what you call American psychology were to listen to you and take what you say to heart, the changed outlook you desire would occur?" There are several parts to my reply, but I put the most important part last because it was the major reason I wrote this book.

I can assure the reader that I was aware of the above question, which is not to suggest that that is an answer. In earlier pages I tried to make clear that by American psychology I meant its organizational components which represent to the larger society what psychology is about. They are components which have platforms, status, and power. I referred to departments of psychology, the American Psychological Association, and the American Psychological Society, which was created because its constituents had concluded that the vastly more large and powerful American Psychological Association no longer represented psychology as a science; a fair number of the members, however, retained membership in the two organizations. And, as the above question clearly indicates, each of these components contains and represents diverse substantive interests and groups. What was important to me was the fact, and I regard it as an obvious fact, that the arena of education and schools is one that is on the priority list of none of them in regard to training and research. If the reader doubts that assertion I suggest that he or she read the course requirements, faculty area of interest, and dissertation abstracts of departments of psychology, as well the convention programs of the two national associations. As I said earlier, there are psychologists in schools of education, and there is a National Association of School Psychologists, many members of which cannot be members of the American Psychological Association or the

American Psychological Society because they do not have a doctoral degree. They are not only held in low regard by the members of the two national psychological associations but, as I can attest from personal experience, the existence of the National Association of School Psychologists is not even known to most of the membership of the two national organizations of psychologists. None of this is truly understandable without taking one other fact into consideration: In the American university schools of education are, so to speak, low man on the totem pole in regards to respect, status, and funding. And in many universities schools of education are called "cash cows" because they bring in more money than the university allots them. I in no way wish to convey that I speak from a Manichean, good guy-bad guy perspective as if schools of education, the practicing school psychologists, and national professional educational associations are a persecuted lot or that there is no justification for being critical of them; to say that would be stupid and a denial of reality. What I have tried to convey is the obvious fact that American psychology has little interest in education or schools, even though as citizens, parents, and avid observers of their local and national scene, every psychologist will say that the failure to change and improve schooling will mightily determine the strength of this society's social fabric. Now, what if you ask, as I have over the decades asked, psychologists: In light of American psychology's deep and sincere interest in child development, the learning process, intelligence, attitude formation, group dynamics, and motivation, why is it that so few psychologists have a sustained theoretical or research interest in schools or no personal-professional interest at all, as that interest is reflected in what they do as psychologists?

That question began to be answered at the Boulder Conference in 1949, which is why I devoted Chapter 3 to that conference. However varied they were (and they varied) in background, status, and interests, almost all of the participants gave short schrift to my suggestion that American psychology should forge a closer relationship with education and schools. Their rhetoric (then and now) aside, they had little interest in schools; schools were not places in and about which psychological theory and research would further the field's development. I could talk about the participants at that conference as if they were one person. Let me give another illustration which sheds light on another facet of the problem in that it helps to explain the stance of departments of psychology toward education.

What I have to say in this chapter derives from much more than my years at Yale. I am quite aware that Yale's very negative view of the field and people in education is unusually strong, snobbish, and longstanding; yet it is a matter of degree compared to other universities. I would not argue strenuously against the judgment that Yale's negativity is atypically extreme and that its history supports that judgment. But over nearly 6 decades I have come to know scores of universities where the negativity is less and did or does not get manifested as at Yale. The fact remains that I can think of at most one or two where that negativity was not palpable and a source of festering discontent and derisive rumor. Disinterest is one thing, derision is quite another. Yes, Yale is a textbook case, which is to say that the negativity has taken forms which are painfully clear. In other universities it has taken less obvious forms, but the "symptoms" are there, and no part of the university recognizes those symptoms as quickly and poignantly as the faculty in departments or schools of education. In thinking about this chapter, I made a list of universities I have come to know well over the decades, and for each one I noted specific events or occasions or policy decisions reflective of the negativity. It is not a short list. I saw no point in devoting pages in this book to what I believe is a glimpse of the obvious.

Seventy years ago the president of Yale proposed the creation of a graduate department of education. The Yale faculty was less than lukewarm about the proposal. If he had proposed a school of education, the faculty would have revolted, and that would have been the end of the matter. But the president knew what he was up against and realistically proposed a relatively small graduate department, the faculty and students of which would be selected by the same stringent standards all Yale departments had to meet: Faculty with a record of quality research, students of unquestionable ability and commitment to a research area, and placing those students in highly respected research universities. Although publicly the faculty was decidedly cool to the proposal, in private they regarded the move as a major mistake and departure from its traditions. But as in the politics of all universities, the faculty has to pick its spots for opposing the administration. By throwing a sop to the president, they could exert more pressure to get support for programs they really wanted. During all of its existence that department was, to put it mildly, in a hostile environment. In the late 1950s the department was by fiat eliminated by President Griswold whose major claim to fame was oral and written denunciation of educators, schools of education in general, teachers in particular, and the quality of schools. It was a most unusual, unilateral act. The Yale faculty could not have been more happy. A cancer in the Yale body had been excised. If my colleagues in psychology reacted with subdued approval, they also could not be less interested. (Six decades later a Yale president proposed the elimination of a department, in this case sociology. The faculty publicly opposed, voted no confidence in him, the proposal died, and not long after the president resigned.) The point, of course, is that negative attitudes in the university toward education and schools are reflected in and absorbed by members of psychology departments. Absorbed is, I suppose, somewhat misleading because members of psychology departments were trained and educated in such departments. They were already indoctrinated in what was tradition and mainstream psychology.

One more Yale example. As I mentioned in Chapter 2, in 1961 I decided to create a psycho-educational clinic as a means to study the culture of the school (I have discussed this in detail in my 1988 autobiography *The Making of an American Psychologist*). I presented my proposal to the psychology faculty. There was and is a tradition at Yale that professors can and should be able to go where their interests take them as long as it did not require significant outlays of departmental resources. The faculty heard me out and with no display of enthusiasm or opposition supported the proposal. In short order it was referred to as Seymour's clinic, it was not a departmental clinic. Several factors made things easy (relatively speaking) for me. First, and most important, was the chairman, Claude Buxton, who had a deep interest in teaching. More specifically, he felt that the quality of college teaching was pretty poor and that it was no better or worse in the public schools. Indeed, he later wrote a book on college teaching and was asked by the university to offer an informal seminar to young instructors. He also conducted a major study (1973) on attitudes of high school students to learning and schooling. Claude was very supportive of what I wanted to do. Another unusual factor was Kingman Brewster who was then provost and soon became president after the death of President Griswold, the person who eliminated the graduate department of education. When Claude told him of my plans and that I would need space, Kingman gave us a three story, old brownstone, and *only after* he gave it to us, did he inform the president. Ordinarily, where space is concerned, especially if it is a house, it has had to receive prior approval from the president. I have to assume that Kingman knew what he was doing. He was the most unusual president ever, and that holds for him as a person. So the Yale Psycho-Educational Clinic came to be, not because Yale University wanted to do something about education and schools but because I wanted the clinic and Claude and Kingman made that possible. In a basic sense Yale—by which I mean almost all of the faculty—had not undergone a change in attitude toward the arena of education. To elaborate on that conclusion, let me describe another experience 5 years later when the clinic had become an intellectually exciting and thriving place and attracted the attention of people far beyond New Haven. Given the cast of characters who were there, that was no surprise.

The federal Office of Education (now the Department of Education) had created a TTT program: Training the Teachers of Teachers. The program was recognition of the inadequacies of preparatory programs of teachers and had already conducted long summer workshops for the continuing education of faculty in those programs. Donald Bigelow of the Office of Education had become knowledgeable about what we were doing at the clinic. Would the clinic be willing and able, he asked, in each of 5 years to have a dozen or so faculty of preparatory programs spend a semester at the clinic? They would be given the title of Visiting Fellow; the substance of the program would be completely up to us, no questions asked. He had read the book *The Preparation of Teachers: An Unstudied Problem in Education* (Sarason, Davidson, & Blatt, 1962) and knew that the preparation of teachers was critical to my interests. I pointed out to Don that the funding would be for the purpose of *training, not research,* and unless we could use part of the funding to research what we would do, I was not interested. His unambiguous reply was, "You do with the money what you decide you have to do. Yes, it would officially be designated a training grant; there is no way around that. But you spend the money as you see fit." The funding would be well above a million dollars.

Claude Buxton was no longer chairman of the department. The new chairman, Donald Taylor, was a very decent guy who had little or no interest in education. He had never visited the clinic three blocks away from the department. I wrote an annual report each year detailing the activities of the clinic and how we were funding them. Several things troubled him about the TTT proposal. First, the designation Visiting Fellow in Psychology might be interpreted by the visitors and later used by them, as indicating they had had some kind of faculty status at Yale. Coming as they would from far-less academically prestigious colleges or universities, that was a real danger. Second, he was sure that the administration and even our own department would balk. Third, it was morally unacceptable to accept training funds and then use a significant part of it for research purposes, even if the research would be about training. Taylor was as risk aversive a person as I have ever known. We had a long, non-rancorous talk. I am no shrinking violet, and I made it unmistakably clear that it was precisely because it made no sense to use training funds and not to evaluate what you were doing that I wanted to go forward. He said he would meet and discuss the proposal with the provost.

The provost asked to meet with me. A word about the provost, John Perry Miller, a professor of economics. In later years we became quite friendly. No one was more devoted to Yale than he was, no one ever understood Yale better than he did, and no one was more critical of Yale's sense of preciousness of tradition, and risk aversiveness. It was John who, after he ceased being provost, together with Kingman Brewster, maneuvered (and that is the right word) to create a School of Organization and Management despite the unverbalized but strong reluctance of the faculty. Unlike the chairman he liked our proposal. In fact, he agonized over it because he wanted Yale to be more involved in matters educational. But he said it was doomed because when faculty from other colleges and universities are to be given some kind of official title, for a semester or a year, their appointment must go through the appointments committee consisting of faculty from different parts of the university. And given the fact that these proposed appointees were very likely not to have scholarly and research credentials, they would be turned down, embarrassing my department, and feeding the critical fires of the faculty who looked upon educators as mindless drones. Years later he told me that having to say no to me had been most painful for him. The fact is that I agreed (inwardly) with his analysis and that was the end of the proposal. Up to that time I had been very critical of Yale's derogation of and lack of relationship to the field of education. I had to change my mind. The best thing Yale could do for the field of education was to stay away from it. Yale was inhospitable soil for such a relationship. And that statement applies in spades to departments of psychology.

Some might say Yale is atypical and one cannot generalize from it. They could point to equally prestigious universities who have graduate schools of education. But no one has seen fit to study—it would not be an easy study—how these schools of education are regarded by all other departments, by the university administration, and how all this impacts on the education faculty. The kind of study I am suggesting should be developmental—historical, and anthropological in substance and methods. You cannot go by appearances, organizational charts, or even budgets. Why, for example, is it so frequently the case— I would say almost always—that in schools of education teacher education is the responsibility of faculty who have the least status and voice, in contrast to those whose expertise is in areas that are regarded as more "researchy," scientific, or "social sciencey" (e.g., the arena of policy)? It is as if it is not known that the relationship between policies and what goes on in classrooms is so slight. I assume that the kind of study I am suggesting will never be done. All institutions, least of all the university, steer clear of serious self-scrutiny. On the surface you get one picture; when you start to peel away the surface layers, you begin to see the clash of values and power.

That is predictable whether it is a school, a university, any of its departments, a hospital, a marriage, a family, a church, and of course our political groupings. It takes an unusual set of circumstances to remind us of what we already know but manage to ignore. The most recent example is when the University of Chicago terminated the existence of its program in education. That would be a good place to pilot a study!

I have characterized American psychology as I have in relation to schools because as individuals and organized professional collectivities they have little interest in schools. I am quite aware that in so characterizing American psychology I could be criticized as indulging in overgeneralization. My personal response to that is that I have been in the field for more than 60 years from a time when the annual convention of the American Psychological Association could be held in scores of cities having one modestly sized hotel until today when only six or seven cities have enough hotels and a convention hall to hold the gathering. (In fact, until the late 1940s the annual convention was held on university campuses.) During all of those years I met scads of psychologists, only very few of whom had an interest in education and schools. That is a personal reply. To the doubting reader I suggest perusing all of the many journals and books published by the American Psychological Association to determine what proportion of them concern education and schooling. The percentage will tell you the story.

It is a truism that the university, no less than any other societal institution, reflects its time and the larger society. That is clearly the case in American psychology. So, for example, if you peruse those many publications of the American Psychological Association in the post World War II era, you will find many scores of articles, in the form of essays and formal research, on race, gender, ethnicity, gay and lesbian issues, and health care and health policy. About schools you will find very little if by "schools" you mean why and how and when they are organized as they are; who has what degree of power to do this or that; why classrooms in schools are organized as they are and the implicit and explicit conception of learning held and implemented; how to account for unsatisfactory educational outcomes; why educational reform has been so paltry or non-existent in its consequences; the nature of the system in which the single school is embedded; the preparation of educators in relation to the tasks and problems which confront them; and more, much more. You will find a spate of articles after the 1954 desegregation decision about bussing, but they hardly discuss what goes on in a complicated, social psychological place we call a school or the more complicated thing we call a school system which is embedded in a more complicated system of official stakeholders.

How might we begin to account for this discrepancy? There are two reasons, both external to American psychology. In the case of mental health, American psychology was asked by governmental agencies to become a player by creating programs for the training of clinical psychologists (see Chapter 3). Granted that there were psychologists who played a significant role in convincing federal agencies that psychology had a role to play, an important one, the fact remains that these agencies were confronted with a mammoth social and professional set of problems and needs and, therefore, required little convincing that American psychology could make a potentially significant contribution. American psychology took the matter seriously, and its character changed dramatically.

If the creation of modern clinical psychology had a potent external stimulus, what about the other arenas of societal problems I listed above? In none of those instances did any external agency ask American psychology as a field to do anything. In each of those instances federal agencies and foundations did fund research on those problems, and psychologists sought to be recipients of those funds. Why? There are several reasons but two are truly major. The first is that these problems had obvious moral and legal components causing controversy and divisiveness in the society. For example, gay and lesbian issues are so controversial because they involve moral, legal, constitutional, and religious principles. Precisely because the nature and vicissitudes of sexuality are of obvious centrality to psychological theory, it is not surprising that gay and lesbian issues play such a role in the field. But that was not always the case; it began to pick up steam after World War II, and if you had to pinpoint when the spark lit the fire, it would be the uproar and furor aroused by the first Kinsey report.

The second reason is that in all of these areas the problems are ones with which many psychologists had and have direct experience either through direct observation or personal identity or clinical work. The American Psychological Association has a fair number of gays and lesbians, racial and ethnic minority individuals, and many mental health clinicians; somewhat more than half of the membership are women. When you take note of the fact that, as a group, psychologists tend to be a very politically liberal group, active not passive advocates, it should occasion no surprise that they entered the public arena in the post World War II era as never before. They needed no prompting. And they will say, correctly, that they act consistently with its mandate: to contribute to the advancement of psychology as a science and the public welfare.

So, again, why so little interest in education and schools? The most obvious reason is that in the course of their training they have had no direct and very little indirect experience with these arenas. But the obvious is just that: obvious. Not so obvious is that psychologists are unable to use their very personal experience *as students in schools* to begin to ask why schools are not what they should be or why changing schools has so little to show for such efforts. Relevant here is a series of questions I would put to graduate students. In one or another way they concerned student memories of their schooling: teachers who turned them on or off, their level of interest in and enthusiasm for what they were required to learn, and the like. By far the most frequent response was that school was a "kind of game"—that was the way more than a few put it—in which you learned what you were required to learn even though you soon forgot what you learned. They did not see the point of it all. The second most frequent reaction was that the number of "good" teachers (undefined) they had in 12 years of schooling was about two. The last question I asked was: on a scale of 1 to 10, one being stimulating, exciting, and memorable, and 10 being boring and uninteresting, how would you rate your school years? The average rating was between eight and nine. If you left out the extreme rating (1 and 2, 9 and 10) the modal rating was 7.5. I should note that when we discussed these findings which I put on the black board, the students never or rarely expressed disdain or hostility toward teachers but rather amusement. It was in discussion that the characterization "kind of a game" was expressed.

Memory is a sometime thing, and Yale graduate students are an atypical group on the basis of which one should not generalize. So let me tell you about two groups of teachers with whom I met once a week over 10 weeks in a suburban school system. It was during the turbulent sixties. Somewhere between the middle and the end of our meetings, at a time when I thought it appropriate to the discussion—discussions ranged over many topics and problems—I asked the following question: "During your schooling can you recall and describe one instance, an experience when you learned something or understood something you did not know or understand before? Try to describe why that was so important in your development." At least half of the teachers had difficulty coming up with one instance, for reasons about which I can only speculate, but I will refrain from speculation. But about half of them overcame their reluctance and were able to respond. The instances they described *never* involved a school experience. I was surprised because I had expected that they would interpret my question as requiring that they relate a classroom experience, although I deliberately posed the question somewhat ambiguously. It was as if an interesting, important learning experience was in their minds (their memories) not at all highly associated with classroom experience. Teachers, like psychologists, do not use their school experience better to understand school experience. For more formal and systematic research that throws light on what I have said is Buxton's 1973 study of the attitudes of adolescents toward their school experience and the 1996 study by Steinberg and colleagues.

In the concluding pages of this book I shall assume that there will be readers who will say that my critique of American psychology is justified, which does not mean that I expect that they will agree with all of its particulars. If that assumption is correct, I will also assume that these readers are asking how this state of affairs can begin to be altered. That question, of course, confronts us with the general, fascinating, thorny question: How do institutions change? Put in another and more modest way: What is the *minimal* condition which if not existent will defeat the goals of change from the very beginning? That question is in principle identical with one clinical psychologists ask and answer in their endeavor to help individuals with personal problems. The principle is in the form of two maxims or caveats: You can not help someone who is not there, someone who does not show up because he or she does not want to come. You can not help someone who comes because he or she is forced to come against his or her will. In other words, change will not occur unless there is an internal compliance factor.

On the institutional level and specifically in regard to American psychology, the internal compliance factor exists, but it is woefully weak; there are psychologists who are troubled by their field's lack of relationship to education and schools, but they are few in number. There are many more in number who see their field as no longer possessing a kind of central core or cores which are distinctive and for which there is general agreement that all psychologists should know something about if they identify themselves as psychologists. At the present time there are only two such interrelated cores in psychology, but they are at their roots non-psychological in nature. One is statistics, which is technical in nature and an applied form of mathematics, and by itself not illuminating of human behavior. The other is research design, which derives from logic and the rules of evidence. All psychologists have to have attained a minimal competence in utilizing these cores. Once you go beyond those cores, it will appear on the surface that there are the other cores, e.g., child development, abnormal psychology, psychobiology, clinical psychology, cognitive psychology; they are the course titles of graduate courses. But if you read the psychological literature or the convention program of the American Psychological Association, the surface impression dissolves into a bewildering array of specialties, specialties within specialties, fields within fields, with the consequence that it is not unusual that within any one field or specialty—let alone between fields—one psychologist has little to say to another. I am not bemoaning or criticizing specialization, but when specialization becomes atomization and there are no overarching conceptions that can bring atoms in some degree of relationship to each other, you have a cloud chamber of alienated particles. Or, if you prefer a Tower of Babel. The issue is not specialization, but the absence of any conceptual ties that bind, that provide at least some degree of the sense of shared identity and community.

In keeping with one of the major foci of this book, I suggest that there is a core which has a long history in American psychology but one based on theories and research that essentially went nowhere and after World War II lost whatever distinctiveness and status it had earlier enjoyed. I refer to learning as process, as a developmental phenomenon, as the glue between internal and external world, always in relation to contexts. I describe it that way in order to make a point I discussed in earlier pages. And that is that for more than half of the twentieth century learning theory and research in American psychology was so largely based on work with rats, a mammoth obstacle for the understanding of the role of learning in humans. But if learning theory faded from the scene, the fact is that as a concept learning was and is important, indeed essential, in a variety of psychological specialties, notably child development, social psychology (e.g., attitude formation), personality development, and more. If it was and is central, however, there is no overarching conception of learning which would enable us to determine whether or not they are using similar or conflicting conceptions, or conceptions so implicit, simplistic, and vague as to be no test of any conception even though the conclusions they offer clearly imply a conception of learning. Part, and a large part, of the problem is that each of these fields deals with human behavior in very different contexts, as are the questions for which they seek answers. Context, in my opinion, is the most consequential, and for two reasons. First, anything that can be dignified as a theory of learning has to specify the nature and complexity of the context relevant to the theory. Second, psychologists are not good at describing contexts. That may be unfair to say because editors of journals or books are under pressure to keep publications as brief as possible. That is something psychologists are told and learn in graduate school, which is one reason why dissertations of, say, a hundred or more pages, become ten or so pages as journal articles. As an FBI agent in a TV series used to say, "The facts, ma'am, just the facts." Context is the victim. That, of course, begs the question: What do we mean by context? American psychology has never seriously confronted that question. The only psychologist who did was Roger Barker (1968), who almost single-handedly developed a theoretical rationale for an ecological psychology and spent decades demonstrating and testing it in two field stations, one in America and one in England (see Chapter 5). It is beyond the scope of this book to say more about his work; it even defies an instructive summary. American psychology has yet to take him seriously.

What is meant when it is said that a high school is a context of learning? The conventional answer is that it is context in which students acquire knowledge, cognitive skills, and attitudes deemed by the community to be both important and crucial for the personal and intellectual development of students, enabling them to pursue their life goals whatever they may be. That is no answer to the question; it is a statement of purposes and goals. The word *context* is not like such words as *sticks* and *stones, pillows* and *people.* You cannot see a context, just as you cannot see a culture. Context is literally an abstraction we employ in our effort to make sense of how parts (sub contexts) are related to, impact on, each other, and how the different parts are in the service of purposes and goals. Large urban and regional high schools are very complicated organizations so that it is by no means unusual for teachers to say that they do not know many of their colleagues and given the number of teachers and administrators a general faculty meeting is very infrequent and no forum for discussion.

You do not seek to describe and to understand context as an intellectual exercise but rather to judge it in terms of the achievement of purpose and goals. I have had teachers and administrators describe the high school as a disaster area, a zoo, where the only thing that matters is doing just enough to pass the tests and to be graduated. As one teacher put it, "I taught for 2 years in a ghetto high school, and when I got the opportunity to come here, a nice middle class high school, I was ecstatic. After 5 years here I can tell you that from the standpoint of motivation for learning the students are not dramatically different."

The point here is not to learn the obvious: High schools are not contexts in which productive learning exists for a majority of its students. The point is that no effort to change and improve high schools will get to first base until clarity is attained about two things. First, that the many parts of the present context contribute little or nothing to productive learning of students and teachers. *If contexts of productive learning do not exist for teachers, they cannot create and sustain a context of produc-*

tive learning for students. If teachers are not motivated to change and learn, nei-
ther will those students be so motivated. The second thing is that the existing context will require radical change, not cosmetic ones. And I should
add a third thing: the change will be marked by turmoil, resistance, and
conflicts. Unlearning accustomed ways of thinking and acting is no cup
of tea for individuals and institutions. And at the core of the problem
is, as one could predict, the nature, goals, and context of school learning. It is easy to proclaim the importance of new and high standards. It
is also easy to say that meeting these standards will be judged by tests.
But what can happen if a school is organized around a conception of
learning for which those tests are deemed counterproductive or irrelevant? Let us take a case in point.

The Regents of the State of New York oversee public and private
schools. In an effort to improve educational outcomes of high schools,
the Regents adopted the policy that all high school students who entered the ninth grade in 1996 and who enter in subsequent years must
pass the new Regent's English exam before graduation. This policy is
being contested by the New York Performance Standards Consortium
which represents small schools with unconventional approaches to
learning. They argue that elaborate end-of-the-year portfolios and science experiments are more rigorous and creative than standardized
tests. The following is taken from an article by Holloway in the *New
York Times* of October 20, 1999.

"We've created a culture in our schools that supports a rigorous approach
to learning," said Ann Cook, co-director of the Urban Academy, an alternative school in Manhattan and a member of the consortium. "We require
students to write literary essays, devise original science experiments and
defend them, and produce research papers in the social sciences that use
historical evidence. In fact, the work is more demanding than the Regents'."

Schools like Urban Academy and Beacon High School—along with
hundreds of private and many traditional public schools across the state—
began fighting the new measure last year, but the complaints fell on deaf
ears. Supported by Schools Chancellor Rudy Crew, they complain that the
requirements are one-size-fits-all and will impose uniformity on curricu-
lums and teaching styles, forcing teachers to teach to the test and students
to memorize facts and figures rather than develop in-depth understanding of material.

But state officials argue that granting exemptions could undermine
their efforts to make certain that all schools meet the same high standard
for graduation. They also express concern that allowing variances for
some schools would lead to more requests for exemptions.

The response of the Regents is identical in spirit to Henry Ford's classic remark to the public: "You can have any color Ford you desire as long as it is black." Translated: you can implement a conception of productive learning different from that of larger and conventional schools but your students will not be graduated unless they pass our exam.

Imagine the following scenario. A large corporation has seen its profitability decrease over the years. Its stock holders are complaining and pressing for new leadership. Employee morale is low. Customers are dissatisfied with the products they buy. After long deliberation among the officers of the corporation and outside consultants, they have to decide between two courses of action. The first is that in order to improve the quality and saleability of their product, they must set new standards of quality control and performance for its employees, which if not met by employees would be cause for dismissal. Adherence to quality standards has been lax. The second alternative is based on the diagnosis that the way in which lines of production are organized and managed has two self-defeating consequences: Workers on the production line have no sense of personal relationship or commitment to why things are organized as they are, and any ideas or suggestions that workers may have to improve quality of product are not articulated because the ambiance is such that they anticipate that their suggestions will not be welcomed or discussed. To suggest changes is fraught with danger. You play it safe, no one is interested in ideas that are implicitly critical of the way things are done.

I trust the reader will agree that the two alternatives reflect different conceptions of motivation and learning, just as is the case with the contesting parties in New York. The Regents have responsibility for several thousand schools, and we shall assume that the large corporation has many sites scattered here and there. What that means is that there is a third alternative: You adopt and evaluate both alternatives. The corporation has no more credible evidence that setting rigorous standards and a shape-up or ship-out policy will be more or less productive than the other alternative. Similarly the Regents have no credible evidence that adopting and adhering to its policy on standards will be more or less productive than the relatively small number of schools contesting the policy. *Indeed, the history of educational reform in the post World War II provides evidence that the Regents policy for high schools will have little or no positive results.*

There are two related issues here. The more obvious one is whether innovations should be supported and judged by criteria the innovators deem relevant. That does not mean, of course, that any and all innovations should be supported. But when innovation is proposed and will be implemented by serious and responsible people who are not endangering in any obvious way the development of students, and who request an exemption from a policy on a basis the opposite of frivolous, the rule makers are not, in my opinion, entitled to respond negatively because they do not want to exercise judgment about what is or is not worthy of support. It takes more courage and, yes, wisdom to know when to allow departures from rules and standards than to treat the particular rules and standards as if they had the status of the Ten Commandments.

The second issue is far less obvious and far from more important in its implications. In the New York instance neither the Regents nor the contesting schools have done two things: (1) neither has stated clearly, unambiguously, by what concrete outcomes and data they will judge whether their efforts have the intended post high school consequences they desire and expect, and (2) the efforts of neither of the two parties are accompanied by a program of evaluation, a program which at some future point will be the basis of judgment, a basis other than opinion, selective anecdotes, and passion-dominated beliefs. Let me put it this way: Both parties have their priorities wrong, neither will have credible evidence by which to judge the fruits of their labors. But that is an old story in the history of educational reform. There is heat and little light—the Davids vs. the Goliaths; the progressives vs. the conservatives; those who emphasize subject matter vs. those who emphasize values; those who are for and those who are opposed to block scheduling; proponents for the lengthening the school day vs. those who consider it trivial in its consequences—I can go on and on because in the past 60 years I have witnessed scores of differences of opinion conducted or implemented in ways guaranteeing that both sides of a conflict would never have to change their opinions. To fight for educational reform requires strongly held opinions, beliefs, values, and visions. But it also requires acceptance of the obligation to conduct efforts in ways admissible in a court of evidence, ways as independent as possible of passions and beliefs. It makes no difference if those ways are called evaluation, assessment, or research. None of these labels in themselves confers legitimacy on what is done. There is good and lousy research, relevant and irrelevant research. Research cannot be done in a cook-book approach. Research is conceptually, methodologically, statistically, and analytically a very complicated affair. It is beyond the purposes of this book to say more about this except to note two things which in large measure explain why so much assessment research is unenlightening, let alone convincing. The first is that reformers are activists who avoid or resist the obligation to think through in anything resembling a concrete way the criteria by which they want their efforts to be observed, recorded, and measured. The second is that evaluations far too frequently are done long after the reform effort has been initiated and data relevant to the purposes of reform were not obtained or are of a quality that is unusable.

A case in point is President Nixon's much proclaimed Experiment Schools Program (ESP). It was an expensive program and one of the costly items was evaluation. The ESP was a disaster. Most relevant here is the meeting (which I attended) between the federal overseers of ESP and a private research firm which was seeking the contract to do the evaluation. The researchers were sophisticated people who wanted to and could have done a respectable job. But soon after the meeting had begun, it became obvious to them that the schools, which had been selected and which already were implementing the reforms, had in their applications (each of which weighed several pounds) stated their purpose and methods in such vague, global language that left the reader totally at sea about the feasibility of evaluations. The applications were mammoth ink blots. I felt sorry for the researchers who were torn between wanting the contract and knowing they would be participating in a charade. The whole story is even more disappointing than I can go into here. The ESP cost upwards of $60 million dollars, and its fruitless, undecipherable outcomes are not even fit for the dust bin of history.

The second point is that evaluators have to be knowledgeable about the culture of schools if they are to be helpful to the reformers in gaining clarity about what will constitute usable, concrete data which will confirm or disconfirm the outcomes the reform seeks to demonstrate. You can be an expert in data analysis, statistics, and the rules of evidence, but if you are not knowledgeable about the culture of schools, you are unwittingly colluding to produce a predictable confusion.

Why have I brought up the evaluation of educational reform efforts? The fact is that whatever criticisms I have directed at American psychology do not hold for the research training of psychologists. Generally speaking, they are an ingenious lot when it comes to devising ways to test hypotheses so as to differentiate between credible and appropriate evidence, on the one hand, and murky, uninterpretable data on the other hand. Please note that I said "generally speaking" because I do not wish to convey the impression that because someone has spent 4–6 years of graduate training, a significant portion of which centers on the research enterprise, he is ipso facto a research expert. They predictably vary in this respect. But if you read the research journals in child development and social psychology, you are likely to agree with my generalization that American psychology has a commendable track record when it comes to formulating and testing hypotheses even when the phenomena or context are far from simple. American psychology potentially has much to contribute to school reform, but it remains a potential because they are neither interested in nor knowledgeable about schools. And this in a field in which the psychology of learning was once so dominant and today, for all practical purposes, is moribund. This will not change until the powers that be in the field begin to see that it is in the self-interest of the field to be concerned with the educational enterprise. I am not suggesting a one-way street which American psychology traverses bringing gifts to the educational arena. It is a two-way street which would reinvigorate and rejuvenate psychology as theory, research, and practice. And in saying that I am reflecting the views of more than a few psychologists who view their field as having lost its organizing cores (plural). The psychology of learning is one of those lost cores in a society puzzled (too weak a word) by the inadequacies of an institution so central to the lives of individuals and the society. Indeed, the puzzlement and frustration are so strong as to give rise to "experiments," well intentioned ones, which are as truly innovative and radical as I predict they will be disappointing. So let me turn to charter schools, albeit briefly.

As I pointed out in Chapter 5, the large majority of states have authorized the creation of charter schools which are independent of the local school system. A group consisting of teachers, parents, and interested individuals in the community can apply for a charter. The applicants have to describe and justify why their charter school will provide for its students a more interesting, stimulating, growth-enhancing learning experience than can be provided by the comparable elementary, middle, or high school of the local school district. The charter school will receive the same per capita amount that the local school district is given for each of its students; in some states the amount is somewhat higher for charter school students. Regardless of the form of governance of the charter school, all decisions and policies (fiscal, personnel, curriculum) are determined by those who have been given a charter exempting them from control of the local district. The number of charter schools varies among the states. Their total number is comparatively small but has steadily grown each year. As I write these words, the presidential nominating campaigns for president have begun, and there is already good reason to believe that the aspirants will differ only in how fast they want to increase the number of charter schools, the increases varying from noteworthy to galactic.

In 1998, in my book *Charter Schools: Another Flawed Educational Reform?* I predicted that most charter schools would fall short of their mark. That prediction was based on my 1972 book *The Creation of Settings and the Future Societies,* a book written long before the concept of a charter school was on the horizon. Here I do not want to repeat the arguments on which my prediction was based. (I do want to emphasize that I agree with the rationale justifying charter schools.) My present purposes is two-fold: To indicate the societal significance of charter schools, and why it is unfortunate that American psychology has no interest in them.

Charter schools are not comprehensible unless one makes explicit a conclusion implicit in their creation, a very radical and in my opinion correct conclusion: If you want to improve the learning experience of students, the chances that you can do so within the existing school system are very small. Unless you are freed from the self-defeating features of the existing school system, your innovative ideas about a more productive context of learning had best remain in the realm of unrealized dreams. Charter schools are the most radical critique ever directed at our school systems. This is not cosmetic or tinkering at the edges, which has been the distinctive feature of the history of educational reform.

If, as I have, you read charter school applications and talk with those people who have written them, you will have no doubt that central to their thinking and efforts is the necessity to alter the conventional conception and context of the learning process. Their conceptions vary considerably, but what they have in common is a rejection of learning and its context in the classrooms of existing school systems.

Learning, motivation, group dynamics, intergroup relations, leadership, social-institutional change, program and institutional evaluation—these are some of the problem areas of marked interest in American psychology in terms of theory, research, and practice, and yet, American psychology has shown no interest in a social invention, which charter schools are, that can be an unrivaled laboratory for the field. And when you add the fact that in almost all states the policy is that a significant number of charter schools must be in sites containing racial-ethnic minority and poor populations of long interest to psychologists, it is bordering on the indefensible that they have taken no note of charter schools.

Up until a decade ago funding for breast cancer research by the National Institutes of Health was, relatively speaking, paltry, even less than for research on prostate cancer. That had nothing to do, of course, with the frequency and importance of breast cancer. It had a lot to do with a medical community whose educators and policy makers were dominated by males. That situation did not begin to change until for the first time a female physician was appointed to head the National Institutes of Health. Some day, I would hope, the story of that change will be written up, and if it is, I also assume that it will show that the change had two major sources: pressure from external, but not medical, individuals and groups, and a small, "internal" group of physicians heretofore on the outside looking in at those deciding how research funds are allocated. There is currently no external pressure exerted on American psychology to become more meaningfully interested in and related to education. And for all practical purposes there is no internal pressure.

CHAPTER 9

G. Stanley Hall, Lightner Witmer, William James, and John Dewey

At the end of the nineteenth century a small group (I think it was 16) of psychologists met to create the American Psychological Association. One of them was G. Stanley Hall, who by his research and writings shaped what today could be called the field of adolescent psychology. Neither his theories, research, or writings have stood the test of posterity's judgment. But Hall had no doubt that any field which purported to describe and explain human development had to be interested in schooling: its purposes, curricula, pedagogy, and its knowledge of and sensitivity to the needs and characteristics of students. For Hall education was not a marginal field in psychology, let alone a disclaimed one, but no less important to psychology than the institution we call the family. He was the first president of Clark University and during his tenure in that post created more than a few stellar departments of which the department of psychology was probably the most eminent. He founded the journal *Pedagogical Seminary,* which as the name indicates was an expression of his interest in education.

A second founding father was Lightner Witmer of the University of Pennsylvania. It was he who founded the first Psycho-Educational clinic in the country. Witmer knew the school setting, and the clinic was in a helping relationship to schools in regard to children with learning problems whatever their source or nature. He too founded a journal *Psychological Clinic,* which among other things contained some fascinating and sophisticated accounts of the ways in which educational problems were diagnosed, remedial techniques employed, and even psychotherapeutic rationales. When I founded the Yale Psycho-Educational Clinic in the early 1960s, I selected its name as my way of paying homage to a pioneer who has never received the recognition he deserves from American psychology.

The third person was William James, perhaps the most remarkable American psychologist ever. Especially with James, it is best to let him speak for himself. The following excerpt, written 100 years ago, is from the preface of his book *Talks to Teachers and to Students* (1900).

> In 1892 I was asked by the Harvard Corporation to give a few public lectures on psychology to the Cambridge teachers. The talks now printed form the substance of that course, which has since then been delivered at various places to various teacher-audiences. I have found by experience that what my hearers seem least to relish is analytical technicality, and what they most care for is concrete practical application. So I have gradually weeded out the former, and left the latter unreduced; and now, that I have at last written out the lectures, they contain a minimum of what is deemed "scientific" in psychology, and are practical and popular in the extreme.
>
> Some of my colleagues may possibly shake their heads at this; but in taking my cue from what has seemed to me to be the feeling of the audiences I believe that I am shaping my book so as to satisfy the more genuine public need.
>
> Teachers, of course, will miss the minute divisions, subdivision, and definitions, the lettered and numbered headings, the variations of type, and all the other mechanical artifices on which they are accustomed to prop their minds. But my main desire has been to make them conceive, and if possible, reproduce sympathetically in their imagination, the mental life of their pupil as the sort of active unity which he himself feels it to be. He doesn't chop himself into distinct processes and compartments; and it would have frustrated this deeper purpose of my book to make it look, when printed, like a Baedeker's handbook of travel or a text-book of arithmetic. So far as books printed like this book force the fluidity of the facts upon the young teacher's attention, so far I am sure they tend to do his intellect a service, even though they may leave unsatisfied a craving (not altogether without its legitimate grounds) for more nomenclature, headlines, and subdivisions. (p. iii)

James is not talking down to teachers. He is not saying that teachers should not be interested in what psychology as a science has contributed to an understanding of human behavior. But, as will be clear in a moment, what he is saying is that the science of psychology in no way directs a teacher how to understand or what to say and do with the *concrete*, palpable, visible students in a *concrete* classroom context, students for whom the learning situation is an "active unity" which is that student's and not that of the student sitting next to him. To the extent that a teacher sees the student through the prisms of scientific psychology's laws, generalizations, and abstractions, the teacher is blind to that unity, *the fact of individuality*. Please note that James is aware that his scientific colleagues will look askance at what he says even though he in no way is putting down the science of psychology, a field no one more than James shaped. So, let us listen to him in the chapter titled "Psychology and the Teaching Art":

> The desire of the schoolteachers for a completer professional training, and their aspiration toward the "professional" spirit in their work, have led them more and more to turn to us for light on fundamental principles. And in these few hours which we are to spend together you look to me, I am sure, for information concerning the mind's operations, which may enable you to labor more easily and effectively in the several schoolrooms over which you preside.
>
> Far be it from me to disclaim for psychology all title to such hopes. Psychology ought certainly to give the teacher radical help. And yet I confess that, acquainted as I am with the heights of some of your expectations, I feel a little anxious lest, at the end of these simple talks of mine, not a few of you may experience some disappointment at the net results. In other words, I am not sure that you may not be indulging fancies that are just a shade exaggerated. That would not be altogether astonishing, for we have been having something like a "boom" in psychology in this country. Laboratories and professorships have been founded, and reviews established. The air has been full of rumors. The editors of educational journals and the arrangers of conventions have had to show themselves enterprising and on a level with the novelties of the day. Some of the professors have not been unwilling to co-operate, and I am not sure even that the publishers have been entirely inert. The "new psychology" has thus become a term to conjure up portentous ideas withal; and you teachers, docile and receptive and aspiring as many of you are, have been plunged in an atmosphere of vague talk about our science, which to a great extent has been more mystifying than enlightening. Altogether it does seem as if there were a certain fatality of mystification laid upon the teachers of our day. The matter of their profession, compact enough in itself, has to be frothed up for them in journals and institutes, till its outlines often threaten to be lost in a kind of vast uncertainty. Where the disciples are not independent and critical-minded enough (and I think that, if you teachers in the earlier grades have any defect—the slightest touch of a defect in the world —it is that you are a mite too docile), we are pretty sure to miss accuracy and balance and measure in those who get a license to lay down the law to them from above.
>
> As regards this subject of psychology, now, I wish at the very threshold to do what I can to dispel the mystification. So I say at once that in my humble opinion there is no "new psychology" worthy of the name. There is nothing but the old psychology which began in Locke's time, plus a little physiology of the brain and senses and theory of evolution, and a few refinements of introspective detail, for the most part without adaptation to the teacher's use. It is only the fundamental conceptions of psychology

which are of real value to the teacher; and they, apart from the aforesaid theory of evolution, are very far from being new. I trust that you will see better what I mean by this at the end of all these talks.

I say moreover that you make a great, a very great mistake, if you think that psychology, being the science of the mind's laws, is something from which you can deduce definite programmes and schemes and methods of instruction for immediate schoolroom use. Psychology is a science, and teaching is an art; and sciences never generate arts directly out of themselves. An intermediary inventive mind must make the application, by using its originality.

The science of logic never made a man reason rightly, and the science of ethics (if there be such a thing) never made a man behave rightly. The most such sciences can do is to help us to catch ourselves up and check ourselves, if we start to reason or to behave wrongly; and to criticize ourselves more articulately after we have made mistakes. A science only lays down lines within which the rules of the art must fall, laws which the follower of the art must not transgress; but what particular thing he shall positively do within those lines is left exclusively to his own genius. One genius will do his work well and succeed in one way, while another succeeds as well quite differently; yet neither will transgress the lines.

The art of teaching grew up in the schoolroom, out of inventiveness and sympathetic concrete observation. Even where (as in the case of Herbart) the advancer of the art was also a psychologist, the pedagogics and the psychology ran side by side, and the former was not derived in any sense from the latter. The two were congruent, but neither was subordinate. And so everywhere the teaching must agree with the psychology, but need not necessarily be the only kind of teaching that would so agree; for many diverse methods of teaching may equally well agree with psychological laws.

To know psychology, therefore, is absolutely no guarantee that we shall be good teachers. To advance to that result, we must have an additional endowment altogether, a happy tact and ingenuity to tell us what definite things to say and do when the pupil is before us. That ingenuity in meeting and pursuing the pupil, that tact for the concrete situation, though they are the alpha and omega of the teacher's art, are things to which psychology cannot help us in the least.

The science of psychology, and whatever science of general pedagogics may be based on it, are in fact much like the science of war. Nothing is simpler or more definite than the principles of either. In war, all you have to do is to work your enemy into a position from which the natural obstacles prevent him from escaping if he tries to; then to fall on him in numbers superior to his own, at a moment when you have led him to think you far away; and so, with a minimum of exposure of your own troops, to hack his force to pieces, and take the remainder prisoners. Just so, in teaching, you must simply work your pupil into such a state of interest in what you are going to teach him that every other object of attention is banished from his mind; then reveal it to him so impressively that he will remember the occasion to his dying day; and finally fill him with devouring curiosity to know what the next steps in connection with the subject are. The principles being so plain, there would be nothing but victories for the masters of the science, either on the battlefield or in the schoolroom, if they did not both have to make their application to an incalculable quantity in the shape of the mind of their opponent. The mind of your own enemy, the pupil, is working away from you as keenly and eagerly as is the mind of the commander on the other side from the scientific general. Just what the respective enemies want and think, and what they know and do not know, are as hard things for the teacher as for the general to find out. Divination and perception, not psychological pedagogics or theoretic strategy, are the only helpers here. (pp. 5–10)

With one exception, no one since James has put so clearly that there is no direct pipeline between the science of psychology and the art of teaching. And no one has been more sensitive to how that conception of a pipeline can have negative consequences for the artistry of teaching.

> Least of all need you, *merely as teachers,* deem it part of your duty to become contributors to psychological science or to make psychological observations in a methodical or responsible manner. I fear that some of the enthusiasts for child-study have thrown a certain burden on you in this way. By all means let child-study go on,—it is refreshing all our sense of the child's life. There are teachers who take a spontaneous delight in filling syllabuses, inscribing observations, compiling statistics, and computing the per cent. Child-study will certainly enrich their lives. And, if its results, as treated statistically, would seem on the whole to have but trifling value, yet the anecdotes and observations of which it in part consist do certainly acquaint us more intimately with our pupils. Our eyes and ears grow quickened to discern in the child before us processes similar to those we have read of as noted in the children,—processes of which we might otherwise have remained unobservant. But, for Heaven's sake, let the rank and file of teachers be passive readers if they so prefer, and feel free not to contribute to the accumulation. Let not the prosecution of it be preached as an imperative duty or imposed by regulation on those to whom it proves an exterminating bore, or who in any way whatever miss in themselves the appropriate vocation for it. I cannot too strongly agree with my colleague, Professor Munsterberg, when he says that the teacher's attitude toward the child, being concrete and ethical, is positively opposed to the psychological observer's, which is abstract and analytic. Although some of us may conjoin the attitudes successfully, in most of us they must conflict.
>
> The worst thing that can happen to a good teacher is to get a bad con-

science about her profession because she feels herself hopeless as a psychologist. Our teachers are overworked already. Every one who adds a jot or tittle of unnecessary weight to their burden is a foe of education. A bad conscience increases the weight of every other burden; yet I know that child-study, and other pieces of psychology as well, have been productive of bad conscience in many a really innocent pedagogic breast. I should indeed be glad if this passing word from me might tend to dispel such a bad conscience, if any of you have it; for it is certainly one of those fruits of more or less systematic mystification of which I have already complained. The best teacher may be the poorest contributor of child-study material, and the best contributor may be the poorest teacher. No fact is more palpable than this. (pp. 12–14; emphasis in original)

One more excerpt in order to indicate how well James understood a basic principle of productive learning: You start with where the learner is. It is a principle violated in all but a few classrooms in today's school.

The native interest of children lie altogether in the sphere of sensation. Novel things to look at or novel sounds to hear, especially when they involve the spectacle of action of a violent sort, will always divert the attention from abstract conceptions of objects verbally taken in. The grimace that Johnny is making, the spitballs that Tommy is ready to throw, the dog-fight in the street, or the distant firebells ringing,—these are the rivals with which the teacher's powers of being interesting have incessantly to cope. The child will always attend more to what a teacher does than to what the same teacher says. During the performance of experiments or while the teacher is drawing on the blackboard, the children are tranquil and absorbed. I have seen a roomful of college students suddenly become perfectly still, to look at their professor of physics tie a piece of string around a stick which he was going to use in an experiment, but immediately grow restless when he began to explain the experiment. A lady told me that one day, during a lesson, she was delighted at having captured so completely the attention of one of her young charges. He did not remove his eyes from her face; but he said to her after the lesson was over, "I looked at you all the time, and your upper jaw did not move once!" That was the only fact that he had taken in.

Living things, then, moving things, or things that savor of danger or of blood, that have a dramatic quality,—these are the objects natively interesting to childhood, to the exclusion of almost everything else; and the teacher of young children, until more artificial interest have grown up, will keep in touch with her pupils by constant appeal to such matters as these. Instruction must be carried on objectively, experimentally, anecdotally. The blackboard-drawing and story-telling must constantly come in. But of course these methods cover only the first steps, and carry one but a little way.

Can we now formulate any general principle by which the later and more artificial interest connect themselves with these early ones that the child brings with him to the school?

Fortunately, we can: there is a very simple law that relates the acquired and the native interest with each other.

Any object not interesting in itself may become interesting through becoming associated with an object in which an interest already exists. The two associated objects grow, as it were, together: the interesting portion sheds its quality over the whole; and thus things not interesting in their own right borrow an interest which becomes as real and as strong as that of any natively interesting thing. The odd circumstance is that the borrowing does not impoverish the source, the objects taken together being more interesting, perhaps, than the originally interesting portion was by itself.

This is one of the most striking proofs of the range of application of the principle of association of ideas in psychology. An idea will infect another with its own emotional interest when they have become both associated together into any sort of a mental total. As there is no limit to the various associations into which an interesting idea may enter, one sees in how many ways an interest may be derived.

You will understand this abstract statement easily if I take the most frequent of concrete examples,—the interest which things borrow from their connection with our own personal welfare. The most natively interesting object to a man is his own personal self and its fortunes. We accordingly see that the moment a thing becomes connected with the fortunes of the self, it forthwith becomes an interesting thing. Lend the child his books, pencils, and other apparatus: then give them to him, make them his own, and notice the new light with which they instantly shine in his eyes. He takes a new kind of care of them altogether. In mature life, all the drudgery of a man's business or profession, intolerable in itself, is shot through with engrossing significance because he knows it to be associated with his personal fortunes. What more deadly uninteresting object can there be than a railroad time-table? Yet where will you find a more interesting object if you are going on a journey, and by its means can find your train? At such times the time-table will absorb a man's entire attention, its interest being borrowed solely from its relation to his personal life. *From all these facts there emerges a very simple abstract programme for the teacher to follow in keeping the attention of the child: Begin with the line of his native interests, and offer him objects that have some immediate connection with these.* The kindergarten methods, the object-teaching routine, the blackboard and manual-training work,—all recognize this feature. Schools in which these methods preponderate are schools where discipline is easy; and where the voice of the master claiming order and attention in threatening tones need never be heard.

Next, step by step, connect with these first objects and experiences the later objects and ideas which you wish to instill. Associate the new with the old in some natural and telling way, so that the interest, being shed along from point to point, finally suffuses the entire system of objects of thought.

This is the abstract statement; and, abstractly, nothing can be easier to understand. It is in the fulfillment of the rule that the difficulty lies; for the difference between an interesting and a tedious teacher consists in little more than the inventiveness by which the one is able to mediate these associations and connections, and in the dulness in discovering such transitions which the other shows. One teacher's mind will fairly coruscate with points of connection between the new lesson and the circumstances of the children's other experience. Anecdotes and reminiscences will abound in her talk; and the shuttle of interest will shoot backward and forward, weaving the new and the old together in a lively and entertaining way. Another teacher has no such inventive fertility, and his lesson will always be a dead and heavy thing. This is the psychological meaning of the Herbartian principle of "preparation" for each lesson, and of correlating the new with the old. It is the psychological meaning of that whole method of concentration in studies of which you have been recently hearing so much. When the geography and English and history and arithmetic simultaneously make cross-references to one another, you get an interesting set of processes all along the line.

If, then, you wish to insure the interest of your pupils, there is only one way to do it; and that is to make certain that they have something in their minds to attend with, when you begin to talk. That something can consist in nothing but a previous lot of ideas already interesting in themselves, and of such a nature that the incoming novel objects which you present can dovetail into them and form with them some kind of a logically associated or systematic whole. Fortunately, almost any kind of a connection is sufficient to carry the interest along. What a help is our Philippine war at present in teaching geography! But before the war you could ask the children if they ate pepper with their eggs, and where they supposed the pepper came from. Or ask them if glass is a stone, and, if not, why not; and then let them know how stones are formed and glass manufactured. External links will serve as well as those that are deeper and more logical. But interest, once shed upon a subject, is liable to remain always with that subject. Our acquisitions become in a measure portions of our personal self; and little by little, as cross-associations multiply and habits of familiarity and practice grow, the entire system of our objects of thought consolidates, most of it becoming interesting for some purposes and in some degree. (pp. 92–98; emphasis in original)

I trust the reader agrees with me that if I had tried to summarize what James says, I would have been making precisely the same mistake he so beautifully discusses. Today psychologists do not read William James and the few who may have read him, I am certain did not read his talks to teachers. But they are not alone because I have never met a professional educator who read that book.

The fourth of the "founding fathers" was John Dewey. Early in his long life Dewey had been a school teacher, unlike the first three I have discussed. But unlike all of them Dewey created his own school at the University of Chicago in 1896. Indeed, he left the University of Michigan to go to Chicago because Chicago agreed to his request that there be a single department of psychology and education. For Dewey the school he created was the vehicle for testing his emerging conceptions of child development and school learning. For Dewey, theory and basic research had to be informed by and in turn inform educational practice, precisely the point of view Garner (1972; Garner & Hunt, 1959) so pithily discussed many decades later and which I discussed in Chapter 2. Dewey's influence on psychology has been virtually nil, while his influence on education has been and remains huge. In fact, there are many psychologists who do not know that Dewey's formal training was in psychology and that in 1899 he gave a presidential address to the American Psychological Association on the importance of forging symbiotic relationships among psychology, education, and the social sciences. If the reader consults a book on Dewey (1963), readings of articles concerned with psychology, you will be quite surprised (instructed) by the range, creativity, and relevance of his insights. Dewey had a most sophisticated understanding of students, teachers, classrooms, and schools. What I do want to emphasize, as I did in Chapter 3, is the point he makes in his presidential address which is identical to one James makes. Teachers, Dewey says, cannot be expected to understand, to have a firm grasp of the complexity and findings of psychological research. That was not a put down, but a recognition and acceptance of the limits and depth of preparatory programs. What needs to be developed is a new role which did not and still does not exist. Dewey called it a "middleman" who by training and experience was knowledgeable about the psychological literature and the ways in which it can be made salient and practical for the teacher. Beyond that Dewey did not elaborate. He recognized the problem as James did, but neither he or James provided an answer. When we started the Yale Psycho-Educational Clinic, it was fundamental in our approach to schools that they understood that ours was not a clinic to which they could refer children or teachers who might want to talk with us. We worked in classrooms in regard to any questions directed to us, and whatever suggestions, knowledge, and understandings we thought might be helpful would be the responsibility of the teacher to decide to implement. We had no official power or authority; the teacher could accept or reject our advice. The important point is that what we had to offer was based exclusively on sustained observations of a particular teacher with a particular group of students, and a particular child about whom the teacher was puzzled. We (Sarason et al., 1966) have described our experience in some detail, enough experience to say that the issue James and Dewey raised is a very real one of theoretical and practical importance. I say theoretical because introducing a "middleman" role into the culture of schools and school systems is far more than a matter of engineering or adding a new box in an organizational chart. That is a point Dewey did not appreciate as he looked approvingly at the many school systems which bought the wealth of ideas contained in his writings. Dewey *created* his own school, he never directly experienced what was involved in *changing* an existing one. The process of change, be it in an individual or an institution, always requires unlearning the old and acquiring the new, a very difficult psychological experience. In the post World War II period American psychology has produced thousands of clinical psychologists who understand and are prepared to cope with the turmoil of unlearning in their work with individuals. But American psychology has contributed little or nothing to the comprehension of the mind-boggling difficulties that institutional unlearning and learning confronts. Yet, in principle much of what has been learned about individual change is—I would argue has to be—applicable to institutional change. How much of it is applicable on the level of theory will be determined primarily by the degree to which psychologists willingly and seriously experience the culture of schools. At the present time they are neither willing or serious. Schools are in the realm of foreign affairs.

From the writings of James and Dewey there is a conclusion one can draw that neither makes explicit. And one reason they say nothing about it is that it is a glimpse of the obvious, so obvious that it is taken for granted and its enormous implications go unminded. It is also a conclusion that opens up new vistas about schooling in general and educational reform in particular. And, again, it is about a set of problems with which psychology has had to confront and does so in a way that is at best superficial and desultory and at worst irresponsible. And that set of problems is handled no better in any of the other helping professions, wherein I include teaching. To make the point I need here to repeat an excerpt from the passage from James I quoted earlier.

> This is the abstract statement; and, abstractly, nothing can be easier to understand. It is in the fulfillment of the rule that the difficulty lies; for the difference between an interesting and a tedious teacher consists in little more than the inventiveness by which the one is able to mediate these associations and connections, and in the dulness in discovering such transitions which the other shows. One teacher's mind will fairly coruscate with

points of connection between the new lesson and the circumstances of the children's other experience. Anecdotes and reminiscences will abound in her talk; and the shuttle of interest will shoot backward and forward, weaving the new and the old together in a lively and entertaining way. Another teacher has no such inventive fertility, and his lesson will always be a dead and heavy thing. This is the psychological meaning of the Herbartian principle of "preparation" for each lesson, and of correlating the new with the old. It is the psychological meaning of that whole method of concentration in studies of which you have been recently hearing so much. When the geography and English and history and arithmetic simultaneously make cross-references to one another, you get an interesting set of processes all along the line. (pp. 96–97)

Teaching is a performing art. What is more obvious? This did not hit home to me until I began to write a book *Caring and Compassion in Clinical Practice* (1985). It is a book about physicians in general practice and psychiatrists in particular, clinical psychologists, lawyers in family practice, and school teachers. Two things caused me to write that book. One was what for me had become a glimpse of the obvious: not every psychiatrist should be a psychiatrist, not every clinical psychologist should be a clinical psychologist, not every teacher should be a teacher, and so forth. One of the clearest examples concerns physicians. Every 10 years or so the deans of American medical schools produce a report on issues in medical education. Beginning two decades or so after World War II the reports bemoaned the fact that physicians are increasingly viewed by their "audiences" as lacking caring and compassion. In the past decade such a complaint has appeared frequently in the mass media. From the time I became a psychologist I was very closely involved with the medical community; for several years I taught medical students and nurses who were going into pediatrics and psychiatry. In the first book I ever wrote, *Psychological Problems in Mental Deficiency* (1949), there is a long chapter cataloguing the deficiencies and mistakes of physicians in their dealings with families of mentally handicapped children. Closer to my professional home I was director for 15 years of Yale's graduate program in clinical psychology. I helped select and train scores of very bright, highly motivated students who wanted to become clinical psychologists. Like it or not, and I did not, I was forced to conclude that a significant number of these intellectually gifted students did not possess what I and a lot of other psychologists considered essential personal and stylistic characteristics of people in that role. The second thing that caused me to write the book was another glimpse of the obvious: the criteria for and the nature of the procedures for admission to such programs had, as in the case of medical school admissions, nothing to do with caring, compassion, empathy, and other personal attributes we expect in clinicians.

In the middle of writing that book I stumbled on a book, *The Actor Prepares*, by Stanislavski (1936), the Russian director–teacher who influenced actors and acting more than anyone else in the twentieth century. (My copy was the 36th printing of that book.) What he describes is about the personal characteristics of actors and their obligations to script and audience. The final chapter of my book was devoted to Stanislavski. And years later it led me to write *Teaching as a Performing Art* (1999), a title reflecting what William James says in his *Talks to Teachers*, and he says it with a literary panache not since rivaled.

I have written a fair amount about educational reform. I have come to several conclusions. First, the educational reform movement has been, relatively speaking, a failure (1990b; 1996b). Second, it will continue to be ineffective as long as clarity and general agreement are not obtained about the differences between contexts of productive and unproductive learning. Third, there is no one explanation or factor for this state of affairs, if only because what we call a school system is part of a larger system containing parts (teachers, parents, and communities; colleges and universities; state departments of education; the local, state, and federal political systems), which are not only poorly coordinated but in practice are in an adversarial relationship to each other. Fourth, among all the possible starting points for reform, *none* will be productive unless the preparation of teachers and administrators is radically transformed. Fifth, that teachers should have a firm grasp of subject matter goes without saying, but unless that grasp is accompanied by or suffuses the nature of the psychological artistry teaching requires, reforms will be minimal or an outright failure in their outcomes.

Dr. Kenneth Wilson, a physicist whom I introduced in Chapter 4, put the issue this way (paraphrased): "If I went to the Julliard School and said I wanted to learn to play the violin, they would take me by the hand, show me the door, possibly saying that I should come back when I thought I could demonstrate that *perhaps* I had what it takes to become a professional violinist. I could leave Julliard immediately after the rejection, go to several colleges and universities in New York City, tell them I wanted to become a teacher, and the odds are very high that by the end of the day I would be enrolled in each of the programs. Given my college and graduate performance record, and my research accomplishments in physics, they would express no doubts about whether I could teach physics to high school students." (Remember that Wilson is a Nobel laureate in physics.)

In *Teaching as a Performing Art* I attempt to confront the issue Wilson poses. It is a beginning attempt and, given my advanced age and life circumstances, undoubtedly the last. I refer to that book only to emphasize a point central to the concerns of American psychology. The selection and preparation of teachers and administrators contain issues—theoretical, research, practical—that are challenges to every part of psychology concerned with human development and relationships. Learning, cognitive processes, child development, child-child and child-adult relationships, personality theory and measurement, troubled individuals and families, group dynamics, socialization and cultural variations—all of these are implicated in that place called school, the one and only place society requires each person to experience for at least 12 years, a place intended to forge and influence a student's sense of worth, competence, personal identity, and a view of or perspective on an inevitably complicated and murky future. We expect and should expect a lot from schools even though we know that realistically they will always fall short of the ideal. No psychologist will say that American psychology exists for him or her. They will say it exists to discharge an obligation to contribute to the public welfare by credibly deepening understanding of why and how people learn and adapt in the different ways they do to an array of contexts containing obstacles and opportunities. How does an infant become an adult? The key word is "become" because the name of the game is, so to speak, becoming, changing and that is most obvious in the pre-adult years. For American psychology to be as unrelated as it is to schools would not be all that serious if that field had little to contribute to school. But its potential contribution is enormous because there is no laboratory in the real world better than schools to study and test theories and concepts now largely studied in contrived contexts which set drastic limits to the range of permissible generalizations and even their validity. I am not saying there is no value in using contrived contexts as a starting point, but just as medical researchers have learned that a procedure, or medication, or treatment that works in mice does not mean that it will work in humans, one should not assume that what seems to work or to be predictable in contrived contexts has explanatory or predictive value in the normally occurring contexts in the quotidian world in which we live. For psychology the proof of the pudding is not in the laboratory or contrived contexts, but in what rightly can be termed the real world. As Garner pointed out (see Chapter 2), cognitive psychology changed in theory and direction when some very well known research psychologists were confronted with practical problems they confronted in the real world.

How come, the reader might ask, that the four "fathers" I briefly discussed, who had more than a passing interest in schools (to indulge understatement), did not see that interest move into or anywhere near the mainstream of American psychology? I can assure the reader that it was not because the other founding luminaries saw no value in relating the field to schools and education generally. As a group they were the opposite of parochial, they were not snobs, they were steeped in the history of philosophy from which psychology emerged. But that emergence was at a time when the indubitable significance of science was clear and influential. And that meant that for psychology to exploit its potentials and to be recognized as a science, to deserve that appellation, it had to adopt the letter and spirit, the methods, the theories of science, as well as the dichotomy of basic and applied research. The fruits of basic research would be the foundation for applications to the public welfare. The imagery of the laboratory and the lonely, dedicated researcher were quintessential characteristics associated with the scientific endeavor. One consequence of all this was the focus on the decontextualized, controllable, manipulatable organism, human or otherwise, the simple organism. There was little or no place for complicated contexts, the problems they contained. The answers they required could only come after basic research had produced the appropriate golden nuggets of the basic laws of human behavior. So, for example, no one disputed that the nature of human learning should be a major focus of American psychology. That was a glimpse of the obvious, but it was regarded as equally obvious that the first step to ascertain the basic laws of learning in the single organism, human or animal, was in the laboratory where conditions were controllable.

That development was not and is not without merit. There are, after all, rules of evidence, there is a difference between opinion and replicable phenomena, there are times and problems which initially require simplification or restriction of scope in order to get your bearings, to get a sense of the complexity you are up against. But in the case of learning, American psychology forgot the "from what to what" issue: How appropriate and valued are laboratory findings in the complicated, naturally occurring contexts in which humans learn? You *hope* that they are appropriate and valid. Hope does spring eternal, just as reality so frequently exposes what a mischievous need hope is in human affairs.

What was understandable and even commendable in the way the founding fathers of American psychology sought to steer the field took on in subsequent decades a narrowness, a rigidity, a snobbishness, a derogation of psychologists with applied interests, an outlook that permeated the graduate training programs in psychology. Graduates were trained to regard psychology as a science, but, unfortunately, that training was accompanied by an indoctrination of values that demeaned the psychologist with applied interests and responsibilities. There was no symbiotic relationship between the two; there was no relationship to speak of. Select and train psychologists to work in schools? That never happened in departments of psychology, and it is not happening today. If you want such training you go to a school of education which mainstream psychologists in the same university look down upon from their elevated heights, deeming themselves fortunate that they do not have to train "those" kinds of psychologists, especially those who want to become school psychologists for which the doctorate is not required. But, as I pointed out earlier, even in schools of education there is a pecking order: Those who have the status and power in colleges of education are those who are researchers or policy theorists; they have little or no interest in or relation to the preparation of teachers and some interest in and relation to the preparation of school administrators whom they see as somewhat more like themselves in status, power, and ability. I am not being polemical, I am being descriptive, just as I have been in regard to psychology. The university, like school systems, is comprised of enclaves varying in status, power, and resources.

CHAPTER 10

An Imaginary Course in Religion

I did not write this book as a way of preaching a sermon with a moral purpose, as if the "conscience" of American psychology needed a sermon from me. I had two overwhelming, interrelated purposes. The first was to examine the question: Why has American psychology had so little interest in schools to which potentially it has so much to contribute? A critic can retort that American psychology has the potential to contribute to many societal institutions and that it is a reflection of grandiosity or professional imperialism to suggest that the field cover, so to speak, the societal waterfront, running from one pier to another in discharging its obligation to be socially responsible. Resources are limited, problems are not, and the field has to decide how best to allocate those resources. And the critic would be right, of course, in asserting that not all problem areas are equally productive to the development of psychology as a science and its applications. However, that assertion, which in the abstract is obviously true, too frequently is not examined in the concrete in order to determine why this road and not another was taken and with what consequences. That kind of *historical* reflection or reexamination rarely takes place in American psychology or any other discipline. So, when in 1993 the American Psychological Association celebrated its centennial, there was no discordant note to suggest that American psychology may have made some decisions that had untoward consequences, that its history may not have been on an onward-and-upward course, that there was times, eras, and unexamined values that retarded or misdirected the field. You get ready assent to the caveat that history is *not* bunk, and although we know that is true when we try to understand individuals or nations, it is a truth that tends not to be much in evidence in the authorized histories of professional organizations. Voltaire said that history is written by the victors. There is truth to that, but in this book I do not attribute to American psychology nefarious reasons for ignoring a history that was not without mistakes and the ignoring of which negatively affected (and still affects) psychological theory and research. Let me give an example.

I was asked to give an address at the centennial convention of the American Psychological Association. The title of the paper was "American Psychology and the Needs for Transcendence and Community" (Sarason, 1993). For my present purposes I wish only to note one thing I reported: In 14 of the 15 most-used texts on child development, only one had religion in the index. The one exception referred the reader to one paragraph which essentially said nothing. How, I asked, can you develop a theory that purports to explain human development, and leave religion out of the picture? Religion, I argued, has been a millennia-old "variable" that even today influences and is absorbed by different individuals to different degrees in families, and larger collectivities. It should make no difference whether psychologists are or are not religious or even anti-religious. You do not ignore an important variable—and in the mind of the young child it is an omnipresent one—on the basis of personal stance or opinion. It is like writing a history of American psychology and never mentioning the role of religious affiliation in determining who would be admitted to a graduate program in psychology. I should emphasize that I am not talking only about religious discrimination but rather how people, especially children, learn and unlearn, formally and informally, conceptions about and attitudes toward religious questions: Who created the world? For what purposes? Is there life after death? These are questions young children struggle to answer just as they struggle to understand why the sky is blue, why boys have a penis and girls do not, how babies are created and how they live inside the mother, and so on. Children are quintessentially question-asking organisms, and some of the questions they ask are what we call religious in nature.

In the contemporary world of nations and states we have absolutely no doubt that religion is a potent factor one cannot ignore. That is no less the case on the level of the single individual, but the origins, context, substance, and vicissitudes of religious sentiments and beliefs have received little attention in American psychology. To me, at least, that lack impoverishes both developmental theory and research.

I said that the first reason I wrote this book was to try to understand the gulf between American psychology and schools. The second reason was the conviction that American psychology potentially has much to contribute to the improvement of schooling, just as the participants at the Boulder Conference (see Chapter 3) believed that American psychology had much to contribute to the arena of mental health, a belief that if not wholly confirmed has been significantly justified.

Frankly, I never anticipated that in bringing up religion as an ignored factor in development, it also could serve as an example of how

American psychology can potentially contribute to schooling. The reader does not have to be told that both because and despite of the constitutional separation of church and state, schools have been embroiled in religious issues. That was true even before there was compulsory education. Indeed, the Catholic parochial schools were started in the nineteenth century as a reaction to fears about the indoctrination of Catholic children in matters deemed inconsistent with or inimical to the faith. Today those same issues exist although the actors may be different: Creationism vs. Darwinian evolutionary theory, school prayer silent or not, saluting the flag, displays about religious holidays, and most recently whether prayer at high school football games is prohibited by the Constitution. Controversies about multi-cultural curriculum also have raised religious questions. Courts, schools, and religions have long been a triad.

In the spirit of full disclosure I should tell the reader that I am an agnostic, well aware that religion has always been a source of controversy and wars which have killed millions upon millions of people; the twentieth century is the latest instance, and in human history it is but an instance. There is more than one way to seek to ameliorate such instances. To ignore the problem during those years in which children become adults is not one of those ways. We hope and expect that parents and church will inculcate knowledge and attitudes that will have salutary effects, that the process of indoctrination will also serve the purposes of education in that it broadens and deepens a child's knowledge and attitudes toward religions other than one's own. That is asking a lot, and some will say that it is unrealistic to expect parents and church both to indoctrinate and educate in religious matters. If it is not unrealistic, in some measure at least, it has not been a robust need on which to base our hopes and expectations in regard to the educational purpose. But there is another way from which you can come to the educational purpose: How can you teach history and allied subjects and ignore why different religions differ in their basic tenets? How can ignoring such differences be educationally justified? Religion, like it or not, is in the contemporary world more than as a matter of individual adherence to doctrine; it is a fact of social living, ignorance about which makes the contemporary world incomprehensible. The usual answer to why teaching about religion is absent from history courses is the constitutional one: The government is enjoined from doing anything inimical to existing (or future) religions; religion is off limits for secular government. What *historical knowledge* did the founding fathers possess that compelled them to put that prohibition into the Constitution? Not many high school students could answer that question, and there are some who do not even know of the existence of the prohibition, just as there are students who do not know or believe in what the Constitution says about free speech. The Constitution is a statement of *political doctrine*, and there are many countries that have not or do not buy its doctrinal aspects. If it is a doctrinal statement, it is also an educational one in that it protects the duty and right of people to seek knowledge, to acquire it. So, the Constitution does not imply that you are justified to teach history in ways that deprive students of knowledge conducive to becoming informed and responsible citizens. If you are opposed to that, you are free to enroll your child in a parochial school. The public school is an educational institution, not an indoctrinating one that justifies ignoring knowledge that has played a crucial role in history, past and contemporary.

The reader may be puzzled about why at the end of this book I am talking about teaching the tenets of the different religions in high schools. One reason is that the teaching of American history is more than inadequate. It is taught in ways that confuse information with education (this is true not only in history). All states require the course to be taught in high schools. It is a course about the past, but it is a past that suffuses the present. Generally speaking, it is taught in ways that leave students cold, a collection of facts that they relegate to the file-and-forget category once the course exam is over. If I choose to comment on the religious aspects of the course, it is because it permits me to raise questions very relevant to the contents of earlier chapters. What are the nature and goals of teaching? What is a context of productive learning? What preparation do teachers get that sensitizes them to the phenomenology and content of the developing mind of students? How do you select and train teachers who have the style and temperament, and knowledge of subject matter that will do justice to the subject matter and to the curiosity of students, a curiosity they had before they came to school? These are questions that have concerned American psychology in diverse arenas but not in the school one. That is certainly the case in clinical psychology, and most obviously so in the case of child clinical psychologists. That is why I have said that American psychology has the potential to contribute to the improvement of schools.

When you take on the responsibility of helping someone with incapacitating personal problems, you are assuming an awesome responsibility. Students are not patients, they are people in transit trying to make sense of themselves, others, and the world. To take on the responsibility of making that transit personally meaningful and intellectually stimulating is also awesome, especially because the power relationship between teachers and students is incomparably less equal than in the case of the clinician and the patient. And unlike the clinician, the teacher is responsible for an organized group of students, a fact that exponentially complicates discharging that responsibility. I chose to discuss the teaching of the basic tenets of the major religions as a way of directing attention to psychological issues familiar to an American psychology aloof from any meaningful involvement in schooling.

My interest in these matters began two decades ago when I sat in on high school courses about American history and perused a variety of textbooks used in schools. The only conclusion I came away with was that I now understood why these courses were so dull and why they were so forgettable for students. It took me years to realize that these courses in American history said next to nothing about religion. In fact, in all of the books there was nothing about why the founding fathers prohibited the government from supporting or intruding into the religious domain. I am quite aware that high school texts had for long said little about many important issues in our history: For example, the role of women, the horrors of slavery, the treatment of American Indians and more. (You can write two histories of the United States: One would celebrate its adherence to and protection of individual liberty, and the other would condemn its failure to be consistent with those principles. Both would be correct and blatantly incomplete.) But these omissions have at least been recognized and attempts to deal more forthrightly with them have been made, although, for reasons I will shortly give, they will fall far short of the mark. Religion, however, remains a no-no; a more realistic, factual history is trumped both by a constitutional barrier and fear of indoctrination.

Let us imagine the following scenario. You are a part of a group that has been asked to develop and evaluate a one-semester course for high school seniors on several of the major religions. You are enjoined from developing a course that smacks in any way of indoctrination, and you are required to admit to the course any student whose parents will give written consent. Furthermore, before giving consent, parents will be given the syllabus as well as the opportunity themselves to take the course. You have been told that the course has several purposes, all of which must be objectively evaluated. First, the course is educational in that it has caused students not only to learn a subject matter but to have found it sufficiently interesting to say they would want to learn more and they would recommend that their friends take the course. Second, students should know by the end of the course the difference between education and indoctrination; they in no way have been persuaded to change their affiliation (if they have one) or to adopt another. Third, on before and after measures there is evidence that students have become more a community of people than of what we call a group of students in a classroom.

I can, but will not, write many pages on what your group will have to do to get to the point of teaching the course. I wish only to list the major issues the scenario clearly presents.

1. This is not a course of lectures by which the teacher parades his or her knowledge and students passively listen and take notes. From the standpoint of a context of productive learning, how would you start? My answer, of course, is that you start where the learner is: What does the learner know about the several religions that will be discussed? How many of their friends or relatives are of this or that religious persuasion? How do they define a religion? Has it puzzled them that each of the major religions has different denominations? What are the things they hope to learn about the different religions? How do they react to the fact that long before the religions to be discussed in this course were created there were other religions, that from the dawn of history there have been religions? Starting where the learner is cannot be counted on to be a simple affair, a "tell me what you think" affair. Psychotherapists know well that asking a client to reveal what he or she thinks and feels is both necessary and easy, at the same time the therapist knows that client has to overcome internal barriers to the request asked by someone who is at that point a stranger. But one thing is for sure: The learner from minute one is sizing up the teacher to determine whether he or she is likeable and trustworthy, someone whose personal style, facial expressions, and body language invite trust.

2. If you start where the learner is, you are obliged to reveal where you are coming from. That is to say, you make clear that your task in this course is a difficult one because you are not there to pass judgment on any religion but rather to discuss some (and only some) basic tenets of these religions, tenets of great personal significance to their adherents. We have to try to understand why these tenets came to have such significance if only because we live in a world populated by people of different religions. We want others to understand our religious beliefs or why we are not adherent to any systematic belief. If you are not an adherent, that does not mean that you are in some ways a superior or better person than one with religious beliefs, and the reverse should also be the case. In this course we shall seek to understand, not to pass judgment. Your religious beliefs are *yours,* and you have no reason whatever to make excuses for them. And, you hope, the students will

learn to feel safe enough to tell you when you are passing judgment, you seem to feel this religion is better than that one. Similarly, I, like you, want to feel that I can tell you when I think you are passing judgment. We have obligations to each other; our relationship is not a one-way street where only I can be critical and you must not be.

Why do I think American psychology can contribute to such a venture? The most general reply is that it is a venture that poses challenges to psychological theory and research in diverse parts of American psychology, and by challenges I mean that it offers a "real life" setting to test the adequacy and generalizabiltiy of findings from contrived settings so frequently different from naturally occurring settings. For example, there is a very large research literature on attitudes: how they are engendered and changed under different conditions. There is an even larger research literature on the relationships between motivation and performance. And there are many psychologists whose major interest is in the origins and consequences of prejudice. And there is a very active division of community psychology in the American Psychological Association, which is concerned with what facilitates and supports cohesiveness in a community and what erects barriers to it. And, as I emphasized in earlier chapters, the concept of learning has always been central to a theory of human learning.

There is another factor crucial to the venture that is, so to speak, old hat to many people in personnel and industrial psychology. How do you match the job and person? What characteristics should a person possess if he or she is to do the job well? The job may be as a CEO or a midline manager or a telephone operator. The higher the position and the larger the company, the more likely the company will hire a "head hunting" service to come up with names where there seems to be a match between person and the job. The maxim among personnel psychologists is that selection reduces by 50% the time required for training.

From my perspective there are several major virtues of the course I propose. The first is reflected in the question: *How can you justify teaching a subject matter like history when you know full well that you avoid discussing a factor crucial to that subject matter?* In the history of criticisms of American schools there has been the constant refrain that subject matter is watered down or "dumbed down," that it does not meet any reasonable standard of adequacy, a mockery of the subject matter that shortchanges students. Those devastating criticisms, with which I tend to agree, have over the decades come from critics in the university, whether the criticism is about the teaching of history, science, or social studies. That is why in the late 1950s and 1960s more than a few academics developed new curricula: the new math, science, history, and social studies. It was as near a total disaster as you can get. Their hearts were in the right place, their goals were valid, but aside from not knowing the culture of schools (a charitable statement), how teachers are selected and prepared, their conception of learning and teaching was at best fuzzy and at worst dramatically misguided. Most of them ended up blaming the victims: schools and teachers in particular and the educational community in general. How to account for what happened? The answer is complicated, but I will now turn to one factor which if it continues to be superficially addressed will defeat any effort at education reform.

The course I sketched will require teachers appreciative of and sensitive to the thoughts, feelings, and questions of students. That, I hasten to add, does not mean that this is a course in psychology but rather that it is one about a subject matter that students already know, in diverse ways from diverse sources and experiences; religion is a fact of social living, a socially troublesome fact. And we can safely assume that it is a subject matter that was and still is of relevance in the teacher's personal existence, that talking about religion is not like talking about the structure of atoms. We would both expect and require that the teacher knows that it is his or her obligation to distinguish between education and indoctrination. (Ironically, one of the frequent criticisms of history courses in schools is that teachers are unaware that the curricula they are required to use are as indoctrinating as they may be educational; for example, the way textbooks treat the role of women, American Indians, antiabolition sentiments in the North, and virulent anti-Catholicism.) Obviously, we want the teacher to start where the students are coming from and to use that starting point in ways consistent with the stated purpose of the course: to understand the basic tenets of the major religions, how those tenets undergird and justify acts of faith. It is a course that demands a lot of the teacher: a conception of productive learning, knowledge of what is in the heart and mind of the learner, and a style and temperament that for the learner makes the teacher believable and interesting, not a lecturer, a reciter of facts, who is insensitive to the needs, questions, puzzlement of the learner. Teaching is a complicated affair, which is why John Dewey said that because it is so complicated and intellectually and personally demanding, school teachers should be paid as much as college professors. I agree. But as Dewey well knew 100 years ago, as is the case today, preparatory programs for teachers are grossly inadequate and misguided, as I have discussed in *Teaching as a Performing Art* (1999). As I said before, unless and until the preparation of teachers is seriously and noncosmetically transformed, do not be hopeful, let alone optimistic, about educational reform.

What can American psychology potentially contribute to the above issues? That question is one of the reasons I devoted Chapter 3 to the Boulder Conference where selection and training for the role of the clinical psychologist were discussed and outlined. What does the clinical psychologist have to know about human development and behavior? How does one gain understanding of another person for the purpose of being helpful? How can the clinical psychologist learn to control his or her personal values, especially when clients differ from the clinician in terms of age, gender, race, background, and more? Can or should a clinician who is religious take on the responsibility of seeking to help someone who is non- or anti-religious? What are the necessary and desirable personal characteristics a clinician should have? The questions are many because it is about an interaction between two people—in group and family therapy there are, to complicate matters, more—seeking to comprehend each other, and that is no simple affair. It goes without saying that teachers and clinicians have different roles and purposes and use different methods in very different contexts. But that does not mean that requirements for their roles do not discernibly overlap; at the point of a gun I would say that in terms of *principles* the overlap is near total. However, if you were to systematically observe the training of clinicians and teachers, you would justifiably conclude that the overlap is very close to zero.

Psychology has learned a lot about these matters, not as much as necessary but enough to justify my assertion that it has the potential to make a very significant contribution to the truly basic problems in schooling. It would be more correct to say to a societal problem which if not addressed and studied will be a source of an increasing disillusionment and social divisiveness. The Boulder Conference was American psychology's recognition that many people had personal problems of such strength as to cause them to lead lives of personal misery and wasted potential that in turn negatively affected the lives of family and friends. The response of American psychology was essentially one of repair, remediation, and containment; it was understandable and justifiable given that in the aftermath of World War II the problems of mental health were a pressing one calling for action. And, I should remind the reader, the warehousing of mentally disturbed people in state hospitals was recognized for what it was—inhumane, immoral, and iatrogenic.

Schools contain generations of students. If they are not to be regarded as clay to be molded, they should be regarded by adults as growing organisms who need to be stimulated and nurtured, even as the serious gardener is ever on the alert to *prevent* stunted growth in his or her flowers and plants. If the problems of mental health were in the minds of people after World War II, the inadequacies of our schools today is at or near the top of the public agenda. If American psychology remains aloof from those inadequacies, the judgment of posterity will be harsh. I did not write this book in the hope that other psychologists will read it and take it seriously. And I also expect that many in the educational community will not take kindly to what I say about them. In 1899, John Dewey said that unless education is viewed as a social science and comes to be regarded as an arena connected to those other fields, the promise of a productive schooling will fall far short of the mark. He did not say that to people in general but on occasion of his presidential address to the then small membership of the American Psychological Association. His fear, unfortunately, turned out to be 100% correct. What I have written in this and previous books derives from that address and my experience as a psychologist trying to understand why schools are what they are. That also explains why I dedicated *Psychology Misdirected* (1981) to the memory of John Dewey. Dewey was a psychologist, educator, and philosopher. To the bulk of psychologists Dewey's name is by no means a familiar one. There are some who know he is categorized as an educator and philosopher, not categories of respect in the psychological community. They do not know how essential he thought it was that the relation between psychology and education be a symbiotic one in which both parties give and get intellectual sustenance. In Garner's (1972) seminal paper, which I discussed in Chapter 2, he had no cause to refer to Dewey. He was writing about the fruitfulness of a symbiotic relationship between basic and applied research. That is precisely the kind of relationship between psychology and schooling Dewey was advocating in his presidential address. What he had to say fell on deaf ears, and this country has paid and is paying a very high price.

I recognize that I have refrained from giving an answer to what today is called "our educational problem." The problem, as I have tried to indicate in previous writings, is mind bogglingly complicated. A very dear colleague was puzzled that I would devote the concluding chapter of this book to teaching a comparative course on religion in high school. Although I have given the reasons for my decision above, when I ruminated about her puzzlement, several things came to mind. The first was the psychotherapeutic maxim that what a client does *not* talk about is frequently more significant than what he or she does talk about. One could say that there are many things that never get talked about in schooling. What is special about religion? For one thing, my answer is it is a crucial component in the shaping of one's world view, of how one understands self and others, how it enters in and affects human relationships, how its content, imagery, and allusions suffuse educational subject matter, how human history is incomprehensible absent knowledge of religions, how religion in the present world is shaping our individual futures. By not talking about it we passively collude in shaping a social future we very likely will regret. Perhaps the wisest thing that John Dewey ever said is that schooling is not a preparation for life but life itself. What we are not sensitized to in schooling, we will likely remain insensitive to after schooling, even though as in the case of religion we know that it is a source of great personal interest and puzzlement to students, frequently in ways that are individually and collectively untoward and counterproductive. To take a hands-off stance toward religion is to ignore the phenomenology of the student learner, to devalue it as a goad to learning.

Why sketch a course in a subject matter that is emotionally loaded and may turn students and parents off? Let me reply with this question: How do we justify teaching math and science in ways that mammothly turn off students, engender anxiety, and close off conceptions? I trust that no one would deny that students know that they live in a world suffused with and explained by math-science concepts and measurements. For most students their initial curiosity, interest, and puzzlements about these subjects had been strong and motivating but steadily become less so as they went through the grades. Why this is so is less important at this point than that it is so. But in the lives of many of these disaffected students religions continue to be a fact in social living, a source of social-doctrinal-political-geographical conflict and divisiveness, even of war. They see and hear about these matters on TV. On a globe of the world many of these students cannot point to the Mideast, Pakistan, India, Northern Ireland, Croatia, Bosnia, Kosovo, Albania, but in some inchoate way they know that religious differences are differences that make a difference in this world, including the United States. For example, they know that John F. Kennedy was the first non-Protestant to become a president and that religious prejudice was and is a part of American history which we should try to overcome. But how and where? Is there no justifiable, non-indoctrinating role schools can play to provide students with a better, more factual basis for understanding religions other than their own? Do we continue to preach sermons on religious tolerance without providing a concrete basis for comprehending why the major religions are both similar and different? Students know that these religions have different names, but they cannot tell you why they are so similar and why they became different. Tolerance requires, among other things, some understanding of why others do not share your beliefs or point of view. Absent such understanding tolerance is an empty concept.

We tell students that math and science are necessary for them if they are to adapt to and exploit an everchanging, increasingly complicated, technical-scientific world. We then proceed to teach these subjects in ways that defeat our stated purposes. We change curricula, we require teachers to take more courses, but to no general avail. In fact, the major problem schools face today is finding teachers who *want* to teach math and science even if their credentials hardly justify hiring them. The number of people who enter a preparatory program because they want to become math or science teachers is piddling. By the time students are graduated from high schools their interest in math science is not much above zero.

Before saying more about these matters I need briefly to return to what happened when after World War II American psychology embraced clinical psychology with the hope and strong belief that it could make a distinctive contribution to the remediation of disabling mental problems. I say "hope and belief" advisedly because from a historical perspective the field had little to go on; basically it was unprepared. Within a matter of a few decades clinical psychologists played a major role in developing a plethora of different (and often competing) rationales for developing and researching the efficacy of psychotherapies. That psychotherapeutic arena was transformed, and no one had predicted it. Three things marked that transformation. One was that no one psychotherapeutic rationale was effective with all problems but rather with a limited range of problems. The second was that the most effective psychotherapies were those whose rationales were relatively clear about how symptoms are learned and unlearned. The third was that independent of rationale a key ingredient of efficacy were certain attributes of the therapist: he or she possessed qualities which engendered in patients the feeling they were understood and respected, that they could trust the therapist, that they were safe in revealing their inadequacies. And I am not alone in concluding that the personal qualities of the therapist cannot be overestimated. The point of all this is that the psychotherapy is a highly personal and interpersonal encounter for therapist and client; it is a learning and unlearning experience for both. The effective therapist is one who does not treat diagnostic categories but an alive, thinking, feeling person as aware of the therapist as the therapist is of him or her.

Far too many teachers teach subject matter, not students, and that is why math and science teaching is so ineffective and counterproductive. That, of course, is not the whole story, but it certainly is a large part of it and that is why in my writings I have been so critical of preparatory programs. Teachers share kinship with clinical psychologists in that their task is to understand students, to go beyond what students say and do, beyond surface appearances, beyond the impersonal. It will be argued that I am asking a lot of teachers, too much of people who already feel harassed, pressured, misunderstood. In saying what I have I am only repeating what educators and policy makers say in their mission statement: To help each individual student realize his or her potential, that every child can learn, and that children should learn to tolerate and respect others who are different in some ways than they are. My criticism has been that the rhetoric is belied by the realities of classroom living and unlearning. Some people may accuse me of being impractical, a utopian, out of touch with what our schools confront and, therefore, unsympathetic to the plight of educators and schools. What I would find ironic about such criticisms is that they concede my major point: There is an obvious disconnect between what is said about the purposes of schooling and the realities and outcomes of schooling.

My imaginary course in comparative religions has the virtue of containing every important aspect of learning and social living. If I would single out the most crucial aspect, it would be: How would you select and prepare those who would teach such a course? If I tackle that aspect succesfully, and the results of the course were even moderately positive (the first time given), the practical implications for the selection and preparation of teachers would become evident. But there is also a tactical virtue to creating and developing such a course: We would not be changing curricula, we would not have to overcome how this or that subject matter has been taught before, we would not encounter the resistances that derive from past imprisonment in the tradition of how to teach (and where) and to evaluate what we teach by criteria that are only very distantly related, if at all, to contexts of productively learning. Creating a new subject to be taught in schools will confront many problems, but they will not be those that confront any educator or external reformer whose proposals for change require teachers or administrators to alter significantly how they think, practice, and relate to each other, what I have called the behavioral and programmatic regularities which have characterized the culture of schools for at least a couple of centuries.

I finished this book and was ready to send it to the publisher after the coming Memorial Day weekend during which time I visited New York to see the new Planetarium in the American Museum of Natural

History. I never expected that I would feel compelled to add my reactions to the new Planetarium.

The new structure is striking to the eye. In fact, even before it opened the national media waxed ecstatic about the architectural feat, which cost upwards of $150 million. It was predicted that it would become the No. 1 tourist attraction, and that prediction is being confirmed. But I was bored throughout the visit. It was in all respects like a lecture; more correctly, it reminded me of Groucho Marx's question: Do you want to learn French in ten easy lessons or five hard ones? What was to be the most enlightening and distinctive experience of the visitors—the visual display of the ever-changing universes—took about 20 or so minutes. It undoubtedly raised dramatically more questions in viewers than it answered. Following the visual display of the heavens, visitors walked along elevated walkways looking at and reading material (factual) intended to give them an idea of comparative time and sizes of celestial objects. I tried carefully to observe the viewers to see how much interest they manifested and how long they stayed at each display. They showed little evidence of interest, of engagement. I cannot be accused of seeing what I wanted to see because I and my family came to the site with much curiosity and eagerness. I was not prepared for what I personally experienced. I did not come with any expectation that it would be relevant to my thinking about learning and educational reform. I never, but never, expected to be bored. For example, I expected, correctly it turned out, that the audio for the heavenly display would say something about the big bang theory of the start of the world, about why that theory explained what heretofore had been unsatisfactory explanations. I know a little something about the big bang theory, and I was eager to see how the detection and measurement of an expanding universe would be conveyed. Nothing of the sort was conveyed. What the viewer "learned" was that there was a big bang, period.

In the week after the visit I had occasion to be at several informal gatherings, and I made it my business to ask people if they had been to the Planetarium. Two had been there. I asked each what their reactions had been. Their immediate response was one of awe and admiration for the striking architecture. Neither of them spontaneously said anything about "subject matter." So I asked: "How did you find what you saw and heard there?" A look of thoughtful puzzlement came to the fore, and after a pause of 5–10 seconds each of them said that what they saw and heard aroused little interest in them and that they had learned little.

Several questions occurred to me:

1. What did the creators of the Planetarium want viewers to learn? Granted that visitors would be a very heterogenous group in terms of age, education, interest, social class, etc., how did they arrive at the "solution" they did? What was the universe of alternatives they considered? What evidence did they have for the efficacy of the plan they adopted? As in the case of too many educational reforms, was the Planetarium a place where empty buckets would be filled and no fires lit?

2. Before the Planetarium was open to the public was an effort made to bring in discrete samples of people in order to determine what questions they would want the Planetarium to answer, and why? After they had seen the exhibits, to what extent were these questions addressed? Leaving their expectations aside, was an attempt made to determine what visitors said they learned? On a scale of 1 (uninteresting) to 10 (thrilling), how would they rate the experience? Would they pay the not-small entry fee to see it again? Would they recommend their friends see it?

3. Does the Planetarium have any plans to study and analyze visitor reactions? Is its "curriculum" locked, so to speak, in concrete like curricula in our schools? And again like schools, is the Planetarium exempt from the obligation of instituting self-correcting forums and mechanisms?

The Planetarium is not a context of productive learning. There are no "teachers" with whom to interact, there is no one to whom one can address questions or express opinions, no one is really interested in what you think and feel. The only thing I learned is something I already knew: Let the buyer beware! It takes years for students in our schools to learn that, by which time many of them will buy nothing educational. A fact: The head of the American Museum of Natural History, a driving force for the Planetarium, is a psychologist.

References

Aiken, W. A. (1942). *The story of the eight year study with conclusions and recommendations.* New York: Harper Collins.

Angier, N. (1999, June 17). Do primates think? *New York Times.*

Barker, R. G. (1968). *Ecological psychology.* Stanford, CA: Stanford University Press.

Barker, R. G., & Gump, P. V. (1964). *Big school, small school.* Stanford, CA: Stanford University Press.

Brown, J. F. (1936). *Psychology and the social order.* New York: McGraw Hill.

Buxton, C. (1973). *Adolescents in schools.* New Haven, CT: Yale University Press.

Cutts, R. (1997). *An empire of schools.* Armonk, NY: M. E. Sharpe.

De Tocqueville, A. (1956). *Democracy in America.* New York: New American Library. (Original work published 1835–40)

Dewey, J. C. (1963). The concept of the reflex arc in psychology. In *J. Dewey, philosophy, psychology, and social practice* (J. Ratner, Ed.). New York: Capricorn.

Dewey, J. C. (1978). Psychology and social practice. In E. Hilgard (Ed.), *American psychology in historical perspective.* Washington, DC: American Psychological Association.

French, H. V. (1999, December 7). Exam wars, prepping and other nursery crimes. *New York Times.*

Felix, R. (1988). Opening address to Boulder conference on clinical psychology. In S. B. Sarason, *The making of an American psychologist.* San Francisco: Jossey-Bass.

Garner, W. R. (1972). The acquisition and application of knowledge: A symbiotic relationship. *American Psychologist, 27*(10), 941–946.

Garner, W. R., & Hunt, H. F. (1959). Education for research in psychology. *American Psychologist, 14,* 167–179.

Ginzberg, E. & Bray, D. (1953). *The uneducated.* New York: Columbia University Press.

Goodlad, J. (1984). *A place called school.* New York: McGraw Hill.

Goodnaugh, A. C. (1999, December 8). Investigator says teachers in city aided in cheating. *New York Times.*

Holloway, L. (1999, October 20). Parents and educators seek Regents test exemption. *New York Times.*

James, W. (1900). *Talks to teachers and to students.* New York: Henry Holt.

Kamii, C., & DeVries, R. (1993). *Physical knowledge in preschool education: Implications for Piaget's theory.* New York: Teachers College Press. (Original work published 1978)

Köhler, W. (1925). *The mentality of apes.* New York: Harcourt, Brace.

Kounin, J. S. (1967). *Observations and analysis of classroom management.* Paper presented at the annual meeting of the American Educational Research Association.

Kounin, J. S., Friesen, W. V., & Norton, A. E. (1966). Managing emotionally disturbed children in regular classrooms. *Journal of Educational Psychology, 55*(1), 1–13.

Kounin, J. S., Gump, P. V., & Ryan, J. J. (1961). Explorations in classroom management. *Journal of Teacher Education, 12,* 235–246.

Myrdal, G. (1944). *An American dilemma.* New York: Harper Collins.

National Commission on Teaching and America's Future. (1996). *What matters most: Teaching for America's future.* New York: Author.

Pauly, E. (1991). *The classroom crucible: What really works, what doesn't and why.* New York: Basic Books.

Raimy, V. (Ed.) (1950). *Training in clinical psychology.* Englewood Cliffs, NJ: Prentice-Hall.

Sarason, S. B. (1949). *Psychological problems in mental deficiency.* New York: Harper.

Sarason, S. B. (1965). The school culture and processes of change. In S. B. Sarason & F. Kaplan (Eds.), *The Psycho-Educational Clinic: Papers and research studies (1966).* Boston: Department of Mental Health.

Sarason, S. B. (1971). *The culture of the school and the problem of change.* Boston: Allyn and Bacon.

Sarason, S. B. (1972). *The creation of settings and the future societies.* San Francisco: Jossey- Bass.

Sarason, S. B. (1975). To the Finland station in the heavenly city of the eighteenth century philosophers. *American Psychologist, 30*(5), 584–592.

Sarason, S. B. (1981). *Psychology misdirected.* New York: Free Press.

Sarason, S. B. (1985). *Caring and compassion in clinical practice: Issues in the selection, training and behavior of helping professionals.* San Francisco: Jossey-Bass.

Sarason, S. B. (1988). *The making of an American psychologist.* San Francisco: Jossey-Bass.

Sarason, S. B. (1990a). *The challenge of art to psychology.* New Haven, CT: Yale University Press.

Sarason, S. B. (1990b). *The predictable failure of educational reform.* San Francisco: Jossey- Bass.

Sarason, S. B. (1993a). American psychology and the needs for transcendence and community. *American Journal of Community Psychology, 21*(2), 185–202.

Sarason, S. B. (1993b). *The case for change: Rethinking the preparation of educators.* San Francisco: Jossey-Bass.

Sarason, S. B. (1993c). *You are thinking of teaching?* San Francisco: Jossey-Bass.

Sarason, S. B. (1995). *Parent involvement and the political principle: Why the existing governance structure of schools should be abolished.* New York: Jossey Bass.

Sarason, S. B. (1996a). *Barometers of change.* San Francisco: Jossey-Bass.

Sarason, S. B. (1996b). *Revisiting "the culture of the school and the problem of change."* New York: Teachers College Press.

Sarason, S. B. (1998a). *Charter schools: Another flawed educational reform?* New York: Teachers College Press.

Sarason, S. B. (1998b). *Political leadership and educational failure.* San Francisco: Jossey-Bass.

Sarason, S. B. (1999). *Teaching as a performing art.* New York: Teachers College Press.

Sarason, S. B., Davidson, K., & Blatt, B. (1962). *The preparation of teachers: An unstudied problem in education.* New York: John Wiley.

Sarason, S. B., Davidson, K. S., Lighthall, F. F., Waite, R. R., & Ruebush, B. K. (1960). *Anxiety in elementary school children.* New York: John Wiley.

Sarason, S. B., Levine, M., Goldenberg, I., Cherlin, D., & Bennett, E. (1966). *Psychology in community settings.* New York: John Wiley.

Slavin, R. E., Madden, N. A., Dolan, L. J., & Wasik, B. (1996). *Every child, every school: Success for all.* Thousand Oaks, CA: Corwin Press.

Stanislavski, C. (1936). *The actor prepares.* New York: Theater Arts.

Steinberg, J. (1999, September 15). Idea of rewarding "strivers" is opposed by College Board. *New York Times.*

Steinberg, L. D., with Brown, B., & Dornbusch, S. (1996). *Beyond the classroom.* New York: Simon and Schuster.

Susskind, D. (1969). *Questioning and curiosity in the elementary school.* Unpublished doctoral dissertation, Yale University.

Veblen, T. (1957). *The higher learning in America.* New York: Sagamore.

Waller, W. (1932). *The sociology of teaching.* New York: John Wiley.

Wigdor, A. K., & Garner, W. R. (1982). *Ability testing.* Washington, D.C.: National Academy Press.

Wasserstein, W. (1999, June 20). Bringing students to the theater. *New York Times.*

Wertheimer, M. (1945). *Productive thinking.* New York: Harper.

Wilson, K., with Daviss, B. (1996). *Redesigning education.* New York: Teachers College Press.

Wilson, K., with Barsky, C. (1998). Applied research and development. *Daedalus, 127,*(4), 233–258.

About the Author

Seymour B. Sarason is professor of psychology emeritus in the Department of Psychology and at the Institution for Social and Policy Studies of Yale University. In 1962 he founded and directed the Yale Psycho-Educational Clinic, one of the first research and training sites in community psychology. Fields in which he has made special contributions include mental retardation, culture and personality, projective techniques, teacher training, anxiety in children, and school reform. His numerous books and articles reflect his broad interests.

Dr. Sarason received his Ph.D. degree from Clark University in 1942 and holds honorary doctorates from Syracuse University, Queens College, Rhode Island College, and Lewis and Clark College. He has received awards from the American Psychological Association and the American Association on Mental Deficiency.